The Complete Prophecies
of
Nostradamus

"Up! Flee! Out into broad and open land!
And this book full of mystery,
From NOSTRADAMUS' own very hand,
Is it not sufficient company?
The stars' course then you'll understand
And Nature, teaching you, will then expand
The power of your soul, as when
One SPIRIT to another SPEAKS."

Faust, act I, scene I.

The Complete Prophecies of

Nostradamus

Translated, Edited and Interpreted by
Henry C. Roberts

NEW REVISED EDITION

Re-edited by
Lee Roberts Amsterdam
and
Harvey Amsterdam

GRANADA
London Toronto Sydney New York

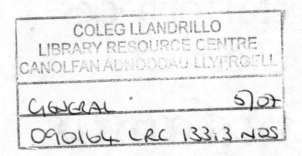
Granada Publishing Limited
8 Grafton Street, London W1X 3LA

Published by Granada Publishing 1984

Copyright 1947, 1949, © 1962, 1964, 1966, 1968, 1969 by
Henry C. Roberts
Copyright © 1982 by Lee Roberts Amsterdam and Harvey Amsterdam

British Library Cataloguing in Publication Data

Nostradamus
    The complete prophecies of Nostradamus.
    1. Prophecies (occult sciences)
    I. Title   II. Roberts, Henry C.
    133.3   BF1815.N8

ISBN 0-246-12303-6

Printed in Great Britain by
Billing & Sons Limited
Worcester and London

Table of Contents

Introduction to Third Edition

In the forty-five years that have passed since my father, Henry C. Roberts, wrote this book, there has been a renewed interest in the writings and prophecies of Nostradamus. Since my father's death several years ago, I have tried to carry on his work and interest in Nostradamus and with my husband, Harvey Amsterdam, have continued my father's research into Nostradamus's writings and the effect of his prophecies on the present generation.

Through the years many people from all over the world have written to me to express interest and offer suggestions for a new edition. It is for this reason that we have re-edited this book in the light of events that have transpired in recent years, and we have made every attempt to incorporate ideas from our readers and answers to their questions. We have updated some of the interpretations and included an index to facilitate ready reference to all material. In every instance, we have endeavoured to maintain the continuity and format of my father's writing and we add our 'blessing' to that of my father's to all readers who wish to make their own interpretations and analyses.

Will mankind heed the warnings that Michael Nostradamus gave to the world more than 400 years ago or will we continue to make his most dire prophecies come true? That depends, of course, upon the actions of our world leaders and whether each of us is willing to follow them blindly in the path of destruction that seems to lie before us.

LEE ROBERTS AMSTERDAM

Oyster Bay, N.Y.
July 28, 1982

Introduction

Nearly everyone, at one time or another, has heard or read something about Nostradamus and his prophecies. Yet, the astonishing fact is that not since 1672 has there been printed an English edition of his complete quatrains. As a bookseller, I was struck by this lack because of the great number of people, interested in predictions and other phenomena of this nature, who had come to me over a period of years, inquiring for the complete works of Nostradamus in English. As a student of the occult, always seeking materials on the subject, I too was anxious to procure the unabridged work of the man who is acknowledged as one of the greatest seers in the history of occult science.

Spurred on by these incentives, I began to search the field for all books, old and new, pertaining to Nostradamus. The reward was scanty. The current available books on Nostradamus dealt with but a few of his more noted quatrains, discussing them at length, but making no attempt to bring to light more than a few hundred out of the thousand he had purportedly written.

At long last I obtained, at an almost prohibitive price, a copy of the afore-mentioned 1672 edition: *The True Prophecies or Prognostications of Michael Nostradamus*, translated and annotated by Theophilus de Garencieres. I had perused but a few pages when I was struck by the sense of familiarity that these verses seemed to hold for me. Words that the author claimed held no significance for him, took on for me a definite meaning, became clearly focused into patterns of events – past, present and future. Here, I felt, was *my* book.

Such being the case, I determined to start the long and arduous task of making available a new complete edition of Nostradamus, using all the materials at hand, bringing to them new interpretations in the light of recent events, taking as much as possible the same position as if Nostradamus were alive today – speaking with both our voices.

Avoiding the hitherto lengthy explanations that, I felt, bewildered rather than enlightened the reader, I have tried to make the interpretations concise and simple; I have also, as much as was feasible, tried to preserve the spirit and cadence of the original quatrains. The present text is the result, and I believe it to be clean

and true. At all times, where there were discrepancies or ambi-
guities in the French text, I have accepted the oldest versions,
especially considering Garencieres' book as the most authoritative.

From the time of the Delphic Sibyl it has been the characteristic
of occult prophecies and utterances, often to seem unintelligible
and garbled to the uninitiated. The strange, broken, and often
incoherent nature of the quatrains, both in French and English, is
the hallmark of prophetic media.

Nevertheless, at this point, I feel that a few words of explanation
are necessary with regard to certain questions that may arise in the
reader's mind. Primarily, we must clear up the fact that the word
'prophecy' does not, in its literal sense, apply to every one of these
quatrains. A good number of the verses have reference to events of
the days before and during the time of Nostradamus – events that
distressed, pleased, or shocked him, and which he considered
important enough to record for posterity. But the bulk of his work
was based upon his awesome gift of prognostication, and it is this
that we are mainly concerned with. Even after deep study and wide
consultation of occult materials, it was not always possible to
assign these predictions to definite places or people. It would have
been an easy matter to lightly attribute certain doings to certain
people, but that would have taken on the nature of 'guessing' and
we say, in closing, that we prefer to leave that to the reader; for he
will inevitably attempt to do so, and we urge him so to do – with
'our' blessing.

HENRY C. ROBERTS

New York, N.Y.
November, 1946

Introduction to Second Edition

Beyond a shadow of doubt, the methods employed and results obtained by Nostradamus in looking into the future were outside of the physical framework.

What to the contemporary critics of his day, for want of a better term they chose to call magic or occult, we today now recognize as the operation of certain tenuous and imponderable laws that permeate the entire Cosmos. These intangible but all-pervading forces we group today under the general title of 'Extra Sensory Perception.'

Such startling and apparently miraculous phenomena as mediumism, telepathy, telekinesis, etc., are today the serious subject of study by such accredited scientists as Dr. Rhine of Duke University and Prof. Gardner Murphy of New York University. An entirely new line of investigation is in progress in this new science of 'Para-psychology' which promises rich rewards for mankind.

Who knows? Perhaps some day this new line of scientific activity may be developed to a point where it will have a practical application to our everyday life and make possible a revolutionary concept of nature's forces.

HENRY C. ROBERTS

New York, N.Y.
March 2, 1949

Who Was Nostradamus?

Much of the information known about Nostradamus is apocryphal but there are certain facts that have been documented. It is known that he was a French physician of Jewish descent who was born in Provence on December 14, 1503. Michael was born within the sphere of the Catholic Church and spent his childhood under the guidance of his grandfathers, who instructed him in the rudiments of the classic languages and in Hebrew and astrology. When he was an adolescent he was sent to Avignon, where he studied philosophy, and then to the University of Montpelier in 1522 to begin his study of medicine. After spending three years at this institution renowned for its training of doctors, he graduated with a bachelor's degree.

Shortly after receiving his licence to practise medicine in 1525, he interrupted his studies to concentrate on the practical applications of his knowledge. An outbreak of the plague at Montpelier, and later at Narbonne, first earned him a reputation as a 'healer of the afflicted ones,' and his courage, combined with his unorthodox and successful treatments, led to his initial recognition and following. Using his own formulas and psychological guidance he was able to cure many patients who had been regarded as incurable.

Did an insight into human needs, motives, and failings, and where they could lead, begin at this time, or was it later, during his studies at the library at Avignon, when he began to read books on alchemy, magic, and the occult? It is impossible to say, but he had been regarded as a bright child with a penchant for learning, and it is said that he 'soaked up knowledge of all kinds like a sponge.'

After further treatment of victims of the ever-present plague, he returned to Montpelier where he obtained his doctoral degree in medicine. Despite what many doctors regarded as his unorthodox treatments, his refusal to 'bleed' patients in accord with the customs of the time, and his 'home-made remedies,' he was asked to join the faculty, a position that he kept for only a year; he soon found it confining and decided to leave Montpelier in order to travel. While he was travelling through Bordeaux, La Rochelle, and Toulouse, he received a summons to visit with the learned Jules-Cesar Scaliger. Nostradamus enjoyed sharing confidences and knowledge with this eminent physician and philosopher and decided to settle in Agen, where he married a beautiful young woman of 'high estate' and proceeded to raise a family.

Did forebodings of coming disaster trouble the prophet at this time of bucolic domesticity? The plague struck once again, this time in Nostradamus's own family. What a paradox! The esteemed physician who had saved the lives of so many 'afflicted ones' was unable to prevent the death of his own young wife and children. To compound his misfortune, this tragedy was followed by a quarrel with his friend Scaliger and by a lawsuit from his wife's family to regain her dowry. The old adage 'troubles come in threes' proved true; at this time Nostradamus was summoned before the Inquisitor at Toulouse. This was the result of a chance remark made to an artisan, regarding a bronze model he was making of the Virgin, which the artisan mistakenly claimed to be heretical. Rather than appear before the Inquisitor, Nostradamus resumed his travels and spent the next six years wandering and practising medicine until he decided to settle in Salon, a town situated in the south. This became his home until his death in 1566.

In Salon in 1550 he published his first almanac containing prophecies for the coming year. This proved so successful that he continued to publish a new almanac containing predictions every subsequent year.

It was about this time, too, that Nostradamus conceived the grandiose plan that occupied him for the next two years: writing the *Centuries*. This was a complete series of prophecies dealing with events from his time to the end of the world in the year 3797. It is these prophecies, translated into English, which are printed in this book. They were written in 'quatrains,' or verses of four lines, with their meaning purposely obscured in order to prevent his being labelled a magician. The *Centuries* referred not to calendar years but to the fact that there were a series of 100 quatrains to each section; thus, a century of quatrains means 100 verses.

The fame of Nostradamus spread to the royal court, and no less a person than the Queen, Catherine de Medici, summoned him to the court to plot the horoscopes of the king and the royal children. The queen held Nostradamus in high esteem throughout her life and in 1564 visited him in Salon.

Nostradamus spent his remaining years in Salon with his second wife, who had been a well-to-do widow. His fame as a prophet led to much controversy. His detractors claimed that he represented the devil, but his followers visited him from all parts of France.

Several famous anecdotes about the seer help to account for the reputation as a prophet that he enjoyed during his lifetime.

While travelling through Italy, he is said to have bowed before a passing young Franciscan monk, addressing him as 'His Holiness.' The astounded onlookers could not understand this strange behaviour, but years later that Franciscan monk, the former swineherd Felice Peretti, became Cardinal Peretti and in 1585 was elected by the College of Cardinals to become Pope Sixtus V. This occurred years after Nostradamus's death.

Another famous legend concerns the tale of the black pig and the white pig. While walking in the courtyard of the château of a certain Monsieur de Florenville, Nostradamus came upon two suckling pigs, a black one and a white one. He was asked by Monsieur de Florenville what would become of the two pigs. Nostradamus replied with alacrity, 'We will eat the black one, and the wolf will eat the white one.' To prove Nostradamus a liar and to discredit him, the lord ordered the chef to roast the white one on the spit and to serve it for their dinner. At dinner, Florenville again asked Nostradamus about the fate of the white and black pigs and Nostradamus maintained that what he had said earlier was true: They ate the black pig and the wolf had eaten the white one. The chef was called in to refute Nostradamus's statement. All were astounded when the chef admitted that a tame wolf cub had nibbled at the white pig while it was roasting on the spit and that he had served them the black one instead.

Nostradamus's fame lives on today despite vilifiers and detractors during his lifetime and in the centuries that have followed. Some have claimed that his 'prophecies' were no more than 'ambiguous guesswork,' but many of the prophecies that are included in this book seem too precise and accurate to be dismissed as mere guesswork. Four centuries after they were written, we can judge for ourselves whether they have proved true and whether they will continue to anticipate events yet to occur.

Preface to First Edition

A Letter of Dedication to his son, Caesar Nostradamus

Thy late coming, Caesar Nostradamus, my son, hath caused me to bestow much time in continual and nocturnal watchings, that I might leave a memorial of me after my death, to the common benefit of mankind, concerning the things which the Divine Essence hath revealed to me by astronomical revolutions. Since it hath pleased the immortal God that thou art come late into this world, and canst say that thy years are but few, and thy months incapable to receive into thy weak understanding what I am forced to define of futurity; since it is not possible to leave thee in writing what might be obliterated by the injury of time, for the hereditary gift of occult prediction shall be locked up in my breast; considering also that events are definitely uncertain, and that all is governed by the power of God who inspired us not by a Bacchic fury nor yet by Lymphatic motion, but by astronomical effects – *'Soli numine divino afflati praesagiunt et spirito prophetico particularia.'**

Although I have often foretold long before what hath afterwards come to pass, and in particular regions, acknowledging all to have been done by divine virtue and inspiration, I was willing to hold my peace by reason of the injury – not only of the present time, but also of the future – because to put them in writing, the Kingdoms, Sects, and Regions shall be so diametrically opposed, that if I should relate what shall happen hereafter, those of the present Reign, Sect, Religion and Faith, would find it so disagreeing with their fancies, that they would condemn that which future ages shall find and know to be true. Consider also the sayings of our Saviour, *'Nolite sanctum dare canibus neque mittatis margaritas vestras ante porcos, ne forte conculcent eas pedibus suis, et conversi dirumpant vos.'* (Matt. vii. 6)

For this reason I have withheld my tongue from the vulgar, and my pen from paper. But, afterwards, I was willing for the common good to enlarge myself in dark and abstruse sentences, declaring the future events, chiefly the most urgent and those which I foresaw (whatever human mutation happened) would not offend

---

* 'Such alone as are inspired by the divine power can predict particular events in a spirit of prophecy.'

the hearers, all under dark figures more than prophetical. Although '*Abscondidisti hoec à sapientibus, et prudentibus, id est,
potentibus et regibus, et enucleasti ea exiguis et tenuibus.*'* The
prophets, by means only of the immortal God and good Angels,
have received the spirit of vaticination, by which they foresee
things, and foretell future events. For nothing is perfect without
Him, whose power and goodness are so great to His creatures, that
though they are but men, nevertheless by the likeness of their good
genius to the Angels, this heat and prophetical power draws near
us, as do the rays of the sun, which cast their influence alike upon
bodies that are elementary and non-elementary. As for us, who are
but men, we cannot attain anything by our natural knowledge, of
the secrets of God our Creator. '*Quia non est nostrum noscere
tempora, nec momenta,*' etc. (Acts i. 7)

There are, or may come some persons, to whom God Almighty
will reveal by impressions made on their understanding some
secrets of the future, according to judicial astrology, as it hath
happened in former times, when a certain power and voluntary
faculty possessed them as a flame of fire. So by His inspiration they
were able to judge of divine and human things, for the divine
works that are absolutely necessary, God will complete.

But, my son, I speak to thee a little too obscurely. There are
secrets that are received by the subtle spirit of fire, by which the
understanding is moved to contemplate the highest celestial
bodies, being active and vigilant to the very pronunciation without
fear or any shameful loquacity; all of which proceeded from the
divine power of the Eternal God, from whom all goodness flows.

Now, my son, although I have inserted the name of prophet
here, I will not attribute to myself so sublime a title, for '*Propheta
dicitur hodie, olim vocabatur videns,*'† and prophets are those
properly, my son, that see things remote from the natural knowledge of mankind. Or, to put the case, the prophets, by the means
of the perfect light of prophecy, may see divine things as well as
human (which cannot but be seeing the effects of future predictions) and do extend a great distance, for the secrets of God are
incomprehensible, and their efficient power is far remote from the
natural knowledge, taking their origin in the free will, causing
those things to appear which otherwise could not be known,
neither by human auguries nor by any hidden knowledge or secret

---

* 'Thou hast hidden these things from the wise and prudent and hast
revealed them to the small and weak.'

† 'He who is called prophet now, once was called seer.'

virtue under Heaven. Only by the means of some indivisible eternal being, and by Herculean agitation the causes come to be known by the celestial motion.

I say, therefore, my son, that you may not understand me well, because the knowledge of this matter cannot yet be imprinted in thy weak brain. Future causes afar off are subject to the knowledge of human creatures, if (notwithstanding the Creator) things present and future were neither obscure nor hidden from the intellectual seal; but the perfect knowledge of the cause of things cannot be acquired without the divine inspiration, seeing that all prophetical inspiration received hath its original principle from God the Creator, next, from good luck, and afterwards from nature. Therefore, causes, independently produced or not produced, the prophecy partly happens where it hath been foretold, for the understanding being intellectually created cannot see occult things, unless it be by the voice coming from the limbo, by the means of the thin flame, to which the knowledge of future causes is inclined. And, also, my son, I entreat thee not to bestow thy understanding on such fopperies which dry up the body and damn the soul, and bring vexation to the senses. Chiefly abhor the vanity of the execrable magic forbidden by the Sacred Scriptures and by the Canons of the Church; except from this judicial astrology by which, and by the means of divine inspiration, with continual calculations, we have put in writing, our prophecies.

Although this occult philosophy was not forbidden, I could never be persuaded to meddle with it, although many volumes concerning that art, which hath been concealed a great while, were presented to me. But fearing what might happen, after I had read them, I presented them to Vulcan and, while he was devouring them, the flame mixed with the air, there was an unwonted light more bright than the usual flame and it was as if there were lightning, shining all the house over, as if it had been all in a flame. Therefore, that henceforth you might not be abused in the search of the perfect transformation, as much lunar as solar, and to seek in the waters uncorruptible metal, I have burnt them all to ashes. But as to the judgment which cometh to be perfected by the help of the celestial judgment, that I will manifest to you that you may have knowledge of future things; rejecting the fantastic imaginations that may arise, and limiting the particularity of places which were arrived at by divine and supernatural inspiration, according to the celestial figures, by an occult property, and by a divine virtue, power and faculty – in the presence of which the three aspects of time are comprehended by eternity, an evolution that ties into one the cause that is past, present, and future; '*quia omnia sunt nuda et aperta* . . .'*

Therefore, my son, thou mayst, notwithstanding thy tender brain, comprehend things that shall happen hereafter, and may be foretold by celestial natural lights, and by the spirit of prophecy, not that I will attribute to myself the name of a prophet, but as a mortal man, being no farther from Heaven by my sense than I am from Earth by my feet. '*Possum non errare, falli, decipi,*'† (albeit) I am the greatest sinner of the world subject to all human afflictions. But being surprised sometimes by a prophetical mood, and by a long calculation, pleasing myself in my study, I have made Books of Prophecies, each one containing a hundred Astronomical Stanzas, which I have joined obscurely, and are perpetual prophecies from this year to the year 3797, at which some perhaps will frown, seeing so large an extension of time, and that I treat of everything under the Moon. If thou livest the natural age of a man thou shalt see in thy climate, and under the Heaven of thy nativity, the future things that have been foretold.

God only knoweth the eternity of the light proceeding from Himself, and I say freely to those to whom His incomprehensible greatness hath by a long melancholic inspiration revealed, that by the means of this occult cause, divinely manifested, chiefly by two principal causes, there is comprehension and understanding in him that is inspired and prophetic. One is that which cleareth the supernatural light and foretelleth by the doctrine of the planets, and the other forecasts by inspired revelation, which is a kind of participation in the divine eternity, by means of Him, of God the Creator. And by these means he knows that what is predicted is true, and hath taken its original from above, and such light and small flame is of all efficacy and sublimity, no less than the natural light makes the philosophers so secure, that by the means of the principles of the first cause, they have attained the greatest depth of the profoundest sciences.

But I must not wander too far, my son, from the capacity of thy sense. I find that learning shall be at a great loss, and that before the universal conflagration shall happen so many great inundations, that there shall scarce be any land that shall not be covered with water, and this shall last so long, that except for Ethnographies and Topographies all shall perish. Before and after these inundations in many countries there shall be such scarcity of rain

---

* 'For all things are naked and open.'
† 'I am able not to err, be deceived nor fail.'

and such a great deal of fire, and burning stones shall fall from Heaven, that nothing unconsumed shall be left. All this shall happen a little while before the great conflagration.

Although the planet Mars makes an end of his course, and is come to the end of his last period, nevertheless he shall begin it again. Some shall be gathered in Aquarius for many years, others in Cancer also for many years. Now we are governed by the Moon, under the power of Almighty God; which Moon before she hath finished her circuit, the Sun shall come, and then Saturn. According to the celestial signs, the reign of Saturn shall come again, so that all being calculated, the world draws near to its anaragonic revolution (death-dealing).

From this present time that I write this, before 177 years, three months, eleven days, through pestilence, famine, war, and for the most part, inundations, the world between this and that prefixed time, before and after, for several times shall be so diminished, and the people shall be so few, that they shall not find enough to till the ground, so that they shall remain fallow as long as they had once been tilled. We are now in the seventh millenary, which ends all and brings us near the eighth, where the firmament of the eighth sphere is, which, in a latitudinary dimension, is the place where the Great God shall make an end of this revolution, where the celestial bodies shall move again, and the superior motion that maketh the Earth firm and stable, *'non inclinabitur in seculum seculorum,'** unless His will be accomplished and not otherwise.

Although by ambiguous opinions exceeding all natural reasons by Mahometical dreams, also sometimes God the Creator by the ministers of His messengers of fire and flame, shows to our external senses, and chiefly to our eyes, the causes of future predictions, signifying the future event, that will manifest to him that prophesies. For the prophecy that is made by the internal light, comes to judge of the thing partly with and by the means of external light, although the part which seemeth to come by the eye of understanding, comes only from the lesion of its imaginative sense. The reason is evident why what he foretelleth comes by divine inspiration, or by the means of an angelical spirit, inspired into the prophetic person, anointing him with vaticinations, moving the fore part of his fancy, by divers nocturnal apparitions, so that by astronomical administrations, he prophesies with a divine certitude, joined to the holy prediction of the future, having no other regard than to the freedom of his mind.

* 'Whence it shall not deviate from age to age.'

Come now, my son, and understand that I find by my revelations (astrological), which agree with the divine inspiration, that the swords draw near to us now, and the plague and the war more horrid than hath been seen in the life of three men before, and also famine, which shall return often, for the stars agree with the revolution, *'Visitabo in virga ferrea iniquitates eorum, et in verberibus percutiam eos.'** For the mercies of God shall not be spread for a while, my son, before most of my prophecies shall come to pass, thus oftentimes shall happen sinister storms, *'Conteram ego, et confringam,'* (said the Lord) *'et non miserebor.'* † And a thousand other accidents shall happen by waters and continual rains, as I have more fully at large declared in my other Prophecies, written *in soluta oratione,* limiting the places, times and prefixed terms, that men coming after, may see and know that those accidents are certainly come to pass, as we have marked in other places, speaking more clearly, although the explication be involved in obscurity: *'Sed quando submoventa erit ignorantia'*;‡ the case shall be made more clear. Making an end here, my son, accept this gift of thy father, Michael Nostradamus, hoping to expound to thee every prophecy of these quatrains, praying to the Immortal God that he will grant thee a long life in felicity.

From Salon, this 1st of March, 1555.

---

* 'I will visit their iniquities with a rod of iron, and with blows will strike them.'
  † 'I will trample them and break them, and not show pity.'
  ‡ 'When the time arrives for the removal of ignorance.'

The Complete Prophecies
of Nostradamus

CENTURY
I

1

Estant assis, de nuit secrette estude,
Seul, repose sur la selle d'airain,
Flambe exigue, sortant de solitude,
Fait proferer qui n'est a croire vain.

Seated at night in my secret study,
Alone, reposing over the brass tripod,
A slender flame leaps out of the solitude,
Making me pronounce that which is not in vain.

Nostradamus clearly shows his method of preparing for a nocturnal visitation from divine sources, from which he shall gain the knowledge of future events for the benefit of Posterity.

2

La verge en main, mise au milieu des
branches,
De l'onae je mouille & le limbe & le
pied,
En peur j'escris tremissant par les
manches;
Splendeur Divine; le Divine prez
s'assied.

With divining rod in hand, I wet the limb and foot,
Set in the middle of the branches.
Fearsome awe trembles my hand, I await,
Heavenly Splendour! The Divine Genius sitteth by.

Evidently our author employed an instrument similar to the present forked divining rod, now used for locating water. In a large brass bowl filled with water, various segments were marked off and, as the rod dipped to the proper significant areas, messages would emanate.

3

Quand la littiere du tourbillon versee,	When the litter shall be overthrown by a gust of wind,
Et seront faces de leurs manteaux couvers,	And faces shall be covered with cloaks,
La Republique par gens nouveaux vexee,	The Republic shall be vexed by new people,
Lors, blancs & rouges jugeront a L'envers.	Then shall White and Red judge wrongly.

Nostradamus here forecasts the Russian Revolution of 1917 with the subsequent strife between the Red and White Russians.

4

Par l'Univers sera fait un Monarque,	In the world shall be a Monarch,
Qu'en paix & vie ne sera longuement,	Who will not leave peace, nor be long alive,
Lors se perdra la Piscature Barque,	Then will be lost the Fishing Boat,
Sera regie en plus grand detriment.	And shall be governed to its great detriment.

The Roman Catholic Church is often compared to a ship or boat, by Nostradamus. At a time when a Temporal Ruler shall reign over the entire earth, the Church shall be conspicuous by its absence.

5

Chassez seront sans faire long combat,	They shall be driven away without great fighting.
Par le pais seront plus fort grevez,	Those of the country shall be greatly grieved,
Bourg & Cite auront plus grand debat.	Town and City shall have a mighty debate,
Carcas, Narbonne auront coeurs esprouvez.	Carcassone, Narbonne shall prove their heart.

Here is nothing mysterious. It must be borne in mind that Nostradamus was a devout Catholic, and in keeping with the then current struggle between the Protestants and Catholics for power, he foretells a fraternal melee, centring about Carcassone and Narbonne in Languedoc.

6

L'oeil de Ravenne sera destitue,	The eyes of Ravenna shall be desti-
Quand a ses pieds les aisles sailliront;	tute,
Les deux de Bresse auront constitue,	When the wings shall rise at his
Turin, Verceil, que Gaulois fouleront.	feet.
	The two of Brescia shall have estab-
	lished Turin and Venice,
	Which the French shall have trod
	upon.

One who lives in Ravenna shall not find time for the pursuit of riches when the wings of inspiration arise.

The French shall ultimately have sovereignty.

7

Tard arrive, l'execution faite,	One arriving too late, the execution
Le vent contrare, lettres au chemin	will take place,
prinses,	The wind being contrary, and let-
Les conjurez quatorze d'une secte,	ters intercepted on the way.
Par le Rousseau seront les entreprin-	The conspirators fourteen of a sep-
ses.	arate body,
	By the Red One, the enterprise
	shall be undertaken.

Reference is made here to the assassinations of Nicholas and Alexandra with their royal children and fourteen retainers by the Reds.

8

Combien de fois prinse cite solaire,	How often taken, O city of the Sun
Seras, changeant les loix barbares &	shall thou be?
vaines,	Changing thy vain and barbarous
Ton mal s'approche, plus seras tribu-	laws,
taire,	Thy Evil groweth nigh, Thou shalt
Le grand Adrie recouvrira tes veines.	be more tributary,
	The great Venice shall recover thy
	veins.

Heliopolis, or Baalbec, an ancient city in Syria near Damascus, famous for its ruins, is used symbolically by Nostradamus to indicate the growing evil in the world.

9

De l'Orient viendra le coeur punique,	From the East of Africa shall come the Lion-Heart,
Fascher Adrie, & les hoirs Romulides,	To vex Venice and the heirs of Romulus,
Accompagne de la classe Libique	Accompanied by the Libian Tribe,
Trembler Melites, & proches Iles vuides.	Malta shall tremble and the neighboring islands shall be empty.

A remarkably prophetic description of the role of Emperor Haile Selassie, in World War II, who reconquered Ethiopia, in East Africa, and sent an expedition to aid the Allied Cause, eventually defeating the Fascists of Italy, self-styled 'Heirs of Romulus.'

10

Sergens transmis dans la Cage de Fer,	Sergeants sent into the Cage of Iron,
Ou les enfans septains du Roy sont pris,	Where the seven children of the King are,
Les vieux & peres sortiront bas d'enfer,	The old men and fathers shall see the death and cries of their first fruit,
Ains mourir voir de son fruit mort & cris.	And before they die, shall go through Hell.

A description of the incidents that came to pass during the 'Reign of Terror' in the French Revolution. The daily roll calls of those proscribed for the guillotine are graphically portrayed.

11

Le mouvement de sens, coeur, pieds, & mains,	Naples, Spain and Sicily shall agree To the movement with heart, feet, hands and sense,
Seront d'accord, Naples, Leon, Sicile,	Swords, Fires, Water, then to the Noble Romans,
Glaives, Feux, Eaux, puis au Noble Romains,	Plunged into death by a weak brain.
Plongez, Tuez, Morts, par cerveau debile.	

The active cooperation of Fascist Italy and Falangist Spain is foretold, predicting dire results to both Mussolini and his cohorts.

12

Dans peu ira fauce brute fragile,	In a little while a treacherous brute
De bas en haut ensleve promptement,	shall be raised,
Puis en estant desloyal & labile,	Quickly from a low to high estate,
Qui de Verone aura gouvernment.	Unfaithfully and swiftly,
	He shall have the government of Italy.

A continuation of the previous quatrain, this depicts the rise of Mussolini from an insignificant rabble rouser to Duce, or Leader of the Italian State.

13

Les exiles, par ire, haine intestine,	The exiles, by anger, shall spread
Feront au Roy grand conjuration,	internal strife,
Secret mettront ennemis par la mine,	And make against the King a great
Et les vieux siens, contre eux sedition.	conspiracy,
	Secret enemies shall they put in the mine,
	And raise the old ones against them by sedition.

The progress of the Italian conspiracy is indicated – the rise of a fifth column rife with internal dissensions, culminating with a plot against King Victor Emmanuel.

14

De gens esclave, chansons, chants, & requestes,	Being kept prisoners, by Princes and Lords,
Captifs par Princes, & Seigneurs aux prisons,	The slavish people petition for songs and books,
A l'aduenir idiots sans testes,	For the future, idiots without heads
Seront receus par divins oraisons.	Shall be received by divine prayers.

The forecast of a revolution in Russia. The Russian, or Slavonic, people, held in subjection by their rulers, will seek enlightenment and surcease from oppression.

15

Mars nous menace par la force beli-que,	Mars threatens us with a warlike force,
Septante fois fera le sang respandre,	Seventy times he shall cause blood to be shed,
Auge & ruine de l'Ecclesiastique,	Causing the ruin of the Clergy
Et par ceux qui d'eux rien ne voudront entendre.	And those who will hear nothing from them.

The Damoclean Sword of War shall hang over Humanity for a period of Seventy Great Wars, eventually causing a debacle among the heedless mortals as well as the Church.

16

Faux a l'Estang, joints vers la Sagit-taire,	When a fish pond that was a meadow shall be mowed,
En son haut auge de l'exaltation,	Sagittarius being in the ascendant,
Peste, Famine, Mort de main mili-taire,	Plague, Famine, Death by the military hand,
Le Siecle approcher de renovation.	The Century approaches renewal.

In 1999, as the old century is about to expire, between November 23rd and December 21st, the climactic War of Wars shall be unleashed.

17

Par quarante ans l'Iris n'apparoistra,	For forty years the rainbow shall not appear,
Par quarante ans tous les jours sera veu,	For forty years it shall be seen every day.
La Terre aride en siccite croistra,	The parched earth shall wax drier and drier,
Et grand deluge quand sera apparceu.	And a great flood when it shall appear.

A continuation of the preceding stanza – the prediction depicts conditions during the Armageddon and forecasts the wasteland produced by nuclear warfare and ultimate destruction.

18

Par la discorde, negligence Gauloise,
Sera passage a Mahomet ouvert,
De sang trempe la terre & mer Sen-
oise,
Le Port Phocen de voiles & nefs
couvert.

Through the discord and negligence of the French,
A passage shall be opened to Mahomet,
The land and sea of Italy shall be
bloody,
And the harbour of Marseilles shall
be covered with sails and ships.

The Arab Mohammedan Confederacy, dominated by the Mohammedan Church, shall find an entering wedge into geopolitics largely through French aid. There was the Moslem revolution in Iran in 1980, the construction of the nuclear reactor in Iraq, with French aid, in 1981, and its eventual destruction by the Israeli Air Force. Aggravation of the Middle East strife will bring warfare between the Moslems and non-Moslems of the world.

19

Lors que serpens viendront circuir
l'air,
Le sang Troien verse par les Espag-
nes,
Par eux; grand nombre en sera fait
tare,
Chef fuit, cache aux marets dans les
saignes.

When the serpents shall come to
encompass the air,
The French blood shall be angered
by Spain,
By them, a great number shall
perish,
The chief flies, and hides in the
rushes of the marshes.

At the beginning of World War II, the air superiority of the Nazis was clearly demonstrated much to the chagrin of the French, who, threatened by Spain, were forced to maintain a strong force at their border. Eventually, the French President and his entourage were forced to fly from Paris.

20

Tours, Orleans, Blois, Angers,
Reimes & Nantes,
Cites vexees par soudain changement,
Par langues estranges seront tendues
tentes,
Fleuves, Darts, Rennes, Terre & Mer
tremblement.

Tours, Orleans, Blois, Angers,
Rheims and Nantes,
Cities vexed by sudden change,
By strange languages tents shall be
set up,
Rivers, Darts, Rennes, Land and
Sea shall tremble.

The German invasion continues, and the above-named cities are quickly changed over to Nazi rule. The strange German language becomes the official speech, and the rest of France trembles under bombardment from the air.

21

Profonde argile blanche nourrit rocher,
Qui d'un abysme istra l'acticineuse,
En vain troublez ne l'seront toucher,
Ignorant estre au fond terre argileuse.

A deep white clay a rock supports,
Which shall break out of the deep like milk,
In vain people shall be troubled, not daring to touch it,
Being ignorant that in the bottom there is a milky clay.

A prediction of a new and as yet undiscovered method of utilization of Nature's resources, producing powerful actinic properties, and also the mining of radioactive elements, and the development of water pollution by industrial waste disposal.

22

Ce qui vivra & n'aura aucen sens,
Viendra le fer a mort son artifice,
Autun, Chalons, Langres, & les deux Sens,
La guerre & la glasse fera grand malefice.

That which shall live shall leave no direction,
Its destruction and death will come by stratagem,
Autun, Chalons, Langres, and from both sides,
The war and ice shall do great harm.

A forecast of the use of supersonic weapons, travelling in the near absolute zero temperature above the stratosphere, i.e., satellites armed with nuclear warheads.

23

Au mois troisiesme se levant le Soleil,
Sanglier, Leopard, aux champs Mars pour combatre,
Leopard lasse au Ciel esttena son oeil,
Un Aigle autour du Soleil voit ses-batre.

In the third month at the rising of the sun,
The Wild Boar and Leopard in the fields of Mars battle,
The Leopard weary, lifts his eyes to Heaven
And seeth an eagle playing about the Sun.

The English *Lion*, or *Leopard*, doggedly holds off the German *Boar*, as the American Eagle gains altitude for his fateful swoop.

24

A Cite Neuve pensif pour condamner,	In the New City, to condemn an idea,
Loisel de Proie au ciel se vient offrir,	
Apres Victoire a captifs pardonner	The Bird of Prey shall offer himself to the sky,
Cremone & Mantoue grands maux auront ouffert.	After Victory the prisoners shall be forgiven,
	After Cremona and Mantua have suffered much.

After many cities have received severe damage, and victory is achieved, a trial shall be held in New City (Nu-Rem-Burg). Most of the prisoners shall be given light sentences.

25

Perdu, trouve cache de si long siecle	Lost, found again, hidden so great a while,
Sera Pasteur demy-Dieu honore,	
Ains que la Lune acheve son grand Siecle,	A Pasteur as Demi-God shall be honoured,
Par autre vents fera dishonore.	But before the moon her great cycle ends,
	By other ancient ones shall be dishonoured.

Louis Pasteur, the great French physician, is shown here to be worshipped almost as a demi-god for his discoveries, until a resurgence of an older school.

26

Le grande du Fondre tomb d'heure diurne,	The great man falleth by lightning in the day,
Mal & predit par porteur populaire,	An evil foretold by the postulant one,
Suivant presage tombe d'heure nocturne,	According to the forecast, another falls in hours of the night,
Conflict Reims, Londres, Etrusque, Pestifere.	A conflict at Rheims and London, and a plague in Tuscany.

The taking over of Czechoslovakia by Hitler, the resignation of President Benes, the dissensions over the matter between France and England, and the dire warning of the consequences of this betrayal, are all remarkably outlined in this prophecy.

27

Des soubs le chesne Guyen du ciel frappe,	Underneath the cord, Guien struck from the sky,
Non loin de la est cache le thresor,	Near where is hid a great treasure,
Qui par long siecles avoir este grappe,	Which has been many years a-gathering,
Trouve mourra, l'oeil creve de ressor.	Being found, he shall die, the eye put out by a spring.

Paratroopers alight near the Nazis' plunder hoard and, captured, they are executed.

28

La Tour de Bouk craindra fuste barbare,	The Tower of Bouk shall be in awe of barbarous musty odour,
Un temps, long temps apres barque Hesperique,	For a while, and a long time after afraid of Spanish craft,
Bestial, gens, meubles tous deux feront grand tare,	Cattle, people and goods, both shall receive a great damage,
Taurus & Libra quelle mortelle pique.	Taurus and Libra, oh, what a deadly feud!

The Tower of Bouk is a fortified place at the mouth of the Rhone. It shall be attacked by gas, discharged from craft flying the Spanish flag sometime in April or October.

29

Quand le poisson, terreste & aquatique,	When the fish, that is both terrestrial and aquatic,
Par forte vague au gravier sera mis,	By a strong wave shall be cast upon the shore,
Sa forme estrange suave & horrifique,	With his strange, fearful, horrid form,
Par mer aux murs bien tost enemies.	Soon after the enemy shall come to the walls by the sea.

A clear account of the D-Day Invasion of the Normandy beaches, with an exact description of the amphibious tanks and ducks employed by the Allies.

30

La Nef estrange par le tourment Marin,	The strange ship by the Sea's torment,
Abordera pres le port incognu,	Shall come near the unknown port,
Nonobstant signs due remeau palme-in.	Notwithstanding the signs given to it of the bows and palms,
Apres mort, pille, bon advis tard venu.	It shall die, be plundered, a good advice come too late.

A prophetic description of France in the days preceding the War, when the Ship of State was sabotaged and plundered by avaricious, selfish, factional disputes.

31

Tant d'ans les guerras, en Gaule dureont,	So many years the wars shall last in France,
Outre la course du Castulon Monarque,	Beyond the course of the Castilian monarch,
Victoire incerte trois grands couroneront,	An uncertain victory three great ones shall crown
Aigle, Coq, Lune, Lion Soleil en Marque.	The Eagle, the Cock, the Moon, the Lion leaving the sun in its mark.

At the conclusion of the war, an insecure truce is declared between the victors – United States, France, China, and England – all of whom will exact a penalty from the Land of the Rising Sun, or Japan.

32

La grand Empire sera tost translate,	The great Empire shall soon be translated
En lieu petit qui bien tost viendra coistre,	Which shall grow soon into an inferior place of small account,
Lieu bien infime d'exigue comte,	In the middle of which he shall come,
Ou au milieu viendra poser son scepter.	To lay down his sceptre.

A continuation of the previous stanza. Great Japan will degenerate into a minor power, with the Emperor abdicating the throne.

33

Pres d'un grand pont de plaine spa-cieuse,	At a great bridge, near a spacious plain,
Le grand Lion par force, Cesarees,	The great Lion, by Caesarous forces,
Fera abatre hors cite, rigoureuse,	Shall come to be pulled down before the rigorous city,
Par effroy portes luy seront reserrees.	The gates which shall be shut to him.

Winston Churchill will re-enter English politics to save the Tory Party from Labour, but, by a coalition, shall be defeated.

34

L'oiseau de proye volant a la fenestre,	The bird of prey flying to the window,
Avant conflict, fait au Francois parure,	Before battle shall appear to the French,
L'un bon prendra, l'autre ambigue sinistre,	One shall take good omen of it, the other, an ambiguous one,
La partie foible tiendra pour bonne augure.	The weaker party shall hold it a good sign.

A foreign Demagogue will cause intrigue by dividing the various parties, and the faction weakest in numbers will be spurred to action.

35

Le Lion jeune le vieux surmontera,	The young Lion shall overcome the old one
En champ bellique par singulier duelle,	In martial field by a single duel,
Dans cage d'or loeil il lui crevera,	In a golden cage he shall put out his eye.
Deux plays une puis mourir mort cruelle.	Two wounds from one, then he shall die a cruel death.

One of the most famous of Nostradamus's prophecies: – The Young Lion, a Scottish Knight, in a tournament with King Henry II, the Old Lion, accidentally pierced his golden helmet with a splinter of his wooden lance, putting out his eye and penetrating his brain, causing the King to die 'a cruel death.'

36

Tard le Monarque se viendra repentir.
De navoir mis a mort son adversaire,
Mais viendra bien a plus haut consen-
  tir,
Que tout son sang par mort fera def-
  faire.

The Monarch shall repent too late,
That he has not put his adversary to
  death,
But he shall give his consent to a
  greater thing than that,
Which is, to kill all his adversary's
  kindred.

Toussaint L'Ouverture, the great leader of the blacks of Haiti, and his connection with Napoleon I, is here foreseen. Despite his fight on the side of the French, L'Ouverture was eventually deposed as Governor of Haiti by Napoleon, and brought to France where he died in prison.

37

Un peu devant que le Soleil sabaconse
Conflict donne, grand peuple du-
  bieux,
Profligez, port-marin ne fait responce,
Pont & sepulchre en deux estranges
  lieux.

A little before the sun sets,
A battle shall be given, a great
  people shall be doubtful,
Of being foiled, the sea port makes
  no answer,
A bridge and sepulchre shall be in
  two strange places.

One of the numerous prophecies that refer to the events in the great Armageddon.

38

Le sol & l'aigle victeur paroisstront,
Response vain au vaincu lon asseure,
Par Cor ne cris, harnois n'arresteront,
Vindicte paix, par mort lacheve a
  l'heure.

The sun and eagle shall appear to
  be victorious,
A vain answer shall be made good
  to the vanquished,
By no means, arms shall not be
  stopped,
Peace, prosecuted by death, it shall
  be achieved.

A movement shall arise for the suppression of armament and wars. War in itself will become so terrible that nations will achieve peace through fear of Universal Death.

39

De nuit le lit le supresme estrange,	By night, in the bed, the chief one shall be strangled,
Pour avoir trop suborne blonde esleu,	For having corrupted too much the fair elect,
Partrois l'Empire subroge exancle,	By three the Empire subrogate ex- ancle,
A mort metra, carte ne pacquet leu.	He, devoted to death, reading neither card nor packet.

The author purposely obscured this prophecy in the third line, because the persons concerned were then alive, viz. King Philip II of Spain, who caused his only son, Don Carlos, to be strangled in bed, for suspicion of being intimate with his wife, Elizabeth of France and daughter of Henry II.

40

La tourbe fausse dissimilant folie	The false troupe dissembling their folly,
Fera Bizance un changement de loix,	Shall make in Constantinople, a change of laws,
Istra d'Egypt qui veus que l'on deslie,	One shall come out of Egypt who will have untied the edict,
Edict, changant monnoys & alloys.	Changing the money and the stan- dards.

At a convention held in the Near East, the Nations will attempt to draw up an economic and financial formula for the free flow of world trade. Note the OPEC (Organization of Petroleum Exporting Countries) meetings and their regulation of oil prices and consequent alteration of the flow and value of money throughout the world.

41

Siege a cite & de nuit assaille,	A siege laid to a city, and assaulted by night,
Peu eschapez non loing de Mer con-flict,	A few shall escape to fight not far from the sea,
Femme de joys, retour fils, de faillie	A woman swoons for joy to see her son returned,
Poison & lettres cache dedans le plic.	A poison hidden in the fold of letters.

The siege of Leningrad brought starvation and death. A few escaped to the Baltic Sea and Finland. 'Woman' is Mother Russia. 'Son' is victorious Stalin, who later became a 'poison' to Russia and was subsequently downgraded.

42

Les dix Calendes d'Avril de fait Gothique,	The tenth of the Calends of April, Gothic account,
Rescuscite encor par gens malins,	Raised up again by malicious persons,
Le feu estaint, assemblee diabolique,	The light put out, a diabolical assembly,
Cherchand les os de d'amant & Psellin.	Seek for the bones of the lovers and Psellus.

An account of a witches' assembly, on the twenty-third of April, old style – evil persons assemble and various diabolical acts are performed in the dark, all according to Psellus, a famed Byzantine writer on Black Magic.

43

Avant qu'avien le changement d'Empire,	Before the change of Empire comes,
Ill adviendra un cas bien merveilleux,	There shall be a strange accident,
Le champ mue, le pilier de Porphyre,	A field shall be changed, and a pillar of Porphyry
Mis, translate sur le Rocher Noileux.	Shall be transported upon the chalky cliffs.

England will change its course of Empire, when upon the chalky cliffs of Dover, shall appear a pillar, or adherent, of Porphyry (a famous anti-Christian philosopher of ancient Rome, A.D. 233–305).

44

En bref seront de retour sacrifices,	In a short time sacrifices shall return again,
Contrevenans seront mis a martyre,	Opposers shall be put to martyrdom,
Plus ne seront moins, abbez ne novices,	There shall be no more monks, abbots, nor novices,
Le miel sera beaucoup plus cher que cire.	Honey shall be dearer than wax.

A period of persecution against the Catholic Church is foretold, when Protestants will forbid the use of wax candles in the Catholic ritual.

45

Secteur de Sectes, grand paine au delateur,	Followers of Sects, great pains to the informer,
Beste en theatre, dresse le jeu scenique,	A beast on the stage prepares the scenes,
Du fait antique ennobly l'inventeur,	The inventor of that iniquitous fact shall be famous,
Par sectes, monde confus & schismatique.	By sects the world shall be confused and schismatic.

Nostradamus, a confirmed Catholic, and a believer in the infallibility of the Church, releases a blast of condemnation at Martin Luther, whose appearance divided the Christian World into innumerable Sects.

46

Tout aupres d'Auch, de Lectoure & Mirande,	Near Auch, Lectoure and Mirande,
Grande feu du ciel en trois nuits tombera,	A great fire shall from the sky for three nights fall,
Chose adviendra bien stupende & mirande,	A thing shall happen stupendous and wonderful,
Bien peu apres al terre tremblera.	And shortly after the ground shall quake.

The forecast is of an extra-terrestrial sighting and landing with subsequent benefits to earth people.

47

Du Lac Lemans les sermons fascheront,	The sermons of the Leman Lake shall be troublesome,
Des jours seront reduit par des sepmains,	Some of the days shall be extended to weeks,
Puis mois, puis an, puis tous dafalliront,	Then into months, then into years, when they shall fail,
Les Magistrats damneront leurs Loix vaines.	The magistrates shall condemn their own inept laws.

Lake Leman is the ancient name for Geneva. Here is clearly foretold the efforts and final failure of the League of Nations.

48

Vingt ans du regne de la lune passez,	Twenty years of the reign of the moon having passed,
Sept mil ans autre tiendra sa monarchie,	Seven thousand years another shall hold his monarchy,
Quand le soleil prendra ses jours laissez,	When the sun shall resume his days past,
Lors accomplit a fine ma Prophecie.	Then is fulfilled and ends my prophecy.

The end of the world is here explicitly prophesied by Nostradamus. In the year 7000 the Sun will destroy the Earth and again resume its undisputed sway.

49

Beaucoup, beaucoup avant telles menees,	Much, very much before these doings happen,
Ceux d'Orient par la vertu Lunaire,	Those of the East by virtue of the Moon,
L'An mil sept cens feront grands emmenees,	In the year 1700, shall carry away great multitudes,
Subjugant presque le coin Aquilonaire.	And shall subdue almost the whole northern section.

In the year 2025, by ritual, China, having completed her industrial and economic expansions, will absorb almost the whole of Northern Russia and Scandinavia.

50

De l'aquatique triplicite naistra,	From the aquatic triplicity shall be born,
Un qui fera Jeudy pour sa feste,	One who shall make Thursday his holiday,
Son bruit, loz, regne & puissance croistra,	His fame, praise, rule, and power shall grow,
Par Terre & Mer, aux Orients tempeste.	By Land and Sea to become a tempest to the east.

Nostradamus predicts the origin of the United States 200 years before it existed. The 'aquatic triplicity' refers to the Atlantic, the Pacific, and the Gulf of Mexico. Also the national holiday of Thanksgiving, always on Thursday (Thor), is noted.

51

Chef d'Aries, Jupiter and Saturn,
Dieu Eternal quelles mutations!
Puis apres long siecle son malin temps
*   retourne,*
Gaule & Italy quelles emotions!

Heads of Aries, Jupiter and Saturn,
O Eternal God, What changes there
   shall be!
After an era his evil time returns,
Gaule and Italy, what commotion!

A period of unrest in Italy shall culminate in the intervention of the French and a complete change in the social order.

52

Les deux malin de Scorpion conjoint,
Le Grand Seigneur meurtry dedans sa
*   salle,*
Peste a l'Eglise par le nouveau Roy
*   jonts,*
L'Europe basse & Septentrioanle.

The two evils of Scorpion being
   joined,
The Grand Seignior murdered in
   his hall,
Plague to the Church by a King
   joined to it,
Europe in the depths and dismem-
   bered.

The Church, as well as all Europe, is to be cut up by one born a member of the Catholic Church.

53

Las qu'on verra grand peuple tour-
*   mente,*
Et la Loy Saincte en totale ruyne,
Par autres loix toute la Chrestiente,
Quand d'or, d'argent trouve nouvelle
*   mine.*

Alas, how a great people shall be
   tormented
And the Holy Laws in total ruin,
By other laws, all Christianity
   troubled,
When new mines of gold and silver
   will be found.

The industrial revolution, the discovery of gold mines in Africa, Australia, etc., the rise of the God of Mammon, shall bring grief to all of Christendom.

54

Deux revolts faits du malin falcigere	Two revolts shall be made by the evil torch bearer,
De regne & siecles fait permutation	Which shall make a change of the reign and age,
Le mobil signe en son endroit s'ingere,	The mobile sign to right shall meddle,
Aux deux esgaux & d'inclination.	And shall have an inclination to the two equals.

The evil genius of the age shall instigate two revolts, in the name of enlightenment; the Swastika shall make concessions to the right and to both leaders.

55

Soubz l'opposite climat Babylonique,	In the climate opposite to the Babylonian,
Grands sera de sang effusion,	There shall be a great effusion of blood,
Que terre & mer, air, ciel sera inique,	So that the land and sea, air and heaven shall seem unjust,
Sectes, faim, regnes, pestes, confusion.	Sects and famine shall rule over plague and confusion.

Cataclysmic destruction, with great loss of life, is promised to the land of the Pacific, far in the East (the antipodes of the Near East or Babylonia).

56

Vous verrez tost & tard faire grand change	Sooner or later, you shall see great changes,
Horreurs extresmes & vindications,	Extreme horrors and persecutions,
Que si la lune conduite par son ange,	The moon led by her angel,
Le ciel s'approche des inclinations.	The heaven draws near its inclination.

This quatrain reflects, as do so many of Nostradamus's prophecies, his repeated prophetical conviction of the great changes to take place in the future, most of which will lead to strife among humans and the ultimate destruction of the Earth.

57

Par grand discord la trombe tremblera,	By great discord, the trumpet shall vibrate,
Accord rompu, dressant la teste au ciel,	Agreement broken, lifting the head to heaven,
Bouche sanglante dans le sang nagera,	A bloody mouth shall swim in blood,
Au sol sa face oingte de laict & miel.	The face turned to the sun anointed with milk and honey.

A clear and forthright prediction. Japan will treacherously break her agreement with the United States and, plunging into the bloody war, she will embark on her East Asia Co-Prosperity scheme, promising a future land of milk and honey to her cohorts.

58

Trenche le ventre, naistra avec deux testes	Slit in the belly, it shall be born with two heads,
Et quatre bras, quelques ans entiers viura,	And four arms, and shall live a few years,
Jour qui Aquilare celebrera ses festes,	The day that Aquila shall celebrate his feasts,
Foussan, Thurin, chef Ferrare suyura.	Fossan, Turin, the chief of Ferrara shall run away.

A monstrous thing shall be brought into being, but shall not exist long. When Aquila (a Jewish Proselyte who literally translated the Hebrew Scriptures into Greek) celebrates his feast, the Italians shall have much sorrow.

59

Les exilez deportez dans les Isles,	The exiles that were carried into the Isles,
Au changement d'un plus cruel Monarque,	At the whim of a most cruel monarch,
Seront meurtris, & mis deux des scintilles	Shall be murdered, and put in the sparks of fire,
Qui de parler ne seront este parques.	Because they had not been sparing of their tongues.

Hitler's wholesale extermination of the Jews and Poles, followed by the infamous cremation of their bodies, is indicated in this quatrain.

60

Un Empereur naistra pres d'Italie,	An Emperor shall be born in Italy.
Qui a l'Empire sera vendu bien cher,	Who shall cost the Empire dear,
Diront avec quels gens il se ralie	They shall say, with what peoples
Qu'on trouvera moins Prince que	he keeps company!
boucher.	He shall be found less a Prince than a butcher.

A presage of the coming of Napoleon, born in Corsica (then an Italian possession), and the subsequent wars and destruction he will bring to Europe.

61

La republique miserable infelice,	The miserable and unhappy republic
Sera vastee du nouveau Magistrat,	Shall be wasted by the new Magistrate,
Leur grand amas de l'exil malefice,	Their great number of broken refugees,
Fera Sueve ravir leur grand contract.	Shall cause Sweden to break her contract.

This refers to the dissipation of the resources of France, and the repudiation by Sweden of her treaty with France in favour of a Russian alliance, on December 3, 1804.

62

La grande perte las! que feront les lettres	Alas, what a great loss shall learning suffer
Avant le cicle de laton a parfaict,	Before the cycle of the moon is accomplished,
Feu, grand deluge, plus par ignares sceptres	By fire, great flood, and ignorant sceptres,
Que de long siecle ne se verra refaict.	More than can be made good again in a long age.

The cycle of the moon shall end when, on the last cataclysmic day, it shall fall on the earth; until then much misery shall happen due to the ignorance of men.

63

Les fleaux passees diminue le monde,
Long-temps la paix, terres inhabitees,
Seur marchera par le ceil, terre, mer
& Onde,
Puis de nouveau les guerres suscitees.

The scourge being past, the world
shall be made smaller,
Peace for a long time, lands in-
habited,
Everyone safe shall go by air, land
and sea,
And then the wars shall begin
anew.

In the period after the great influenza epidemic, that followed World War I, great progress was made in air travel, etc.; then after a brief time, World War was renewed.

64

De nuict soleil penseront avoir veu,
Quand le porceau demy homme on
verra,
Bruit, chant, bataille au Ciel battre
apperceu
Et bestes brutes a parler on orra.

They shall think to have seen the
sun in the night,
When the hog half a man shall be
seen,
Noise, singing, battles in the sky
shall be perceived,
And brute beasts shall be heard to
speak.

This presages modern mechanized warfare: searchlights, baby tanks, whistling bombs, dog fights in the air, and radio equipment.

65

Enfant sans mains, jamais veu si
grand foudre
L'enfant Royal au jeu d'esteuf blesse,
Au puy brisez, fulgures allant
moudre,
Trois sur le chaines par le milieu
trousse.

A child without hands, lightning
never so great was seen,
The Royal child, wounded at the
tennis court,
Bruised at the well, lightning going
to the ground,
Three in the midst of the field shall
be struck thereby.

An allegorical attempt to show that when the 'Oath of the Tennis Court' was taken by the French Revolutionists, the *Royal Three* were irretrievably struck down, viz. Louis XVI, Marie Antoinette, and the Dauphin.

66

Celuy qui lors portera les nouvelles,	He that then shall carry the news,
Apres un peu il viendra respirer,	A little while after shall draw his
Vivers, Tournon, Montferrant &	breath,
Pradelles,	Viviers, Tournon, Montserrant,
Gresle & tempeste, les fera souspirer.	and Pradelles,
	Hail and storm shall make them
	sigh.

A continuation of the preceding quatrain – the mounting storm of the Revolution rolls over all France.

67

La grand famine que je sens approcher,	The great famine do I see drawing near,
Souvent tourner puis estre universelle,	Turning from one way to another
Si grande & longue qu'on viendra arracher,	and then becoming universal,
Du bois racine, & l'enfant de mamelle.	So great and long, that they shall come to pluck
	The root from the wood and the child from the breast.

Famine and drought are very prominent in the late twentieth century in Europe, India, and Africa.

68

O quel horrible & malheureux tourment!	O what a horrid and sad torment
Trois innocens qu'on viendra a livrer,	Shall be put to three innocents,
Poison suspecte, mal garde tradiment	Poison shall be suspected, evil
Mis en horreur par bourreaux enyvrez.	guards shall betray them.
	They shall be put to horror by
	drunken executioners.

Three innocent persons shall be suspected of a poison plot, and they shall be tortured and put to death by drunken executioners.

69

La grand montagne ronde de sept estades,	The great mountain encompasses seven stadia,
Apres paix, guerre, faim, inondation,	After peace, war, famine, and inundation,
Roulera loing, abysmant grand contades,	Shall tumble a great way, sinking great countries,
Mesmes antiques, & grand fondation.	Even ancient houses and their great foundations.

Great institutions, after surviving the vicissitudes of war, etc., shall go down, carrying with them the long established order and the ruling castes.

70

Pluys, faim, guerre, en Perse non cessee,	Rain, famine, war in Persia having not ceased,
La foy trop grande trahira le Monarque,	Too great credulity shall betray the Monarch,
Par la finie en Gaule commencee,	Being ended there, it shall commence in France,
Secret augure pour a un estre parque.	A secret omen to one that he shall die.

The weak, vacillating policy of Louis XVI, and his too great faith in advisers, bring France to the brink of disaster, and an unheeded omen to the King himself.

71

La tour marins trois fois prinse & reprinse	The sea tower three times taken and retaken,
Par Espagnols, Barbares, Ligurins,	By Spaniards, Barbarians, and Italians,
Marseille & Aix, Arles par ceux de Pise	Marseilles, and Aix, Arles by those of Pisa,
Vast, feu, fer, pille, Avignon des Thurins.	Waste, fire, iron, pillage, Avignon by Piedmont.

Confirmation of Quatrain 28, Century One – wherein France is attacked by the Axis.

72

Du tout Marseille des habitans changee	Marseilles shall wholly change her inhabitants,
Course & pour fuitte jusques pres de Lyon,	These shall run and be pursued as far as Lyons,
Narbon, Tholose par Bordeaux outragee,	Narbonne, Toulouse shall wrong Bordeaux,
Tuez, captifs, presque d'un million.	Killed and prisoners shall be almost a million.

The Vichy Regime of Marshal Pétain occupied the territory of Toulouse, Lyons, and Narbonne. German troops entered Paris (June 14, 1940) and the government fled to Bordeaux.

73

France a cinq parts par neglect assaillie	France by neglect shall be assaulted by five sides,
Tunys, Argiels esmeuz par Persiens,	Tunis and Algiers shall be stirred by the Persians,
Leon, Seville, Barcelone faillie	Leon, Seville, Barcelona shall be missed,
N'aura la classe par les Venitiens.	And not be pursued by the Venetians.

By the pettiness of her political parties, France will be invaded, and in French Africa the Italians will cause unrest, while the cities of Spain remain untouched.

74

Apres sejourne vogueront en Epire	After a stay, they shall sail toward Epirus,
Le grand secours viendra vers Antioche,	The great aids shall come towards Antioch,
Le noir poil crespe tendra fort a l'Empire,	The black hair curled, shall aim much to the Empire,
Barbe d'airain le rostira en broche.	The brazen beard shall be roasted on a spit.

An Axis expedition will be sent to Epirus (Greece) and the Mediterranean. Mussolini, the Black One, will aim at expansion of the Italian Empire.

75

Le tyran Sienne occupera Savone,
Le fort gaigne tiendra classe marine,
Les deux armees par la marque d'An-
  cone
Par effrayeur le chef s'en examine.

The tyrant of Sienna shall occupy
  Savone,
The fort being won, shall hold a
  fleet,
The two armies shall go by the way
  of Ancona,
Where by fear the chief shall be
  examined.

The tyrant of Italy shall occupy French Savoy, thereby tying up the
British fleet on the coast. Two Italian armies will proceed east, past
Ancona, on the Adriatic Sea. Marshal Balbo will be executed.

76

D'un nom farouche tel profere sera,
Que les trois soeurs auront fato le Nom
Puis grand peuple par langue & fait
  dira,
Plus que nul autre aura bruit &
  renom.

By a wild name one shall be called,
So that three sisters shall have the
  name of Fate
Afterwards a great people by
  tongue and deeds shall say,
He shall have fame and renown
  more than any other.

Nostradamus very definitely feels that a Messiah will come.

77

Entre deux mers dressera promontoire
Que puis mourra par le mords du
  cheval,
Le sien Neptune pliera voille noire,
Par Calpre & classe supres de Roche-
  val.

Between two seas shall a promontory be raised,
By him, who shall die by the biting
  of the horse,
The proud Neptune shall fold the
  black sail,
Through Calpre, and a fleet shall be
  near Rocheval.

In Greek legend, according to the history of Theseus, the Greeks, in
order to please the Minotaur, sent him a tribute of Athenian children in a
ship with black sails.

78

D'un chef vieillard naistra sens hebete,	An old head shall beget an idiot,
Degenerant par scavoir & par armes,	Who shall degenerate in learning and in arms,
Le chef de France par sa soeur redoute,	The head of France shall be feared by his sister,
Champs divisez, concedez aux gens L'armes.	The fields divided and granted to the people's army.

The long reign of Louis XV (1715–1774) yielded to his grandson, Louis XVI, who was weak, irresolute, and awkward. The oncoming French Revolution spurred the rise of power of the masses.

79

Bazax, Lectore, Condon, Ausch, Agine,	Bazax, Lectore, Condon, Auch, Agine,
Esmeus par loix, querelles & monopole,	Being moved by laws, quarrels and monopoly,
Car Bourd, Tholose, Bay mettra en ruyne,	They shall put to ruin Bordeaux, Toulouse, Bayonne,
Renouveller voulant leur tauropole.	Going about to renew their Tauropole.

The Northern industrial districts of France will try to exploit the agricultural regions.

80

De la sixiesme claire splendeur celeste,	From the sixth bright celestial splendour,
Viendra tonner si fort eu la Bourgongne,	Shall come very great lightning to Burgundy,
Puis naistra monstre de tres-hydeuse beste,	After which shall be born a monster of a most hideous beast,
Mars, Avril, May, Juin grand charpin & rongne.	In March, April, May and June shall be great quarrelling and muttering.

The sixth planet from the Sun, or Saturn, shall shed a clear light on horrific events to occur in the above-named months.

81

D'humain troupeau neuf seront mis a part;	Of the human flock, nine shall be set aside,
De jugement & conseil separees,	Being divided in judgment and counsel,
Leur sort sera divise en depart,	
Kappa, Theta, Lambda, morts, bannis, egarez.	Their destiny shall be to be divided,
	Kappa, Theta, Lambda, dead, banished, scattered.

The Supreme Court of the United States, consisting of nine members, is here indicated, as well as the Politburo of the USSR. More than once has death and dismissal involved both bodies.

82

Quand les colomnes de bois grande tremblee,	When the wooden columns shall be shaken
D'auster conduicte couverte de rubriche,	By the stern wind and covered by a ruby hue,
Tant vuidera dehors une grand assemblee,	Then shall go out a great assembly,
Trembler Vienne & le pays d'Austriche.	And Vienna and the land of Austria shall tremble.

In July of 1934 there was an uprising in Vienna, Austria, followed by the assassination of Chancellor Dolfuss. Anschluss followed with the annexation of Austria by Nazi Germany in 1938.

83

La gent estrange divisera butins	The alien agent shall divide booties,
Saturne & Mars son regard furieux,	Saturn and Mars shall have his aspect furious,
Horrible estrange aux Toscans & Latins,	Horrid and strange to the Tuscans and Latins,
Grec qui seront a frapper curieux.	The Grecians shall be curious to strike.

Extra-terrestrial aliens will land on earth and terrify southern Europe.

84

Lune obscur cie aux profondes tenebres,	The moon shall be obscured in the deepest darkness,
Son frere passe de couleur ferrigine;	Her brother shall pass being of a ferruginous colour;
Le grand cache long temps soubs les tenebres,	The great one long hidden under shadows,
Tiendra fer dans la pluie sanguine.	Shall make his iron lukewarm in the bloody rain.

At a time when vision is obscured, the Sun shall take on a tinge of red, or iron rust, and this will be the signal for the great one to rise and whet his sword.

85

Par la response de dame, roy trouble,	A king shall be troubled by the answer of a lady,
Ambassadeurs mespriseront leur vie,	Ambassadors shall despise their lives,
Les grand ses freres contrefera double,	The great one being undecided, shall counterfeit his brothers,
Par deux mourront ire, hain envie.	They shall die by two, anger, hatred, and envy.

Note the mid-twentieth-century abdication of Edward VIII caused by his love affair with Wallis Simpson. Nostradamus also makes his first reference to the assassinations of the Kennedy brothers.

86

Le grande Royne quand se verra vaincue	When the queen shall see herself vanquished,
Fera excez de masculin courage;	She shall do a deed of masculine courage,
Sur cheval fleuve passera toute nue,	Upon a horse, she shall pass over the river naked,
Suitte par fer, a foy fera outrage.	Followed by iron she shall do wrong to her faith.

Here is an early reference to the women's movement and their drive for equality with men.

87

Ennosigee, feu du centre de terre,	Ennosigee, fire of the centre of the earth,
Fera trembler autour de Cite Neufue;	Shall make an earthquake of the New City,
Deux grands rocher long temps ferot la guerre,	Two great rocks shall long time war against each other,
Puis Arethusa rougira nouveau Fleuve.	After that, Arethusa shall colour red the fresh river.

This is a truly shattering prediction. The two great rocks at war can only mean the East and West (the United States and the Soviet Union) and the earthquake and fire in the New City refers to a nuclear holocaust in New York (?) etc. (?). The 'cold war' shall become a hot one.

88

Le divin mal surprendra le grand Prince,	The divine sickness shall surprise a great prince,
Un peu devant aura femme espousee;	A little while after he hath married a woman,
Son puy & credit a un coup viendra mince,	His support and credit shall at once become slender,
Conseil mourra pour la teste rasee.	Council shall die for the shaven head.

Napoleon's desire to found an empire led to his marriage to Marie Louise, who bore him an heir. His quarrels with the Pope are also indicated here.

89

Tous ceux de Ilerde seront dedans Moselle	All those of l'Isle shall be in the Moselle,
Mettans a mort tous ceux de Loyre & Seine,	Putting to death all those of Loire and Seine,
Secours marin viendra pres d'haute velle,	The sea chase shall come near the high city
Quand l'Espagnol ouvrira toute viene.	When the Spaniard shall open all veins.

Quarrels and warfare among the provinces of France are here referred to.

90

Bordeaux, Poitiers, au son de la campane,	Bordeaux, Poitiers, at the sound of the bell,
A grand classe ira jusques a l'Angon,	With a great navy shall go as far as Langon,
Contre Gaulois sera leur tramontane,	Against the French shall their Tramontane be,
Quand monstre hideux naistra pres d'Orgon.	When a hideous monster shall be born near Orgon.

Tramontane, in Italian, is the North Wind; Orgon is a town in Gascony – An implication that France will be pitted against Northern adversaries and native quislings.

91

Les Dieux feront aux humains apparence,	The Gods shall make it appear to mankind,
Ce qu'ile seront autheurs de grand conflit,	That they are the authors of a great war,
Avant ciel veu serain, espee & lance,	The sky that was serene shall show sword and lance,
Que vers main gauche sera plus grand affliction.	On the left hand the affliction shall be greater.

World leaders of East and West move towards confrontation. Air combat and space warfare with leftist (Communist) destruction is predicted.

92

Sous un la paix par tout sera clemence	Under one shall be peace, and everywhere clemency,
Mais non long temps, pille & rebellion	But not for a long while, then shall be plundering and rebellion,
Par refus, ville, terre & mer entammee,	By a denial shall town, land and sea be assaulted,
Morts & captifs, le tiers d'un million.	Dead and taken prisoner shall be the third part of a million.

The sneak attack on Pearl Harbor, by the Japanese, ushered the United States into World War II, resulting in 350,000 American casualties.

93

Terre Italique pres des monts tremb-lera,	The Italian land of the mountains shall tremble,
Lyon & Coq, non trop confererez,	The Lion and the Cock shall not agree very well together,
En lieu de peur, l'un l'autre s'aidera,	And for fear shall help one another,
Seul Castulon & Celtes moderez.	Only Spain and the Celts shall be neutral.

The World War II alliance of France and England against Italy is here foreseen. Also note Spanish and Irish neutrality in WW II.

94

Au port Selin le tryan mis a mort	In the port, Selin the tyrant shall be put to death,
La liberte non pourtant recouvree	And yet, liberty shall not be recovered,
Le nouveau Mars par vindicte & remort,	The new War by vengeance and remorse begun,
Dame par force de frayeur honoree.	A lady by force of fear shall be honoured.

The victorious Prime Minister Margaret Thatcher was honoured after the British and Argentine war in the Falkland Islands in 1982.

95

Devant Moustier trouve enfant besson	Before the monastery shall one twin be found
D'heroicq sang de moyne vestutisque,	From heroic blood of a monk and ancient,
Son bruit par secte, langue & Puissance son,	His fame by sect, tongue and power shall be founded,
Qu'on dira soit efleue le Vospique.	So that they shall say, Vopisk is highly raised.

One of a pair of illegitimate twins, found deserted in a church, shall rise to great heights.

96

Celuy qu'aura la charge de destruire	He that shall be in charge to destroy
Temples & sectes changees par fanta-	Churches and sects changed by fan-
sie,	tasy,
Plus aux rochers qu'aux vivans vien-	Shall do more harm to the stones
dra nuyre,	than to the living,
Par langue ornee d'oreilles ressaisies.	By a smooth tongue filling up the
	ears.

One shall undertake a campaign to destroy the Churches, but will not succeed, due to the firmness of the faithful, more durable than stone.

97

Ce que fer, flamme, n'a sceu para-	What neither iron nor fire could
cheuer,	achieve,
La douce langue au conseil viendra	Shall be done by a smooth tongue
faire	in a council,
Par repos, songe, le roy fera resuer,	In sleep a dream shall make the
Plus l'ennemy en feu, sang militaire.	king to think,
	The more the enemy in fire and
	military blood.

The United Nations is the council predicted as a deterrent to war.

98

Le chef qu'aura conduit peuple infiny	The leader who shall lead an
Loing de son ciel, de moeurs & langue	infinite number of people,
estrange,	Far from their country to one of
Cinq mil en, Crete, & Thessale finy,	strange manners and language,
Le chef fuyant sauve en la marine	Five thousand in Candia and Thes-
grange.	saly finished,
	The leader escaping, shall be safe in
	a barn on the sea.

Nostradamus forecasts a Sino-Soviet conflict. Lines one and two are very clear on this, but which leader, Chinese or Soviet, shall escape in a submarine or capital ship cannot be determined.

99

Le Grand Monarque qui fera compag-
nie,
Avec deux Roys unis par amitie,
O quel souspir sera la grande mesnie,
Enfant Narbon a l'entour quel pitie.

Le Grand Monarque shall keep company,
With two kings united in friendship,
Oh what fights shall be made by their followers,
Children, O what a pity about Narbonne.

'Le Grand Monarque' is Napoleon as Emperor of France. He won the Italian campaign in 1796 and made the King of Sardinia sue for peace. Further, Napoleon's Egyptian campaign ended with his stealthy and secret return to France near Narbonne (Carcassonne).

100

Long temps au ciel veu gris oyseau,
Aupres de Dole & de Tosquane terre,
Tenant au bec un verdoyant rameau
Mourra tost grand, & finira la guerre.

For a long while shall be seen in the air a gray bird,
Near Dola and the Tuscan land,
Holding in his beak a green bough,
Then a great one shall die and the war be finished.

The role of Franklin D. Roosevelt is here clearly prophesied, indicating his untimely and tragic death just a few weeks before the close of the war in Europe.

CENTURY
II

1

Vers Aquitaine pars insuls Britanni-ques	Towards Gascony by English assaults
Et par aux mesmes grandes incursions	By the same shall be made great incursions,
Pluyes, gelees feront terroir iniques	Rains, frosts shall make the ground unrighteous
Port Selyn fortes fera invasions	Port Selyn shall make strong invasions.

The D-Day invasion of Europe in World War II by the Allied Expeditionary Forces took place in June, after winter frosts and spring rains.

2

La teste bleue fera la teste blanche,	The blue law shall do the white law
Autant de mal que France a fait leur bien,	As much harm, as France has done it good,
Mort a l'anthenne, grande pendu sur la branche	Dead on the antenna, a great one hanged on a branch,
Quand des prins siens le Roy dira combien.	When a king taken by his own shall say 'How much?'

Mussolini, radio silenced, was trapped and hanged on a tree in northern Italy at the end of World War II. A plebiscite abolished the monarchy in 1946.

3

Pour la chaleur solaire sur la mer
De Negrepont les poissons demy cuits,
Les habitans les viendront entemer
Quand Rhod & Gennes leur faudra le
biscuit.

By the heat of the sun upon the sea,
At Black Bridge, the fishes shall be
  half broiled,
The inhabitants shall come to cut
  them up,
When Rhodes and Genoa shall
  want biscuits.

Further volcanic eruptions are predicted along the Mediterranean coastline, viz., Vesuvius (1944), Aetna (1951), Stromboli (1951).

4

Depuis Monach jusqu'au pres de
Sicile,
Toute la plage demourra desolee
Il n'y aura faux-bourgs, cite, ne ville,
Que par Barbares, pille soit & vollee.

From Monaco as far as Sicily,
All the sea coast shall be left desolate,
There shall not be suburbs, cities
  nor towns,
Which shall not be pillaged and
  plundered by Barbarians.

The western Italian sea coast from Monaco to Sicily will be invaded and sacked by barbarians.

5

Quand dans poissin fer & lettre enfer-
mee
Hors sortira qui pis fera la guerre,
Aura par mer sa classe bien ramee,
Apparoissant pres de Latine terre.

When in an iron fish, a letter shall
  be shut up,
He shall go out, that shall afterwards make war,
He shall have his fleet by the sea
  well provided,
Appearing by the Roman Land.

In a submarine, one bearing an important letter and military secrets shall land and afterwards lead a nation to victory. Gen. Clark's daring feat – culminating in the North African campaign – is clearly foreshadowed.

6

Aupres des portes & dedans deux citez	Near the gates and within two cities,
Seront deux fleaux onc n'apperceu un tel,	Shall be two scourges, I never saw the like,
Faim dedans peste, de fer hors gens boutez,	Famine, within plague, people thrust out by the sword,
Crier secours au grand Dieu immortel.	Shall cry for help to the great God immortal.

Clearly predicts the Berlin Wall which divides the city in two. 'Two cities near the gate' (Brandenburg).

7

Entre plusieurs aux iles deportes	Among many that shall be transported into the islands,
L'un estre nay a deux dents en la gorge	One shall be born with two teeth in his mouth,
Mourront de faim, les arbres esbroutez.	They shall die of hunger, the trees shall be eaten,
Pour eux neuf Roy nouvel edict leur forge.	They shall have a new king, who shall make new laws for them.

As the British immigrated to Australia the aboriginal natives were downgraded by the government controlled by the British royal house.

8

Temples sacrez prime facon Romaine,	Temples consecrated and the early Roman way,
Rejetteront les goffes fondemens,	Shall reject the tottering foundations,
Prenant leurs loix premieres & humaines	Sticking to their first humane laws,
Chassant, non tout, des saincts les cultemens.	Expelling, but not altogether, the worshipping of saints.

The rise of the Reformation and split from the Catholic Church is here predicted; and the retaining in Protestant litany of only a few of the Saints.

9

Neuf ans le regne le maigre en paix tiendra	Nine years shall the lean one keep the kingdom in peace,
Puis il cherra en soif si sanguinaire	Then he will fall into such a bloody thirst,
Pour luy grand peuple sans foy & loy mourra,	That a great people shall die without faith or law,
Tue par un beaucoup plus debonaire.	He shall be killed by one much wilder than himself.

The references here point to the reign of Louis XVI – the short period of peace at the start of his kingship, the bloody and lawless revolution, and his eventual execution before the eyes of the roaring mobs of Paris.

10

Avant long temps le tout sera range	Before long, all shall be arranged,
Nous esperons un siecle bien senestre	We look for an era most sinister,
L'estat des masques & des seule bien change,	The state of the masks and they alone shall be changed,
Peu trouveront qu'a son rang vueille estre.	They shall find few that will keep their rank.

A continuation of the preceding prophecy, describing the chaotic conditions to prevail during the Revolution.

11

Le prochain, fils de l'asnier paruiendra	The eldest son of L'Aisnier shall prosper,
Tant esleve jusques au regne des forts	Being raised to the degree for the great ones,
Son aspre gloire un chacun la eraindra,	Everyone shall fear his high glory,
Mais ses enfans du regne jettez hors.	But his children shall be cast out.

This is the famous prediction Nostradamus sent to the Lord of L'Aisnier, who had written him to know of his children's future.

12

Yeux clos ouverts d'antique fantasie	Eyes shut, shall be opened by an
L'habit des seules seront mis a neant;	antique fancy,
Le grand monarque chastira leur fre-	The clothes of the solitary shall be
naisie,	brought to nothing,
Ravir des temples le thresor par	The great monarch shall punish
devant.	their frenzy,
	For having ravished the treasure of
	the temple before.

The Goddess of Justice, with blindfolded eyes, will be resurrected, and shall mete out punishment to the ravishers of the people and the temple.

13

Le corps sans ame plus n'estre en	The body without soul shall be no
sacrifice,	more admitted in sacrifice,
Jour de la mort mis en nativite,	The day of death placed on the
L'esprit divin fera l'ame felice	birthday,
Voyant le verbe en son eternite.	The divine spirit shall make the
	soul happy,
	By seeing the voice in its eternity.

Correctly predicts the change in the language of the Mass from Latin to the vernacular by authorization of the Second Vatican Council of 1964.

14

A Tours, Gien, garde gande seront	At Tours, Gienn, on guard shall be
yeux penetrans,	piercing eyes,
Descouvriront de loing la grand'	Who shall discover before long the
sireine,	great queen,
Elle & sa suitte au port seront entrans,	She and her suite shall enter into
Combats poussez, puissance souver-	the port,
aine.	By the fight shall be thrust out the
	reigning power.

Predicts the conflict in the Falkland Islands with Britain entering the port (Stanley) and the queen thwarting the Argentines.

15

Un peu devant monarque trucide,	A little before a monarch is killed,
Castor, Pollux, en nef, astre crainite,	Castor, Pollux, and a Comet in the
L'Arain public, par terre & mer	sky appears,
vuide,	The public Brass, by land and sea
Pise, Ast, Ferrare, Turin, terre inter-	shall be emptied,
dicte.	Pisa, Asti, Ferra, Turin shall be
	forbidden countries.

A time of unrest is prophesied – great disturbances in Castor and Pollux, the constellations of the Twins or Gemini. Before the assassination of Anwar Sadat, Israel and Egypt agreed to maintain peace and thus became the 'twins' of a Mideast accord. Sadat was murdered in a public appearance.

16

Naples, Palerme, Sicile, Syracuse,	Naples, Palermo, Sicily, Syracuse,
Nouveaux Tyrans, Fulgures, faex	New tyrants, Lightnings, Celestial
celestes,	Fires,
Force de Londres, Gand, Bruxelles &	An Army from London, Ghent,
Suise	Brussels,
Grand hecatombe, triomph, faire	And Switzerland, a sacrifice,
festes.	triumph and feasts.

Forecasts many World War II events, viz., the rise of Mussolini, the deployment of the A.E.F., the neutrality of Switzerland, the opening of a second front in Italy with the invasion in the south at Anzio, Naples, etc.

17

Le camp du temple de la vierge ves-	The camp of the temple of the
tale,	vestal virgin,
Non esloigne d'Ethene & monts	Not far from Ethene and the
Pyrenees;	Pyrenees Mountains,
Le grand conduit est cache dans la	The great passage is driven in the
male,	wall,
North, getez, fleuves, & vigues mas-	Rivers overflow in the North and
tinees.	the vines spoiled.

At Tivoli, the site of the antique temple of the Vestal Virgin, a great passage cuts through, and there will be a great flood.

18

Nouvelle pluie subite, impetueuse	A new rain, sudden, impetuous,
Empeschera subit deux excertites,	Shall suddenly hinder two armies,
Pierre, ciel, feux, faire la mer pierreuse	Stone, heaven, fire, shall make the sea strong,
La mort de sept, terre & marin subites.	The death of seven shall be sudden upon land and sea.

At the D-Day Invasion of the Normandy Coast, the rain of missiles fired from new type rocket guns was most intense, also concrete floating docks were sunk at the beaches to form breakwaters and rallying points for the attack.

19

Nouveaux venus, lieu basty sans defence	Newcomers shall build a place without a fence,
Occuper place par lors inhabitable,	And shall occupy a place that was not then habitable,
Prez, maisons, champs villes prendre a plaissance,	They shall at their pleasure take fields, houses and towns,
Faime, peste, guerre, arpent long labourable.	There shall be famine, plague, war, and a long arable field.

Continuing the preceding stanza, the allied invaders occupy the uninhabited fortified coast and advance successfully inward.

20

Freres & Soeurs en plusieurs lieux captifs,	Brothers and sisters shall be slaves in various places,
Se trouveront passer pres du Monarque	And shall pass before the monarch,
Les contempler ses Deux yeux ententifs,	Who shall look upon them with attentive eyes,
Des plaisant voir, meton, frond, nez les marques.	They shall go in heaviness, witness their chin, forehead and nose.

The brutal enslavement of entire populations by the Nazis is explicitly foreshadowed.

21

L'Ambassadeur envoye par Birmes,	The ambassador that was sent in
A my-chemin d'incogneus repoussez,	the small ship,
De Sel renfort viendront quatre	In the middle of the way, shall be
triremes,	repulsed by unknown men,
Cordes & chaines en Negrepont trous-	And from the salt, to his rescue
sez.	shall come four great ships,
	Ropes and chains shall be carried to
	the Black Bridge.

Rudolf Hess, personal aide to the German Fuehrer, flew solo to England to contact influential British leaders with his unofficial peace terms which were rejected in a closed session of Parliament.

22

Le Camp Ascop d'Europe partira,	The Camp Ascop shall go from
S'adioignant proche de l'isle sub-	Europe,
mergee,	And shall come near the submerged
D'Arton classe phalange pliera	Island,
Nombril du monde plus grand voix	From Arton shall a phalange go by
subrogee.	sea and land
	By the navel of the world, a greater
	voice shall be subrogated.

Apparently a reference to the submerged continent of Atlantis, originally the Navel, which nourished all ancient human culture.

23

Palais oyseaux, par oyseau dechasse,	Palace birds, driven away by a bird
Bien tost apres le Prince parvenu,	Soon after that, the Prince is come
Combien qu' hors fleuve ennemy re-	to his own,
pousse.	Although the enemy be driven
Dehors saisi, trait d'oyseau soustenu.	beyond the river,
	He shall be seized without, by a
	trick of the bird.

Parasitic hangers-on will be expelled from the government, by one who is an Eagle, and a master of stratagem.

24

Bestes farouches de faim fleuves tran-
ner,
Plus part du camp encontre Ister sera,
En cage de fer le grand sera traisner,
Quand rien enfant Germain obser-
vera.

Wild beasts for hunger shall swim
over the rivers,
Most of the field shall be near the
Ister,
Into an iron cage he shall cause the
great one to be drawn,
When the child of Germany shall
observe nothing.

A true prediction of the fate of Adolf Hitler. His demise in the bomb
shelter bunker in Berlin is anticipated as his 'iron cage.'

25

La garde estrange trahyra for teresse,
Espoir & ombre du plus haut mar-
iage,
Garde deceue, fort prins dans la
presse,
Loire, Saone, Rhone, Gar a mort
outragez.

The garrison of strangers shall
betray the fort,
Under the game of hope of a higher
union.
The garrison shall be deceived, and
the fort taken quickly
Loire, Saone, Rhone, Garonne,
outraged by death.

A garrison of extra-terrestrials arrives, defects, and seeks asylum in the
'hope of a higher union.' Anticipates the arrival of a breed of extra-
terrestrials.

26

Pour la faveur que la cite fera,
Au grand qui tost perdra champ de
bataille
Puis le sang Pau, Thesin versera
De sang, feux, morts, noyez de coupe
de taille.

Because of the favour, the city shall
show
To the great one, who soon shall
lose the battle,
The Thesin shall pour blood into
the River Po,
Of fire, blood, drowned, dead by
the edge.

Because of disputes, a town on the River Thesin, a river which empties
into the Po, shall see a great slaughter.

27

Le divin verbe sera du ciel frappe
Qui ne pourra proceder plus avant,
Du reserant le secret estoupe
Qu'on marchera par dessus & devant.

The divine voice shall be struck by heaven
So that he cannot proceed any further,
The secret of close-mouthed one shall be closed,
That people shall tread upon and before it.

A voice, of celestial quality which will be perfection itself, shall appear, the secret of which will be inviolate.

28

Le penultiesme du surnom de Prophete,
Prendra Diane pour son jour & repos,
Loing vauera par frenitique teste,
Et delivrant un grand peuple d'imposts.

The last but one, of the surname of Prophet,
Shall take Diana for his day and his rest,
He shall wander far by reason of his raving head,
Delivering a great people from impositions.

Universally, Monday will become a holiday, thereby creating a Saturday-Sunday-Monday, three-day holiday. Also, a demented leader will promote anarchy in a tax-free society.

29

L'Oriental sortira se son siege,
Passer les monts Appenins, voir la Gaule,
Transpassera le ciel, les eaux & neige,
En un chacun frappera de sa gaule.

The Oriental shall come out of his seat,
Shall pass over the Apennine Mountains and see France,
Shall go over the air, the waters and the snow,
And shall strike everyone with his staff.

Nostradamus predicts nuclear bombardment of France and Italy with multi-warheads released from sites beyond the Urals (Orient?).

30

Un qui les dieux d'Annibal infernaux	One that shall cause the infernal
Fera renaistre, effrayeur des humains,	gods of Hannibal
Oncq plus d'horreur, ne plus dire jour-	To live again, the terror of man-
naux,	kind,
Qu'advint viendra par Babel aux	There never was more horror, not
Romains.	to say ill days,
	Did happen, or shall, to the
	Romans by Babel.

Babel refers to Eurasia. Oil-rich kingdoms armed with nuclear weaponry terrorize Italy.

31

En Campania Castulin fera tant	In Campania, the Castilian shall so
Qu'on ne verra que d'eau les champs	behave himself,
couverts	That nothing shall be seen but the
Devant, apres, la pluye de long temps	fields covered,
Hors mis les arbres rien long temps.	Before and after, it shall not rain
	for a long time,
	Except the trees, no green shall be
	seen.

In Campania, the Spaniard will strip the country of all wealth even to the verdure of the fields.

32

Laict, sang, grenouilles escondre en	Milk, blood, frogs shall rain in Dal-
Dalmatie	matia,
Conflit donne, peste preste, de baliene	A battle fought, the plague near
Cry sera grand par toute Esclavonie,	Basel,
Lors naistra monstre pres & dedans	A great cry shall be through all
Ravenne.	Slovakia,
	Then shall be born a monster, near
	and within Ravenna.

Dalmatia shall be in unrest, and Basel (Switzerland) and Czechoslovakia shall be in fear of an Italian monster.

33

Dans le torrent qui descend de Ver-onne,	In the torrent which descends from Verona,
Par lors qu'au Pau guidera son entree,	About the place where it enters into the Po,
Un grand naufrage, & non moins en Garonne,	A great shipwreck, and no less in Garonne,
Quand ceux de Gennes marcheront leur contree.	When those of Genoa shall go into their country.

When the Italians of Genoa invade France, they are foredoomed to destruction and shipwreck.

34

L'ire insensee du combat furieux,	The mad anger of the furious fight,
Fera a table par freres le fer luyre,	Shall cause by brothers the iron to glisten at the table,
Les departir mort blesse curieux,	To part them, one mortally wounded, curious,
Le fier duelle viendra en France nuyre.	The fierce duel shall do harm after in France.

A quarrel between two allies shall be the cause of a misunderstanding that will do France much harm.

35

Dans deux logis de nuict le feu pren-dra,	The fire shall take by night in two houses,
Plusieurs dedans estouffez & rostis,	Many shall be stifled and burnt by it,
Pres de deux fleuves pour seur il adviendra,	Near two rivers it shall for certain happen
Sol, l'Arc & Caper, tous seront amor-tis.	Sun, Arc, Caper, they shall all be mortified.

In a town near two rivers, a momentous decision will be made, and many shall suffer by it – all this to happen when the Sun is in the signs of Arc (Sagittarius), and Caper (Capricorn).

36

Du grand prophete lettres seront prin-
   ses,
Entre les mains du tyran deviendront,
Frauder son roy seront les entreprin-
   ses,
Mais ses rapines bien tost le troubler-
   ont.
	The letters of the great prophet
	   shall be intercepted,
	They shall fall into the hands of the
	   tyrant,
	His undertakings shall be to de-
	   ceive his king,
	But his extortions shall trouble him
	   soon.

Before the great prophet shall triumph, his plans shall be betrayed by selfish, tyrannical interests.

37

De ce grand nombre que l'on envoyera
Pour secourir dans le fort assiegez,
Peste & famine tous les deux de-
   vorera,
Hors mis septante qui seront profligez.
	Of the great number which shall be
	   sent,
	To relieve the besieged in the fort,
	Plague and famine shall devour
	   them all,
	Except seventy that shall be beaten.

A warning that biological warfare and fearful destruction of both plant and animal life is imminent.

38

Des condamnez sera fait un grand
   nombre,
Quand les monarques seront conciliez;
Mais, l'un d'eux viendra si mal en-
   combre,
Que guerre ensemble ne seront raliez.
	There shall be a great number of
	   condemned men,
	When the monarchs shall be recon-
	   ciled,
	But one of them shall come to such
	   a bad obstacle,
	That their reconciliation shall not
	   last long.

Forecasts the Hitler-Stalin non-aggression pact of August 24, 1939, which lasted till June 22, 1941, when Germany attacked Russia.

39

Un an devant le conflit Italique,	One year before the Italian conflict,
Germain, Gaulois, Espagnols pour le fort,	German, French, Spaniards for the fort,
Cherra l'escole maison de republic,	The schoolhouse of the republic shall fall,
Ou, hors mis peu, seront suffoquez morts.	Where except few, they shall be suffocated to death.

One year before Italy enters World War III, Paris will be overwhelmed by a terrific onslaught of atomic-powered rockets.

40

Un peu apres non point longue inter-valle,	A little while after, without any great difference of time,
Par mer & terre sera fait grand tu-multe,	By land and sea shall a great tumult be made,
Beaucoup plus grand sera pugne na-valle,	The sea fight shall be much greater,
Feux, animaux, qui plus feront d'in-sulte.	Fire and beasts, which shall make great affront.

Nostradamus forecasts a global conflict, World War III, with nuclear bombardments from ships and submarines.

41

La grand estoile par sept jours brus-lera,	The great star shall burn for the space of seven days,
Nue fera deux soleils apparior,	A cloud shall make two suns appear,
Le gros mastin toute nuict hurlera,	The big mastiff shall howl all night,
Quand grand pontife changera de ter-roir.	When a great Pope shall change his country.

Pope John Paul II, from Poland, the first pontiff not of Italian birth, was installed in 1978. Also, see V. 79 wherein Nostradamus predicts the selection of a Frenchman as Pope.

42

Coq, chiens, & chats, de sang seront repeus,	A cock, dogs and cats shall be fed with blood,
Et de la playe du tyrant trouve mort,	And with the wound of the tyrant found dead,
Au lict d'un autre jambes & bras rompus,	In the bed of another with legs and arms broken,
Qui n'avoit pu mourir de cruelle mort.	Who could not die before by a cruel death.

The French nation (the Cock), and the rabble of Paris (cats and dogs), were satiated with the blood of the guillotine and the beheading of Robespierre, the tyrant of the Revolution. He had been ordered seized by the Convention, and in the struggle was dangerously wounded, tied on a strange bed and executed the next morning.

43

Durant l'estoille cheuelue apparente,	During the time when the hairy star is apparent,
Les trois grand princes seront faits ennemys,	The three great princes shall be made enemies,
Frappez du ciel paix terre trembulente,	Struck from heaven, place quaking earth,
Pau, Tymbre, Undans, serpens sur le bord mis.	Po, Tiber, full of surges, serpents cast upon the shore.

The reappearance of Halley's Comet, due in 1985, will again presage profound changes in human destiny.

44

L'aigle poussee entour des pavillons,	The eagle flying among the tents,
Par autres oyseaux d'entour sera chassee,	By other birds shall be driven away,
Quand bruit des cymbres, tubes et sonnaillons,	When the voice of cymbals, trumpets, and bells,
Rendront le sens de la Dames insensee.	Shall make sense to the lady who was insane.

The United States planes (eagles) fly over Arab lands (tent dwellers) but are driven away by other nations who come to the aid of the Arabs.

45

Trop le ciel l'Androgin procree	Heaven bemoaneth too much the Androgyn born,
Pres de ciel sang human respandu,	Near heaven human blood shall be spent,
Par mort trop tarde grand peuple recree,	By death too late a great people shall be diverted,
Tard & tost vient le secours attendu.	Late and soon cometh the help expected.

The Islamic revolution is anticipated but there will be much bloodshed after the death of Khomeini in the early- to mid 1980s.

46

Apres grand troche humain, plus grand s'appreste.	After a great human change, another greater is near at hand.
Le grand moteur les siecles renouvelle,	The great motor, reneweth the ages,
Pluye, sang, laict, famine, feu, & pest;	Rain, blood, milk, famine, sword, plague,
Au ciel veu, courant longue estincelle.	In the heavens shall be seen a running fire with long sparks.

After the great industrial age of steam and electricity, another stupendous revolution will be near. A new type of motor power will accelerate all human progress, but before this happens, there will be seen awesome aerial projectiles causing much suffering. Predicts nuclear space warfare.

47

L'ennemy grand vieil, dueil meurt de poison,	The great and old enemy grieveth, dieth by poison,
Les souverains par infinis subjuguez.	An infinite number of sovereigns conquered.
Pierres plouvoir cachez soubs la toyson,	It shall rain stones, they shall hide under rocks,
Par mort articles en vain sont alleguez.	In vain shall death assert articles.

The old enemy of mankind, war, shall no longer exist, nor will poverty and the allied ills. All this will happen after a period of human suffering.

48

La grand coppie quie passera les monts,	The great army shall pass over the mountains,
Saturne en l'arc tournant du poisson Mars,	Saturn, Aries, Mars turning to the fishes,
Venins chachez soubs testes de saulmons,	Poisons hidden in the heads of salmons,
Leurs chefs pendus a fil de polemars.	Their captain hanged with a string of the polemars.

An invasion over the mountains is indicated, with melancholy results, as this force will be driven into the sea and the captain slain.

49

Les conseillers du premier monopole,	The counsellors of the first monopoly,
Les conquerans seduits par la Melite,	The conqueror being seduced by the Melite,
Rhodes, Bisance pour leur exposant pole	Rhodes, Bizance, for exposing their pole
Terra faudra le pour suivants de suite.	The ground shall fail the followers of the runways.

In the Latin tongue, Melites are classified as the inhabitants of the island of Malta. The sense seems to be that Malta will successfully oppose its would-be conquerors who shall not be able to land planes on its runways.

50

Quand ceux d'Hinault, de Gand & de Bruxelles	When those of Hainaut, of Gand and Brussels
Verront a Langres le siege devant mis,	Shall see the siege laid before Langres,
Derriere leurs flancs seront guerres cruelles,	Behind their sides shall be cruel wars,
La pluye antique, fera pis qu' ennemys.	The old wound shall be worse than enemies.

War shall devastate various cities of Holland, Belgium and Northern France.

51

Le sang du juste a Londres sera faute,	The blood of the just shall be dry in London,
Bruslez par foudres de vingt trois les six,	Burnt by the fire of three times twenty and six,
La dame antique cherra de place haute,	The ancient dame shall fall from her high place,
De mesme secte plusieurs seront occis.	Of the same sect many shall be killed.

The great fire of London, 1666, three times twenty and six, with the subsequent falling of the statue of the Virgin from St. Paul's Steeple, is exactly predicted and occurred as forecast.

52

Dans plusieurs nuicts la terre tremblera,	During many nights the earth shall quake,
Sur le printemps deux efforts feront suitte,	About the spring, two great earthquakes shall follow one another,
Corinthe, Ephese aux deux mers nagers,	Corinth, Ephesus shall swim in the twin seas,
Guerre s'esmeut par deux vailants de luitte.	War shall be moved by two great wrestlers.

An era of earth-shaking events will occur in the region of Greece, caused by the action of two great powers.

53

La grand peste de cite maritime	The great plague of the maritime city,
Ne cessera que morte ne soit vengee;	Shall not cease until the death be revenged,
Du juste sang par pris damne sans crime,	Of the just blood by price condemned without crime,
De la grand' dame par fainte n'outrages.	Of the great dame not feigned abused.

The great plague of London, 1665, shall be inflicted on the populace as a revenge for the execution of Charles I.

54

Par gent estrange, & de Romains loingtaine,	By a strange people and a remote nation, ·
Leur grand cite apres eau fort troublee;	The great city near the water shall be much troubled,
Fille sans main trop different domaine,	The girl without great difference for an estate,
Prins, chef terreure n'avoit este riblee.	The chief frightened, at not having been warned.

This is Pearl Harbor of December 7, 1941, prior to which President Roosevelt had been deceived by the Japanese envoys at the White House.

55

Dans le conflit le grand qui peu valloit,	In the fight the great one, who was but little worth,
A son dernier fera cas merveilleux;	At his last endeavour shall do a wonderful thing,
Pendant qu'Hadrie verra ce qu'il falloit,	While Adria shall see what was wanting,
Dans le banquet pongnale l'orgueilleux.	In the banquet he shall stab the proud one.

The arch criminal seeing that the fight is lost shall go down in ruin, and drag his Italian fellow-conspirator with him.

56

Que peste & glaive n'a s'en definer,	He whom neither plague nor sword could destroy,
Mort dans le pluies sommet du ciel frappe,	Shall die in the rain being stricken by thunder,
L'abbe mourra quand verra ruyner	The abbot shall die when he shall see ruined
Ceux au naufrage, l'escueil voulant grapper.	Those in the shipwreck, striving to catch hold of the rock.

The destruction of Nazi Germany with the removal of Hitler to his bunker for his final hours and death.

57

Avant conflit le grand mur tombera,	Before the battle, the great wall shall fall,
Le grand a mort, mort trop subite & *plainte,*	The great one to death, too sudden and bewailed,
Nef imparfaict la plus part nagera,	The boat being imperfect the most part shall swim,
Aupres du fleuve de sang la terre *tainte.*	Near the river the earth shall be dyed with blood.

Anticipates a Sino-Soviet war with destruction of the Great Wall of China. The Yellow River intersects the Great Wall in Shansi Province where, on the outreaches of Peking, the great battle will be fought turning the Yellow River red with blood.

58

Sans pied ne main, dent aygue & forte	Without foot or hand, sharp and strong teeth,
Par globe au fort de port & l'aisne *nay,*	By a globe, in the middle of the port, and the first born,
Pres du portail desloyal se transporte.	Near the gate shall be transported by a traitor,
Seline luyt, petit grand emmene.	The moon shineth, the little great one carried away.

A kidnapping at night, by an alien, of an infant belonging to a great one, shall take place. This, of course, is the kidnapping of the Lindbergh baby allegedly by Hauptmann.

59

Classe Gauloise par appuy de grand' *garde,*	The French Fleet by the help of the great guards,
Du grand Neptune, & ses tridens *soldats,*	Of great Neptune, and his tridented soldiers,
Rongee Provence pour soustenir *grand' bande,*	Shall gnaw Provence by keeping great company,
Plus Mars, Narbon, par javelots & *dards.*	Also, Mars shall plague Narbonne by javelots and darts.

The French Fleet, with the aid of the British Navy, shall invade France, at the same time a heavy bombardment shall be kept up.

60

La Foy Punique en orient rompue,
Grand Jud, & Rhosne, Loyre & Tag,
changeront,
Quand du mulet la faim sera repeve
Classe espargie sang & corps
nageront.

The Punic Faith broken in the east,
Great Jud, and Rhone, Loire and
Tagus shall be changed,
When the mule's hunger shall be
satisfied,
The fleet scattered, blood and
bodies shall swim.

The false faith broken in the East shall unleash a series of changes, while the rivers shall be choked with bodies and the fields shall remain uncultivated.

61

Agen, Tamins, Gironde & la
Rochelle,
O sang Troien mort au port de la
flesche,
Derriere le fleuve au fort mise l'es-
chelle,
Pointes, feu, grand meurtre sur la
breche.

Agen, Tomains, Gironde and
Rochelle,
O Trojan blood, death is at the
harbour of the arrow,
Beyond the river, the ladder shall
be raised against the fort,
Points, fire, great murder upon the
breach.

Civil wars in France, between various cities, are predicted.

62

Mabus puis tost, alors mourra viendra,
De gens & bestes une horrible defaite,
Puis tout a coup la vengeance on
verra,
Sang, main, soif, faim, quand courra
la comette.

Mabus shall come, and soon after
shall die,
Of people and beasts shall be a
horrible destruction,
Then on a sudden the vengeance
shall be seen,
Blood, hand, thirst, famine, when
the comet shall run.

The coming of the comet shall occur in the period of reconstruction, and there will be vengeance for wrongs inflicted on humanity by selfish interests.

63

Gauloise, Ausonhe, bien peu sub-jugera,	The French fleet shall a little sub-due Ausonne,
Pau, Marne, & Seine fera perme l'vrie,	Pau, Marne, and Seine shall make permanent the truth,
Qui le grand mur contre eux dressera,	Which shall raise a great wall against them,
Du moindre au mur le grand perdra la vie.	From the less to the wall the great one shall lose his life.

Bordeaux is called Ausonne by Nostradamus because Ausonius, a Latin poet, was born there. During World War II part of the French fleet was sunk in the harbour of Bordeaux, thereby rendering it unfit for use by the Germans (creating a wall against them).

64

Seicher de faim, de soir gent Genevoise,	Those of Geneva shall be dried up with hunger and thirst,
Espoir prochain viendra au defaillir,	A near hope shall come when they shall be fainting,
Sur point tremblant sera loy Gehenoise,	The Hellish law shall be upon a quaking point,
Classe au grand port ne se peut ac-cueillir.	The navy shall not be able to come into port.

At Geneva men shall almost succeed in outlawing war and dismantling all navies, but those of Geneva shall have no support.

65

Le parc enclin grand calamite,	The park inclineth to great cala-mity,
Par l'Hesperie & Insubre fera,	Which shall be through Hesperia and Insubria,
Le feu en nef, peste & captivite,	The fire in the ship, plague and captivity,
Mercure en l'arc, Saturne fenera.	Mercury in Aries, Saturn shall wither.

Spain and the House of Savoy (Italy) are due for a great calamity when the sun is in Mercury and Aries.

66

Par grand dangers le captif eschappe,	The prisoner escaped through great danger,
Peu de temps grand la fortune changee,	A little while after shall become great, his fortune being changed,
Cans le palais le peuple este attrape,	In the palace the people shall be caught,
Par bon augure la cite assiegee.	And by a good sign the city shall be besieged.

Once again, Napoleon's rise and fall. He escaped from Elba on March 1, 1815, and after 100 days re-entered Paris in triumph. His eventual defeat came at Waterloo on June 18, 1815.

67

La blonde au nez forche viendra com- mettre	The fair one shall fight with the forked nose
Par le duelle & chassera dehors.	In duel, and expel him forth.
Les exilez dedans fera remettre,	The exiles shall be re-established,
Aux lieux marins commettant les plus forts.	Putting the stronger of them in maritime places.

La Belle France – the Fair One – shall expel the intruder, regaining peace and a strong navy.

68

De l'aquilon les efforts seront grande,	The endeavours of the north shall be great,
Sur l'ocean sera la porte ouverte,	Upon the ocean the gate shall be open,
Le regne en l'isle reintegrande,	The kingdom in the island shall be re-established,
Tremblera Londres par voile des- couverte.	London shall quake, for fear of sails discovered.

A very remarkable prophecy. Charles II is re-established on the British throne; and the forays of the Dutch Fleet under Admiral Van Tromp against quaking London are predicted.

69

Le Roy Gaulois par la Celtique dextre	The French King, by the Celtic
Voyant discorde de la Grand Monar-	right hand,
chie,	Seeing the discord of the Great
Sur les trois parts fera fleurir son	Monarchy,
sceptre,	Upon three parts of it, will make
Contre la cappe de la grand Hierar-	his sceptre to flourish,
chie.	Against the cap of the great Hier-
	archy.

Henry II, King of France, seeing the discord in England under the Commonwealth, will aid in the restoration of Charles II.

70

Le dard du Ciel fera son estendue,	The dart of heaven shall make his
Morts en parlant grande execution,	circuit,
La pierre en l'arbre la fiere gent	Some die speaking, a great execu-
rendue,	tion,
Bruit humain monstre, purge expia-	The stone in the tree, the fierce
tion.	people humbled,
	Human noise, a monster purged by
	expiation.

The blitz of London is herewith prophesied – blockbusters, scattering stones into trees, will cause instant death and terror, even to the mightiest.

71

Les exiles en Sicile viendront,	The banished persons shall come
Pour deliverer de la gent faim es-	into Sicily,
trange,	To free the foreign nation from
Au point du jour les Celtes luy faud-	hunger,
ront,	In the dawning of the day, the Celts
La vie demeure a raison Roy se range.	shall fail them,
	Their life shall be preserved, the
	King shall submit to reason.

The United Nations adopts the Palestine partition plan with the creation of the state of Israel. The immigrants (banished) flock to Israel and the King (Great Britain) removes its troops.

72

Armee Celtique en Italie vexee,	The French Army shall be vexed in Italy,
De toutes parts conflit & grande perte,	On all sides fighting, and a great loss,
Romains fuis, ou Gaule repousee,	The Romans run away, and though France, repulsed
Pres du Thesin, Rubicon pugne incerte.	Near the Ticino, by Rubicon the fight shall be doubtful.

A French Army will be routed from Italy. Two great battles will be fought, one by the river Ticino, and one by the Rubicon; but so great will be the slaughter that the victory will be a doubtful one.

73

Au Lac Fucin de Benacle rivage,	At the Fucin Lake of the Benacle shore,
Prins du Leman ou port de l'Origuion,	Near the Leman at the port of Lorguion,
Nay de trois bras predict belliq' image,	Born with three arms, a warlike image,
Par trois couronnes au grand Endymion.	By three crowns to the great Endymion.

Nostradamus confessed his inability to interpret this obscure stanza. In this later day it becomes clearer. Fascism had its birth near Lake Fucino, in Central Italy – the three-armed image indicates the strife and war that will follow.

74

De Sens, d'Autun viendront jusques au Rhosne	They shall come from Sens and Autun, as far as the Rhone,
Pour passer outre vers les monts Pyrenees,	To go further to the Pyrenees Mountains,
La gent sortir de la marque d'Auconne,	The nation shall come from the mark of Ancona,
Par terre & mer le suyvra a grands trainnees.	By land and sea shall follow speedily after.

Sens and Autun, two typical French towns, obviously represent the spirit of the Maquis during World War II. Harassed by the Nazis, the Maquis were forced to scatter, sometimes fleeing to the shelter of the Pyrenees Mountains. The import of the remainder of this quatrain indicates quite clearly the eventual re-birth of France as a united nation.

75

La voix ouye de l'insolit oiseau,	The noise of the unwanted bird
Sur le canon du respiral estage;	having been heard,
Si haut viendra de froment le bois-	Upon the canon of the highest
seau,	story,
Que l'homme d'homme sera Antro-	The bushel of wheat shall rise so
pophage.	high,
	That Man shall be a man-eater.

Nostradamus predicts aircraft and spacecraft with military implications of outer space warfare; worldwide famine, inflation, and eventual cannibalism.

76

Foudre en Bourgongne fera cas por-	Lightning in Burgundy, with mar-
tenteux,	vellous portents,
Que par engin homme ne pourroit	Which never could have been done
faire,	by art,
De leur senat, Sacrifiste fait boyteux,	Of their senate, Sacriste being
Fera scavoir aux ennemis l'affaire.	lamed,
	Shall make known the business to
	the enemies.

The Sacriste, or clergy, shall betray the interests of the state to the enemies at a time of stress.

77

Par arcs, feux, poix, & par feu re-	Being repulsed with bows, fires and
poussez,	pitch,
Crys, hurlemens sur la minuict ouys;	Cries and howlings shall be heard
Dedans sont mis par les ramparts	about midnight;
cassez,	They shall get in through the
Par cunicule les traditeurs fuis.	broken walls,
	The betrayers shall run away
	through the sewers.

By treason, some shall let in the enemy within the fortress, the betrayers themselves shall escape (the 'fifth column' in Madrid).

78

Le grand Neptune du profond de la mer,	The great Neptune, in the deep of the sea,
De gent Punique & sang Gaulois mesle,	Having joined African and French blood,
Les isles a sang, pour le tardif ramer,	The islands shall be put to the sword and the slow rowing
Pluy luy nuira que l'occult mal cele.	Shall do them more harm than the concealed evil.

The threat of invasion of the British Isles by the Nazis in 1942–1943. Actually, their tardiness and turn towards the Russian front cost them the war, since it gave the British time to regroup and provide the United States with air bases from which US aircraft bombarded Germany.

79

La barbe crespe & noire par engin,	The frizzled and black beard by fighting
Subjuguera la gent cruelle & fiere;	Shall overcome the fierce and cruel nation;
Le grand Chyren ostera du longin,	The great Henry shall free from bonds,
Tous les captifs par Seline baniere.	All the captives made by Selin's banner.

In 1571, five years after the death of Nostradamus, the Battle of Lepanto was fought. Don Juan of Austria, called the 'Frizzled and Black Beard,' defeated the Turks. Henry of France also redeemed many of the Christian slaves.

80

Apres conflit du leffe l'eloquence,	After the battle, the eloquence of the wounded man,
Par peu de temps se tramme saint, repos,	Within a little while shall procure a holy rest,
Point on n'admet les grands a delivrance,	The great ones shall not be delivered,
Des ennemis sont remis a propos.	But shall be left to their enemies' will.

More clearly refers to Roosevelt paralyzed ('wounded'), and sustaining a stroke and dying in 1944 (holy rest). The Nazi leaders were left to the will of the victors at the Nuremberg trials.

81

Par feu du ciel la cite pres qu'aduste,	By fire from heaven the city shall be almost burnt,
Urna menace encor Deucalion,	The waters threaten another Deucalion,
Vexes Sardaigne par la Punique fuste,	Sardinia shall be vexed by an African fleet,
Apres qu Libra lairra son Phaeton.	After that Libra shall have left her Phaeton.

Deucalion, a figure in Greek mythology, was the only human left after the great flood.

A city shall be so destroyed from the air as to be nearly lifeless, all this to occur when the sign of Libra has reached its last half.

82

Par faim la proye sera loup prisonnier,	By hunger, the prey shall make the wolf prisoner,
L'assaillant hors en extreme detresse;	Assaulting him then in great distress;
Un nay ayant au devant le dernier,	The eldest having got before the last,
Le grand n'eschappe au milieu de la presse.	The great one doth not escape in the middle of the crowd.

The Wolf (Rome), being hungry, shall snatch at the prey offered to it and become entrapped, while the greatest of all shall not escape the vengeance of the mob.

83

Par le traffic du grand Lyon change,	The great trade of the great Lion altered,
Et la plus-part tourne en pristine ruine,	The most part turns into pristine ruin,
Proye aux soldats par pille vendange,	Shall become a prey to soldiers and reaped by wound
Par jura mont & Sueve bruine.	In Mount Jura, and Suabia great fogs.

The industrial supremacy of the British Lion shall be endangered. England shall become the scene of pillage and the home of wounded soldiers. Mt Jura and Suabia (Germany) shall have some relation to these events.

84

Entre Champagne, Sienne, Flora, Ostie	Between Campania, Sienna, Pisa and Ostia,
Six mois neuf jours ne pleuvera une goutte;	For six months and nine days there shall be no rain,
L'Estrange langue en terre Dalmatie, Courira sus, gastant la terre toute.	The strange language in Dalmatian land, Shall overrun, spoiling all the country.

There shall be a drought along the east coast of Italy; and adjacent Albania, a Soviet satellite, shall overrun Yugoslavia and possibly Greece.

85

Vieux plains de barbe sous le statut severe,	The old plain beard, under the severe statue,
A Lyon fait dessus l'Aigle Celtique,	Made at Lyon upon the Celtic Eagle,
Le petit grand trop outre persevere,	The little great too far perseveres,
Bruit d'armes au ciel, mer rouge Lygustique.	Noise of arms in the sky, and the Ligurian sea made red.

The power of the German Air Force will for a time sustain the big and little Fuehrers (obviously Hitler and his satellites), and war will rage in the air and on the sea.

86

Naufrage a classe pres d'onde Adriatique,	A fleet shall suffer a shipwreck near the Adriatic sea,
La terre esmeu sur l'air en terre mis;	The earthquakes, a motion of air comes upon the land;
Egypte tremble augment Mahommetique,	Egypt trembles for fear of the Mohammedan increase,
L'Heraut se rendre a crier est commis.	The Herald surrendering shall be commissioned to cry.

In the Mediterranean Seas a fleet will be wrecked, the earth will shake with the sound of terrible weapons, and the air will vibrate with a strange whirring. Mohammedan influence will increase to the detriment of the rulers of Egypt. The mouthpiece shall desert to the victor and shall be commissioned under him.

87

Apres viendra des estremes contrees,
Prince Germain sur le throsne dore.
En servitude & par eaux recontrees
La dame serve, son temps plus n'a
  dore.

After that, shall come out of the
  remote countries,
A German Prince upon a gilded
  throne.
The slavery and waters shall meet,
The lady shall serve, her time no
  more worshipped.

The accession of the Hanoverian Kings of England commencing with
George I is here indicated.

88

Le circuit du grand fait ruyneux,
Au nom septiesme le cinqueiesme sera;
D'un, tiers plus grand estrange belli-
  quex,
Mouton, Lutece, Aix garantira.

The circuit of the great deed
  ruined,
The seventh name shall be that of
  the fifth,
From a third person, one greater, a
  warlike man,
Aries shall preserve Paris nor Aix.

The reference here is to the French league against Henry III and Henry
IV, which numbers, being joined together, make seven.

89

Un jour seront amis les deux grands
  maistres,
Leur grand pouvoir se verra aug-
  mente,
La terre neufe sera en ses hauts estres,
Au sanguinaire, le nombre racompte.

One day the two great masters shall
  be friends,
Their great powers shall be in-
  creased,
The new land shall be in a
  flourishing condition,
The number shall be told to the
  Bloody Person.

Nostradamus foresees a détente between East and West. China and the
US become allies against their common enemy, Russia, here represented as
the 'Bloody Person'.

90

*Par vie & mort change regne d'Hon-
 grie,
La loy sera sera plus aspre que service,
Leur grand cite d'Urlemens, plaints &
 cris,
Castor and Pollux ennemis dans la
 lice.*

By life and death the kingdom of
 Hungary shall be changed,
The law shall be more severe than
 the service,
Their great city shall be full of
 howling and crying.
Castor and Pollux shall be enemies
 in the lists.

Hungary is overrun by Soviet might and becomes a satellite with many
repressive laws and civil war.

91

*Soleil levant un grand feu on verra,
Bruit & clarte vers Aquilon tendant;
Dedans le rond mort & cris on orra,
Par glaive, feu, faim, mort les atten-
 dans.*

At the rising of the sun a great fire
 shall be seen
Noise and light tending to the
 north;
Within the round, death and cries
 shall be heard,
Death by sword, fire, hunger
 watching for them.

Predicts the explosion of a nuclear device at sunrise with the attack
coming from the north.

92

*Feu, couleur d'or de ciel en terre veu,
Frappe du haut n'ay, fait cas merveilleux;
Grand meurtre humain, prinse du
 grand veveu,
Morts d'expectacles, eschappe l'or-
 gueilleux.*

Fire the colour of gold, from
 heaven to earth shall be seen,
Stricken of the high born, a
 marvellous event.
Great murder of mankind, great
 loss of infants,
Some dead looking, the proud one
 shall escape.

Continues the previous stanza. The marvellous event refers to fission
and/or fusion and satisfies Einstein's $E = mc^2$ formula. A saviour shall
become a great leader.

93

Bien pres du Tymbre presse la Lybitine,	Near the Tiber, going towards Libia,
Un peu devant grand inondation;	A little before a great inundation,
Le chef du nef prins, mis en la sentine,	The master of the ship being taken shall be put into the well,
Chasteau, palais en conflagration.	And a castle and a palace shall be burnt.

An Italian prophecy. After a great flood the Pope will be disenfranchised and his summer residence, the castle (Gondolfo) and the Vatican will be burned to the ground.

94

Grand Pau, grand mal pour Gaulois recevra,	Great Po shall receive great harm from the French,
Vain terreur au maritin Lyon,	A vain terror shall seize upon the maritime lion,
Peuple infiny par la mer passera,	Infinite people shall go beyond the sea,
Sans eschapper un quart d'un million.	Which shall not escape even a quarter million.

Italian cities shall receive great harm from the French, resulting in an exodus of their inhabitants.

95

Les lieux peuplez seront inhabitables,	The populous places shall be deserted,
Pour champs avoir grand division;	A great division to obtain fields,
Regnes livrez a prudens incapables,	Kingdom given to prudent incapable
Entre les freres mort & dissention.	When the great brothers shall die by dissension.

Civil war will cause the populace to leave congested places and seek rural pursuits.

96

Flambeau ardant au ciel sera veu,	A burning shall be seen by night in
Pres de la fin & principe du Rhosne,	Heaven,
Famine, glaive, tarde le secours	Near the end and beginning of the
poreu,	Rhone,
La Perse tourne envahir Macedoine.	Famine, sword, too late help shall
	be provided,
	Persia shall come against Macedo-
	nia.

Incendiary attacks will strike along the Rhone River in France, at the same time that the war will continue in the East.

97

Romain Pontife garde de t'appocher,	Roman Pontiff take heed to come
De la cite qui deux fleuves arrouse;	near,
Ton sang viendras aupres de la	To the city watered with two rivers,
cracher,	Thou shall spit there thy blood,
Toy & les tiens quand fleurira la rose.	Thou and thine when the rose shall
	bloom.

The attempted assassination of the Pope is forecast at a time when the rose, the symbol of the French Socialist Party (of Mitterrand), assumes power in 1981. The gunshot wound the Pope sustained tore through his colon and caused him to spit much blood.

98

Celuy du sang resperse le visage,	He that shall have his face bloody,
De la victime proche sacrifice,	With the blood of the victims near
Venant en Leo augure presage,	to be sacrificed,
Mais estre a mort lors pour la	The sun coming into Leo shall be
financee.	an augury by presage,
	That then he shall be put to death
	for his confidence.

In the summer, one who is a great oppressor of humanity shall be cut down by death, before his bloody plans fully mature.

99

Terroir Romain qu'interpretatoit augure,
Par gens Gauloise par trop sera vexee,
Mais nation Celtique craindra l'heure,
Boreas, classe trop loing l'avoir poussee.

The Roman country in which the augur did interpret,
Shall be too much vexed by the French nation,
But the Celtic nation shall fear the hour,
The North Wind had driven the navy in too far.

Rome, site of the ancient college of Augurs, shall be at cross swords with the nation of Celts (France).

100

Dedans le isles si horrible tumulte,
Rien on n'orra qu'une bellique brigue,
Tant grand sera des prediteurs l'insulte,
Qu'on se viendra ranger a la grand ligne.

In the islands shall be such horrible tumults,
That nothing shall be heard by a warlike surprise,
So great shall be the assault of the robbers,
That everyone shall shelter himself under the great line.

The London blitz, with all its horrid tumult due to the assault by the Nazis, is clearly foreshadowed even to the seeking of shelter by the populace in the London underground lines.

CENTURY
III

1

A pres combat & bataille navale,	After the fight and sea battle,
Le grand Neptun a son plus haut beffroy,	The great Neptune in his highest steeple,
Rouge adversaire de peur deviendra pasle	The red adversary shall wax pale with fear,
Mettant le grand Ocean en effroy.	Putting the great Ocean in a fright.

Adumbration of the Japanese attack on Pearl Harbor, December 7, 1941. The 'red adversary' is the red circle of the flag of Japan with 'great Neptune' represented by the United States fleet.

2

Le divin verbe pourra a la substance,	The divine word shall give to the substance
Comprins ciel, terre, or occult au fait mystique,	Heaven and earth, and gold hid in the mystic fact,
Corps, ame, esprit ayant tout puissance	Body, soul, spirit, having all power,
Tant soubs ses pieds comme au siege Celique.	As well under his feet, as in the Heavenly Seat.

A hermetic stanza, expounding the secret of the Philosopher's Stone, whereby medieval alchemists sought for a catalyst to convert base metals into gold.

3

Mars & Mercure & l'argent joint ensemble
Vers le midy extreme siccite,
Au fond d'Asie on dit a terre tremble,
Corinthe, Ephese lors en perplexite.

Mars, and Mercury and silver joined together,
Towards the south a great drought,
In the bottom of Asia shall be a great earthquake
Corinthe and Ephesus shall then be in perplexity.

The twentieth century has already seen great earthquakes take their toll: 1935, India, 50,000 dead; 1939, northern Turkey, 100,000 dead; 1950, India, 30,000 dead; 1962, Iran; 1966, Turkey; 1975, Iran. And in the twenty-first century more natural disasters are forecast.

4

Quand seront proches le deffaut des lunaires,
De l'un a l'autre ne distant grandement,
Froid, sicite, danger vers les frontieres,
Mesme ou l'oracle a prins commencement.

When default of the luminaries shall be near,
Not being far distant one from another,
Cold, drought, danger towards the frontiers,
Even where the oracle had his beginning.

When two great lights shall be nearly eclipsed, privations will be increased, even where the oracle (Nostradamus) was born.

5

Pres loing defaut de deux grand luminaires,
Qui surviendra entre Avril & Mars,
A quel cherte! mais deux grande debonnaires,
Par terre & sea secourront toutes parts.

Near the eclipse of the two great luminaries,
Which shall happen between April and March,
O what a dearth! But two great ones bountiful
By land and sea shall succour them on all sides.

Verification of the preceding verse, naming the time of the event, and also the rehabilitation and relief of the stricken areas by two bountiful nations.

6

Dans temples clos le foudre y entrera,	In closed temples the lightning shall fall,
Les citadins dedans leurs forts grevez,	The citizens shall be distressed in their strength,
Chevaux, boeufs, hommes, l'onde leur touchera,	Horses, oxen, men, the water shall touch the wall,
Par faim, soif, soubs les plus foibles armez.	By hunger, thirst, down shall come the worst provided.

The temples of learning shall be destroyed, but the citizens will hold fast, even through much suffering and loss.

7

Les fugitifs feu du ciels aux les piques,	The fugitives, fire of heaven on the pikes,
Conflit prochain des corbeaux s'esta-tans;	A fight near at hand, the ravens croaking,
De terre on crie, aide secours celiques,	They cry from the land, Help, O heavenly powers,
Quand pres des murs seront les comba-tans.	When near the walls shall be the fighting men.

The European theatre of conflict in the late twentieth century with nuclear installations and battles near the (Berlin) Wall. The raven appears on the German emblem along with the black eagle.

8

Les Cimbres joints avec leurs voisins,	The Welsh, joined with their neighbours,
Depopuler viendront presque l'Es-pagne,	Shall come to depopulate most of Spain,
Gens amaffez Guienne & Limousins,	People gathered from French towns,
Seront en ligue & leur feront com-pagne.	Shall be in league with them, and keep them company.

Eighteenth-century colonizing rivalry between France and England. Britain blockades the French channel seaports in 1759 preventing France's reinforcing its troops in America. French and Indian war (seven-years war, 1756–1763) ends with British domination of Canada and the other American colonies.

9

Bordeaux, Rouen, & la Rochelle joints,	Bordeaux, Rouen and La Rochelle joined together,
Tiendront autour de la grand mer Oceane,	Will range about upon the great ocean,
Anglois, Bretons, & les Flamens conjoints,	English, Bretons and Belgians, joined together,
Les chasseront jusques aupres de Rouane.	Shall drive them away as far as Rouane.

The great fleet of France will be driven from the seas by the British and Flemish fleets.

10

De sang & faim plus grand calamite,	Of blood and famine, what a great calamity,
Sept fois s'appreste a la marine plage,	Seven times is ready to come upon the sea coast,
Monech de faim, lieu pris captivite,	Monaco by hunger, the place taken captivity,
Le grand mene, croc, enferree cage.	The great one carried away, and shut up in a cage.

Monaco was annexed to France in 1793 after having been independent for over 800 years.

11

Les armes battre au ciel longue saison,	Armies shall fight in the air a great while,
L'arbre au milieu de la cite tombe,	The tree shall fall in the middle of the city,
Vermine, rongue, glaive en face tyfon,	Vermin, scabs, sword, firebrand in the face,
Lors le Monarque d'Adrie succombe.	When the Monarch of Venice shall fall.

Whatever else may be interpreted, to conceive of air battles and aircraft is remarkable. Nostradamus was aware of the work of Leonardo da Vinci (1452–1519).

12

Par la tumeur de Heb., Po, Tag., Tibre de Rome,	By the swelling of Heb., Po, Tag., Tiber of Rome,
Et par l'estang Leman & Aretin,	And the Lake Leman, and cities of Garonne,
Les deux grands chefs & citez de Garonne,	The two great leaders will be taken,
Prins, morts, noyez, partir, humain butin.	Dead, drowned, the human booty shall be divided.

Heb., is the river Hebrus in Thrace, the river Po is in Italy, and Tag. is the Tagus river in Portugal. Throughout Europe there will be a great disturbance, but the chief instigators will eventually meet violent deaths.

13

Par foudre en l'arche or & argent fondu,	In the ark, lightning, gold and silver melted,
Des deux captifs l'un l'autre, mangera,	Of two prisoners, one shall eat up the other,
De la cite le plus grand estendu,	The greatest of the city shall be laid down,
Quand submergee la classe nagera.	When the navy that was drowned, shall swim.

When the ships that were sunk are afloat again, the greatest of the enemy's cities will be destroyed by a thunderbolt, leaving them with valueless money.

14

Par le rameau du vaillant personnage,	By the branch of the valiant personage,
De France infirme, par le pere infelice,	Of weak France, by the unfortunate father,
Honneurs, richesses, travail en son vieil age,	Honours, riches, labour in his old age,
Pour avoir creu le conseil d'homme nice.	For having believed the counsel of a nice man.

Louis Philippe (whose father, descended from the brother of Louis XIV, was executed during the revolution) conspired with General Dumouriez and was exiled from Paris on the discovery of their plot to overthrow the Republic in 1793. Returning as King in 1830, he later enjoyed great riches and honours.

15

Coeur, vigueur, gloire, le Regne changera,	Heart, vigour and glory shall change the Kingdom,
De tous points, contre ayant son adversaire,	In all points, having an adversary against it,
Lors France enfance par mort sujugera,	Then shall France overcome childhood by death,
Le grand Regent sera lors plus contraire.	The great Regent shall then be most contrary to it.

The courage, vigour and glory of France were reanimated by Napoleon. His greatest adversary was the Pope, 'Regent of St Peter's Temporal Rule.'

16

Le Prince Angloise Mars a son coeur de ciel,	The English Prince Mars has his heart from Heaven,
Voudre pour suyure sa fortune prospere;	Will follow his prosperous fortune;
Des deux duels l'un percera le fiel,	Of two duels, one shall pierce the gall,
Hay de luy, bien ayme de sa mere.	Being hated of him, and beloved of his mother.

Edward VIII, later the Duke of Windsor, abdicated the throne in 1936 in order to marry a commoner.

17

Mont Aventine brusler nuict sera veu,	Mount Aventine shall be seen to burn in the night,
Le Ciel obscur tout a un coup en Flandres;	The Heavens shall be darkened upon a sudden in Flanders,
Quand le Monarque chassera son neveu,	When the Monarch shall expel his nephew,
Lors Gens d'eglise commettront les esclandres.	Then churchmen shall commit scandals.

The burning of Mount Aventine, one of the seven hills of Rome, is probably one of the many symbolizations used by Nostradamus to indicate war.

18

Apres la pluye laict, assez longuette,	After a long rain of milk,
En plusieurs lieux de Reims le ciel touche,	In many places of Rheims the lightning shall fall,
O quel conflit de sang pres d'eux s'appreste!	O what a bloody fight is making ready for them,
Peres & Fils, Roys n'oseront approche.	Father and Son, both Kings, shall not dare to come near.

After a period of peace and plenty, France shall be involved in a bloody war.

19

En Luques sang & laict viendra pleuvoir,	In Lucca it shall rain blood and milk,
Un peu devant changement de preteur,	A little before the change of the magistrate,
Grand peste & guerre, faim & soif fera voir,	A great plague, war, hunger and thirst shall be seen,
Loing on mourra leur Prince & grand recteur.	Along where their Prince and great director shall die.

In Italy, there will be alternating periods of depression and prosperity, then a change of chief magistrate, who will bring a plague, followed by war and hunger. The leader will die near Lucca.

20

Par les contrees du grand fleuve Betique	Through the countries of the great River Betis,
Loing d'Ibere au royanne de Grenade,	Far off from Iberia, in the kingdom of Grenada,
Croix respoussees par gens Mahometiques,	Crosses beaten back by Mohammedan people,
Un de Cordobe trahyra la contrade.	One of Cordoba shall at last betray the country.

The River Betis (Latin name) is the River Guadalquivir in Spain, on whose banks is the city of Seville. There Christians shall be betrayed by a Spaniard of Cordova, who will bring in Moors to slaughter his own people.

21

Au Crustamin par Mer Adriatique,	Among the Crustacea, near the Adriatic Sea,
Apparoistra un horrible poisson,	A horrid fish shall appear,
De face humain & de corps aquatique,	Having a man's face and a fish's body,
Qui se prendra dehors de l'hamecon.	Which shall be taken without a hook.

The Manatee, an herbivorous aquatic mammal, inhabiting the African and Amazonian coasts, often wanders far from its haunts. It was frequently mistaken for a human being, which its upper half resembles.

22

Six jours l'assaut devant citte donne,	Six days shall the assault be in front of the city,
Livres sera forte & aspre bataille,	A great and fierce battle shall be fought,
Trois la rendront & a eux pardonne,	Three shall surrender it, and be pardoned,
Le reste a feu & a sang tranche taille.	The rest shall be put to fire and sword, cut and slashed.

In 1967 Israel threatened retaliation for Syrian border raids, whereupon Syria asked for and received Egyptian aid. On June 5, with simultaneous air attacks against Syrian, Jordanian, and Egyptian air bases, Israel totally defeated her Arab enemies in what was to be called the Six Day War. The three Arab nations surrendered and their prisoners of war were freed and 'pardoned'.

23

Si, France, passe outre me Ligustique,	If France goeth beyond the Ligustic Sea,
Tu te verra en isles & mers enclos,	Thou shalt see thyself enclosed with islands and seas,
Mahomet contraire plus Mer Adriatique,	Mahomet, against thee besides the Adriatic Sea,
Chevaux & d'asnes tu rongeras les os.	Of horses and asses thou shalt gnaw the bones.

A warning to France not to advance beyond Corsica, or she will be attacked on all sides, blockaded and will suffer want of food.

24

De l'entreprinse grande confusion,	From the undertaking great confusion,
Perte de gens, tresor innumerables;	Loss of people and innumerable treasure,
Ty ny dois faire encores tension,	Thou ought not yet to tend that way,
France, a mon dire fais que sois recordable.	France! Endeavour to remember my saying.

A continuation of the preceding stanza, and of the same general tenor.

25

Qui au royanne Navarrois parviendra,	He that shall obtain the kingdom of Navarre,
Quande le Sicile & Naples seront joints,	When Sicily and Naples shall be joined,
Bigorre & Landes par Foix lors on tiendra,	Bigorre and Landes they by Foix shall be held,
D'un qui d'espagne sera par trop conjoints.	Of one who shall too much be joined to Spain.

At a time when Italy is united, one who is deeply involved with Spain shall also obtain his way in France.

26

Des Roys & princes dresseront simulachres,	Some kings and princes shall set up idols,
Augures cruez, esclevez aruspices;	Divinations and hollow raised divinators,
Corne victime doree, & d'azur d'nacre,	Victim with gilded horns, set with azure and mother of pearl,
Interpretez seront les estipices.	The looking into the entrails shall be interpreted.

Oil-rich Arab kings and princes, idolizing modern technology, shall soon be victimized. The kings and princes, with golden horns, shall have their lands uprooted.

27

Prince Lybinique puissant en Occident,	A Libian Prince being powerful in the West,
Francois d'Arabe viendra tant enflammer;	The French shall love so much the Arabian language,
Scavans aux lettres sera condescendent,	That he, being a learned man, shall condescend
La langue Arabe en Francois translater.	To have the Arabian tongue translated into French.

An alliance is forecast between Libya and France with the construction of a nuclear reactor.

28

De terre foible & pauvre parentelle,	One weak in lands and of poor kindred,
Par bout & paix parviendra dans l'Empire,	By thrusting and peace shall attain to Empire,
Long temps regner une jeune femelle,	Long time, shall reign a young woman,
Qu'onc q'en regne n'en furvint un si pire.	Such as in a reign was never worse.

Nostradamus here refers to India in its poverty, ruled by Indira Gandhi.

29

Les deux neveaux en divers lieux nourris,	The two nephews brought up in divers places,
Navale pugne, terre pierres tombees.	A sea fight, fathers fallen to the earth,
Viendront si haut esleve enguerris,	They shall come highly educated and expert in arms,
Venger l'injure ennemys succombez.	To avenge the injury, their enemies shall fall down under them.

Two people of the same blood, from opposite sides of the ocean, shall unite and crush their common enemy. England and the United States fight their common enemy, Nazi Germany.

30

Celuy qu'en luitte & fer au fait belli-
que,
Aura porte plus grand que luy le prix,
De nuit au lit six luy feront la pique,
Nud sans harnois subit sera surprins.

He who in wrestling and martial
deeds,
Had carried the prize before his
better,
By night six shall abuse him in his
bed,
Being naked and without harness
he shall suddenly be surprised.

The Earl of Montgomery, who accidentally killed Henry II of France, in a sporting bout, was afterwards beheaded for being one of the Protestant Party.

31

Aux champs de Mede, d'Arabe &
d'Armenie
Deux grands copies trois fois s'as-
sembleront,
Pres du rivage d'Araxes la mesnie,
Du grand Soliman en terre tomberont.

In the fields of Media, Arabia and
Armenia,
Two great armies shall meet thrice,
Near the shore of Araxes, the
people,
Of great Solyman shall fall down.

In the Near East, two great armies will clash, the net result of which will be that the Jews will suffer thereby.

32

Le grand sepulchre du peuple Aquita-
nique,
S'approchera aupres se la Toscane,
Quand Mars sera pres du coing Ger-
manique,
Et au terroir de la gent Mantuane.

The great grave of the Aquatanic
people
Shall approach to Tuscany,
When Mars shall be in the German
corner,
And in the territory of the Mantuan
people.

When war shall be in Italian territory sponsored by the Germans, then the British shall suffer much loss of life in Tuscany.

33

En la cite ou le loup entrera,	In the city wherein the wolf shall go,
Bien pres de la les ennemis seront;	Near the place the enemies shall be,
Copie estrange grand pays gastera,	An army of strangers shall spoil a great country,
Aux monts & Alpes les amis passeront.	The friends shall go over the mountains of the Alps.

The city of the Italian Wolf shall be besieged and almost overcome by a great army of strangers until assistance shall be rendered by those on the other side of the Alps.

34

Quand le deffaut du soleil lors sera,	When the eclipse of the sun shall be,
Sur le plain jour le monstre sera veu;	At noon day, the monster shall be seen,
Tout autrement on l'interpretera,	It shall be interpreted other ways,
Cherte n'a garde, nul n'y aura pourveu.	Then for a dearth, because nobody hath provided for it.

When the eclipse of Liberty shall be at its zenith, a monstrous movement shall arise, disguised as freedom; running its course it will cause great havoc.

35

Du plus profond de l'Occident d'Europe,	Out of the deepest part of the west of Europe,
De pauvres gens un jeune enfant naistra,	From poor people a young child shall be born,
Qui par sa langue seduira grande trouppe,	Who with his tongue shall seduce many people,
Son bruit au regne d'orient plus croistra.	His fame shall increase in the Eastern Kingdom.

Adolf Hitler, born in Austria of poor parents, with his knowledge of mob psychology and powers of speech, was successful in seducing many people, even in the Eastern Empire of Japan.

36

Ensevely non mort apoplectique,	One burned, not dead, but apoplectical,
Sera trouve avoir les mains mangees,	Shall be found to have eaten up his hands,
Quand la cite damnera l'heretique	When the city shall damn the heretical man,
Qu'avoit leurs loix ce leur sembloit changees.	Who as they thought had changed their laws.

Former President Nixon's downfall predicted with Watergate scandal. His 'hands' repressed his aides, who suffered for his misdeeds.

37

Avant l'assaut l'oraison prononcee,	Before the assault, the prayer shall be said,
Milan prins d'Aigle par embusches deceus,	A kite shall be taken by the eagle, being deceived by an ambuscade.
Muraille antique par cannons enfoncee.	The ancient wall shall be beaten down with cannons,
Par feu & sang a mercy peu receus.	By fire and blood, a few shall have quarter.

A play on words, Milan being both the name of an Italian city and a bird.

38

La gent Gaulois & nation estrange,	The French people and another nation,
Outre les monts, prins & profligez;	Being over the mountains, shall die and be taken,
Au moys contraire & proche de vendange,	In a month contrary to them, and near the vintage,
Par les Seigneurs en accord redigez.	By the Lords agreed together.

In September (grape harvest time), France and Britain give Hitler an ultimatum and then on September 3, 1939, they declare war on Germany only to suffer great defeats and death in the ensuing three years.

39

Les sept en trois mis en concorde,	The seven shall agree together within three months,
Pour subjuguer les Alpes Apennines,	To conquer the Apennine Alps,
Mais le tempeste & ligure courade,	But the tempest and the cowardly Genoese,
Les profligent en subiets ruynes.	Shall sink them into sudden ruin.

Seven persons shall take three months to make an agreement to conquer the Italians, but the invasion shall be held up by bad weather.

40

Le grand theatre se viendra redresser,	The great theatre shall be raised up again,
Le dez jette & les rets ia tendus,	The die being cast and the net spread,
Trop le premier en glaz viendra lasser,	The first too much in toiling shall weary,
Par arcs prostraits de long temps ia fendus.	Beaten down by bows, who long before were split.

Allied reconstruction of Nazi Germany after World War II, United States reconstruction of Japan, as well as Vietnam in the 1970s. So it is with wars and reconstruction. The vanquished are helped by the victors and eventually the victor becomes the vanquished only to recycle the procedure.

41

Bossu sera esleu par le conseil,	Crook-back shall be chosen by council.
Plus hydeux monstre en terre n'aperceu;	A more hideous monster I never saw upon earth,
Le coup volant prelat crevera l'oeil,	The flying blow shall put out one of his eyes,
Le traistre au Roy pour fidele receu.	The traitor to the King shall be admitted as faithful.

A hunchback will be elected to a position of power, but will turn out to be a traitor to the King.

42

L'enfant naistra a deux dents en la gorge,	A child shall be born with two teeth in his mouth,
Pierre en Tuscie par pluye tomberont;	It shall rain stones in Tuscany.
Peu d'ane apres ne sera bled ne orge,	A few years after there shall be neither wheat nor barley,
Pour faouller ceux qui de faim failler-ont.	To feed those that shall faint for hunger.

A world famine will occur after the birth of a prodigy and the falling of bombs in Tuscany.

43

Gens d'alentour de Tarn, Loth, & Garonne,	People that live about the Tarn, Lot and Garonne,
Gardez les monts Apennines passer,	Take heed to go over the Apennine Mountains,
Vostre tombeau pres de Rome & d'Anconne	Your grave is near Rome, and Ancona,
Le noir poil crespe fera trophee dres-ser.	The black-haired ones shall set up a trophy.

The people of France, near the Tarn, Lot and Garonne Rivers, are warned not to go into Italy, the home of the Black Shirts. The 'trophy' refers to the dishonoured corpse of the former Duce – Mussolini.

44

Quand l'animal a l'homme domesti-que,	When the beast familiar to man-kind,
Apres grand peine & saute viendra parler;	After great labour, and leaping shall come to speak,
Le foudre a vierge sera si malefique,	The lightning shall be so hurtful to a virgin,
De terre prinse & suspendue en l'air.	That she shall be taken from the earth and suspended in the air.

The dogs of war will be unleashed and shall come to 'speak.' An explosion in a church shall blow a Virgin skyward, and initiate a period of great uncertainty.

45

Les cinq estrangers entrez dedans le temple	The five strangers having come into the church,
Leur sang viendra la terre prophaner;	The blood shall profane the ground,
Aux Thoulouseins sera bien dure exemple	It shall be a hard example to those of Toulouse,
D'un qui viendra les loix exterminer.	Concerning one that came to break their laws.

In Toulouse, five alien officials will be assassinated in a church, profaning the ground according to clerical opinion. The assassins shall be penalized heavily for it.

46

Le Ciel (de Plancus la cite) nous presage	The Heaven foretelleth concerning the city of Plancus,
Par clairs insignes & par estoilles fixes,	By clear signs and fixed stars,
Que de son change subit s'approche l'aage,	That the time of her sudden change is near at hand,
Ne pour son bien ne pour les malefices.	Neither because of her goodness nor wickedness.

The city of Plancus is Lyons, as Plancus was its founder. She is due for a sudden change in fortune.

47

Le vieux monarque dechasse de son regne,	The old monarch being expelled out of his reign,
Aux Orients son secours ira querre,	Shall go into the East to get assistance
Pour peur de croix ployers son enseigne,	For fear of the crosses he shall fold up his colours,
En Mitilens ira par port & par terre.	He shall go into Mitylene by sea and land.

The monarchy and regime in Greece in the twentieth century are noted for upheavals and change. In 1941 and 1967 the king was replaced by a military junta.

48

Sept cens captifs attachez rudement,	Seven hundred prisoners shall be tied together,
Pour la moitie meurdrir, donne le fort;	To murder half of them, the lot being cast,
La proche espoir si promptement,	The next hope shall come quickly,
Mais non si tost qu'une quinziesme mort.	And not so quickly, but fifteen shall be dead before.

An example of Nazi brutality to both civilians and combatants in World War II.

49

Regne Gaulois tu seras bien change,	French Kingdom, thou shalt be much changed,
En lieu estrange l'Empire translate,	The Empire is translated in another place,
En Autres loix & moeurs seras range,	Thou shalt be put to other manners and laws,
Rouen & Chartres te fera bien du pire.	Rouen and Chartres shall do the worst they can to thee.

A prediction of the change of form of Government in France from Monarchy to Republic.

50

La Republic de la grande Cite	The Republic of the great City,
A grand rigueur ne voudra consentir;	With great harshness shall not consent,
Roy sortir hors par trompette cite,	That the king should go out being summoned by the city's trumpet,
L'eschelle au mur la cite repentir.	The ladder shall be put to the wall and the city repent.

The government of Paris, with great harshness, summons and arrests the King and the Bastille is stormed.

51

Paris conjure un grand meurtre commettre	Paris conspireth to commit a great murder,
Blois le fera sortir en plain effect;	Blois shall cause it to come to pass,
Ceux d'Orleans voudront leur chef remmettre,	Those of Orleans will set up their head again,
Angiers, Troye, Langres leur feront grand forfait.	Angiers, Troyes, Langres will do them harm.

In Paris the Reign of Terror commences, and spreads to all France. The house of Orleans again will ascend the Throne, in the person of Louis Philippe.

52

En la campagne sera si longue pluye,	In the country shall be so long a rain,
Et en l'Apoville si grande siccite,	And in Apulia so great a drought,
Coq verra l'Aigle mal accomplie,	The cock shall see the eagle with his wing injured,
Par lyon mise sera en extremite.	And by him the lion brought to extremity.

The Gallic Cock shall see the American Eagle and the British Lion in great peril, during a long war.

53

Quand le plus grand emportera le pris,	When the great one shall carry the prize,
De Nuremberg, Auspourg, & ceux de Basle,	Of Nuremberg, Augsburg and Basle,
Par Agrippine chef Frankfort repris,	By Agrippina the Chief of Frankfurt shall be taken,
Traverseront par Flamens jusque'en Gale.	They shall go through Flanders as far as France.

When the Commander in Chief shall have captured other German cities, after the blasting of Cologne (ancient name, Agrippina), the German Commander shall be captured and imprisoned in France.

54

L'un des plus grands fuyra aux Espagnes,	One of the greatest shall run away into Spain,
Qu'en longue playe apres viendra feigner,	That shall cause a wound to bleed long,
Passant copies par les hautes montaignes,	Leading armies over high mountains,
Devastant tout & puis en paix regner.	Destroying all, and afterwards shall reign.

Argentina's Juan Peron was sent into exile in 1955 and fled to Spain. Argentina was then thrown into chaos. Peron was brought back to power in 1973 subduing the junta.

55

En l'an qu'un ceil en France regnera,	In the year that one eye shall reign in France,
La court sera en un bien fascheux trouble,	The court shall be in the very same trouble,
Le grand de Bloys son amy tuera,	The great one of Blois shall kill his friend,
Le regne mis en mal & doubte double.	The kingdom shall be in an evil way, and double doubt.

A King blind in one eye shall rule a court that is just as shortsighted.

56

Montauban, Nismes, Avignon, & Besiers,	Montauban, Nismes, Avignon and Besier,
Pest, tonnerre, & gresle a fin de Mars,	Plague, lightning and hail at the end of March,
De Paris pont Lyon mur, Montpelier,	The Bridge of Paris, the Wall of Lyons, and Montpelier shall fall
Depuis six cens et sept vingt, trois parts.	From six hundred and seven score three parts.

Widespread destruction shall befall France in March, in 12,143 parts.

57

Sept fois changer verrez gent Britannique,	Seven times you shall see the English change,
Taints en sang en deux cents nonante an;	Dyed in blood, in two hundred and ninety years,
France, non, point par appuy Germanique,	Not France, by the German support,
Aries double son Pole Bastarnan.	Aries doubles his Bastarnan Pole.

Thought to represent the period from 1555 to 1845, 290 years, and predicts greater English upheavals such as: (1) Protestant reversion under Elizabeth in 1558; (2) Stuart succession in 1603; (3) Commonwealth in 1649; (4) Restoration in 1660; (5) Bloodless revolution in 1688; (6) Hanoverian succession in 1714; and (7) The Reform Bill in 1832.

58

Aupres du Rhin des Montagnes Noriques,	Near the Rhine out of the Norick Mountains,
Naistra un grand de gens trop tard venu,	Shall be born a great one, though come too late.
Qui deffendra Saurome & Pannoniques,	Who shall defend the Poles and Hungarians,
Qu'on ne scaura qu'il sera devenu.	So that it shall not be known what is become of him.

Forecasts the birth and demise of Hitler. His burned body in the Berlin bunker was never found and his 'defence' of Poland and Hungary were, in reality, conquests.

59

Barbare Empire par le iters usurpe,	A Barbarian Empire shall be usurped by a third person.
La plus part de son sang mettre a mort,	Who shall put to death the greater part of his kindred,
Par mort senile, par luy, le quart frappe,	By death of old age, the fourth shall be stricken by him,
Par peur que sang par la sang en soit mort.	For fear that blood should not die by blood.

Iran, under Khomeini, in a blood bath, shall end with the death of Khomeini in old age. Moslem revolution will be followed by a counter-revolution with the restoration of the monarchy.

60

Par toute Asie grande proscription,	Through all Asia shall be a great
Mesme en Mysie, Lysie, & Pamphy-	proscription,
lie;	The same as in Mysia, Lydia, and
Sang versera par dissolution,	Pamphilia,
D'un jeune noir remply de felonnie.	Blood shall be spilled by the de-
	bauchery
	Of a dark young man, full of
	treason.

An Asiatic shall force the hordes of Asia into armies of conquest.

61

La grand bande & secte crucigere	The great band and sect wearing a
Se dressera en Mesopotamie,	cross,
Du proche fleuve compagnie legere,	Shall rise up out of Mesopotamia,
Que telle loy tiendra pour ennemis.	Near the river shall be a light com-
	pany,
	Which shall hold that law for the
	enemy.

A great organization, with some kind of cross as its emblem, shall emerge in a land between two rivers. Near one of these rivers, some traitors shall give the enemy assistance.

62

Proche del Duero par mer Cyrene	Near the Duro, close by the Cyre-
close,	nian Sea,
Viendra percer les grands Monts	Shall come to pierce the Pyrenees
Pyrenees,	Mountains,
Le main plus courte & sa percee close,	The shorter hand and his pierced
A Carcassonne conduira ses menees.	criticism,
	Shall in Carcassone lead his plot.

Near the Duro River, which rises in Spain near the Pyrenees Mountains, the one with a short hand shall lay a plot that will eventually embroil the strongest fort of France, Carcassone.

63

Romain pouvoir sera du tout a bas,	The Roman power shall be quite put down,
Son grand voisin imiter ses vestiges;	His great neighbour shall follow his steps,
Occultes haines civiles & debats	Secret and civil hatreds and quarrels,
Retarderont aux bouffons leurs follies.	Shall stop the buffoon's folly.

The collapse of power under Mussolini, the Roman buffoon, was quickly followed by the downfall of his neighbour, Hitler.

64

Le chef de Perse remplira grands Olchades,	The head of Persia shall fill great merchant ships,
Classe trireme contre gent Mahometique,	A fleet of warships against the Mohammedan folk,
De Parthe & Mede, & pilliers les Cyclades,	From Parthia and Media they shall come to plunder the Cyclades,
Repos long temps au grand port Ionique.	A long rest shall be on the Ionic port.

A great potentate shall send a fleet of warships supported by a well-supplied group of commercial vessels against a Moslem League, and commerce in the Mediterranean shall be stagnant.

65

Quand le sepulcre du grand Romain trouve	When the sepulchre of the great Roman shall be found,
Le jour apres sera esleu pontife,	The next day after a Pope shall be elected,
Du senat gueres il ne sera prouve	Who shall not be much approved by the Senate,
Empoisonne son sang au sacre scyphe.	Poisoned, his blood in the sacred chalice.

On the election of a Pope, great turmoil will arise due to disapproval by the Senate, and he will be assassinated.

66

Le grand Baillif d'Orleans mis a mort,	The great Bailiff of Orleans shall be put to death,
Sera par un de sang vindicatif;	By one of revengeful and vindictive blood,
Demort merite ne mourra ne par fort,	He shall not die of a deserved death nor by chance,
Des pieds & mains mal le faisoit captif.	But the disease of being tied hand and foot, hath made him prisoner.

The grim Rabelaisian humour of the age is well displayed here. A great personage of France will meet an untimely death at the hands of a vindictive enemy.

67

Une nouvelle secte de Philosophes,	A new sect of Philosophers shall arise,
Mesprisant mort, or, honneurs & richesses,	Despising death, gold, honours and riches,
Des monts Germains seront fort limitrophes,	They shall be near the mountains of Germany,
A les ensuyure auront appuy & presses.	They shall have abundance of others to support and follow them.

In Central Germany, near the Alps, a fanatical group shall arise and they will find much support and many followers throughout the world.

68

Peuple sans chef d'Espagne & d'Italie,	A people of Spain and Italy without a head
Morts profligez dedans la Cherrenosse,	Shall die, being overcome in the Crimea,
Leur duict trahy par legere folie,	Their saying shall be betrayed by their folly,
Le sang nager par tout a la traverse.	The blood shall swim all over at random.

The Blue Division, Fascist Spain's contribution to Hitler's invasion of Russia in World War II, was entirely exterminated on this front.

69

Grand exercite conduit par jouvenceau,
Se viendra rendra aux mains des ennemis;
Mais le vieillard nay au demy pourceau.
Fera Chalon & Mascon estre amis.

A great army led by a young man,
Shall yield itself in the hand of enemies,
But the old man born at the sign of the Half Hog,
Shall cause Chalon and Mascon to be friends.

Great French Armies shall be betrayed to the enemy by an inexperienced leader, but the old man shall reunite all.

70

Le grand Bretagne comprinse d'Angleterre,
Viendra par eaux si fort a inondre,
La ligue neufue d'Ausonne fera guerre,
Que contre eux il se viendront bander.

Great Britain including all of England,
Shall suffer so great an inundation of waters,
The new league of Italy shall make wars,
So that they shall stand against them.

Great Britain will be endangered by floods; and at the same time a New League, under Italian leadership, will threaten her shores.

71

Ceux dans les Isles de long temps assiegez,
Prendront vigueur force contre ennemis,
Ceux par behors morts de faim profligez,
En plus grand faim que jamais seront mis.

Those in the Islands that have long been besieged,
Shall take vigour and force against the enemies,
Those without shall die for hunger, being overcome,
They shall be put in greater famine than they were before.

The Dutch, being besieged, shall break the dikes to flood the country, confronting the enemy with great danger and hunger.

72

Le bon vieillard tout ensevely,	The good old man shall be buried
Pres du grand fleuve par faux soup-	alive,
con,	Near the great river by a false sus-
Le nouveau vieux de richesse ennobly,	picion,
Prins a chemin tout l'or de la rancon.	The new old one made noble by his
	riches,
	The gold of his ransom shall be
	taken in the way.

Winston Churchill, after leading Great Britain through its World War II victory, was 'buried alive' by a landslide election after the war. Along the 'great river' (Thames) this was predicted and occurred in 1945 with the ousting of Churchill and the Conservative Party.

73

Quand dans le regne parviendra le	When the lame man shall attain to
boiteux,	the kingdom,
Competiteur aura proche bastard,	He shall have a bastard for his near
Luy & le regne viendront si fort rog-	competitor,
neux	He and his kingdom shall be so
Qu'ains qu'il guerisse son fait sera	scabby,
bien tard.	That before he be cured it will be
	late.

An event that must have taken place in the days of Nostradamus, and which has now lost its meaning.

74

Naples, Florence, Fayence, & Imole,	Naples, Florence, Fayenza and
Seront en termes de telles fascherie,	Imola,
Que pour complaire aux malheureux	Shall be put into so much distress,
de Nole	For being complacent to the un-
Plaint d'avoir fait a son chef mo-	happy one of Nola,
querie.	Who was complained of for having
	mocked his superior.

Italian factional disputes shall flourish because of the lack of unity among the people.

75

Pau, Veronne, Vincence, Saragousse,	Pau, Verona, Vicenza, Saragossa,
De Glaives atteints terriors de sang humides;	Hit by the Sword, the country shall be moist with blood,
Peste si grande viendra a la grande gousse,	So great a plague and so vehement shall come
Proches securs & bien loings les remedes.	That though help be near, the remedy shall be far off.

Italian cities, suffering from plague and famine, shall not be able to avail themselves of assistance, due to lack of organization.

76

En Germanie naistront diverses fectes,	In Germany shall divers sects arise,
S'approchant fort de l'heureux paganisme,	Coming very near to happy paganism,
Le coeur captif, & petites receptes	The heart captivated and small receivings,
Feront retour a payer le vray disme.	Shall open the gate to pay the true tithe.

A prophetic description of the rise of the pagan doctrine of National Socialism.

77

Le tiers climat sous Aries comprins,	The third climate comprehended under Aries,
L'ans mil sept cens vingt & sept en Octobre,	In the year 2025, the 27th of October,
Le Roy de Perse par ceux d'Egypte prins,	The King of Persia shall be taken by those of Egypt,
Conflit, mort, perte, a la croix grand opprobre.	Battle, death, loss, a great shame to the Christians.

In the year 2025, under a special chronology enumerated by Nostradamus, strange events are to take place in the Orient much to the shame of Christians.

78

Le chef d'Escosse, avec six d'Ale-	The chief of Scotland with the six
magne,	of Germany,
Par gens de mer Orientaux captifs,	Shall be taken prisoners by the
Traverseront le Calpre & Espagne,	seamen of the east,
Present en Perse au nouveau Roy	They shall go through the Calpre
craintif.	and Spain,
	And shall be made a present in
	Persia to the new fearful king.

A new King of the East shall arise and conquer many lands, and a British leader and six Germans shall be brought to him as hostages, by way of Calpre (the Straits of Gibraltar).

79

Le grand criard sans honte audacieux,	The great squawker proud without
Sera esle gouverneur de l'armee,	shame,
La hardiesse de son contentieux,	Shall be elected governor of the
Le pont rompu, Cite de peur pasmee.	army,
	The stoutness of his competitor,
	The bridge being broken, the city
	shall faint for fear.

A great demagogue, without shame or conscience, shall obtain control of the army, much to the citizens' helpless fear.

80

Erins, Antibe villes autour de Nice,	Ervins, Antibes, and the towns
Seront vastees fort, par met & par	about Nice,
terre,	Shall be destroyed by land and sea,
Les sauterelles terre & mer vent pro-	The grasshoppers shall have the
pice,	land, the sea and wind favour-
Prins, morts, trossez, pillez sans loy	able,
de guerre.	They shall be taken, killed, thrust
	up, plundered, without law of
	war.

The tremendous air fleets used in the invasions of France are clearly indicated.

81

L'ordre fatal sempiternel per chaine,	The fatal and eternal order by chain,
Viendra tourner par ordre consequent;	Shall come to turn by consequent order,
Du port Phocen sera rompue la chaine,	Of Port Phocen the chain shall be broken,
La cite prinse l'ennemy quant & quant.	The city taken, and the enemy presently after.

Phocen is the ancient name for Marseilles. Her harbour chain shall be pierced by the enemy and the port captured.

82

Du regne Anglois l'indigne dechasser,	From the English Kingdom the unworthy driven away,
Le conseiller, par ire mis a feu;	The councillor through the anger shall be burnt,
Ses adherants iront si bas trasser,	His partners shall creep so low,
Que le bastard sera demy receu.	That the bastard shall be half received.

Rudolf Hess, as peace messenger to the Cliveden Set, was repudiated both by his master and also by his British partners, after the chief councillor of Britain, Winston Churchill, burnt with anger on the notification of his errand.

83

Les longs cheveux de la Gaule Celtique,	The long hairs of the Celtic Gaul, Joined with foreign nations,
Accompagnez d'estranges nations,	Shall put in prison the Aquatanic agent,
Mettront captif la gent Aquitanique,	To make him yield to their intentions.
Pour succomber a leurs intentions.	

The intellectuals of Northern France, with the support of foreign agents, shall stamp out and imprison their opponents that favour the opposite view.

84

La grand cite sera bien desoles,	The great city shall be made very desolate,
Des habitans un seul ny demourra,	Not one of the inhabitants shall be left in it,
Mur, sexe, temple, & vierge violee,	Wall, sex, church and virgin ravished,
Par fer, feu, peste, cannon, peuple mourra.	By sword, fire, plague, cannon, people shall die.

Predicts the destructive removal of the Berlin Wall with fierce consequences.

85

Le Cite prinse par tromperie & fraude,	The City shall be taken by cheat and deceit,
Par le moyen d'un beau jeune attrappe,	By means of a fair young one caught in it,
L'assaut donne, Raubine pres de Laude,	Assault shall be given Raubins near Lande,
Luy & tours morts pour avoir bien trompe.	He and all shall die for having deceived.

A forecast of the Fifth Column as originally conceived during the Spanish Civil War, 1936–1939. Later it was used by Hitler in his invasion of the lowlands of Holland, Belgium, and Luxembourg.

86

Un chef d'Ausonne aux Espagnes ira,	A chief man of Ausonne shall go into Spain,
Par mer fera arrest dedans Marseille,	By sea, he shall stay at Marseilles,
Avant sa mort un long temps languira,	He shall languish a great while before his death,
Apres sa mort l'on verra grand merveille.	After his death great wonders shall be seen.

Nostradamus makes constant reference to happenings connected with Ausonne (the city of Bordeaux), and for the most part they are veiled in obscurity.

87

Classe Gauloise n'approches de Corsegne,	French Fleet, do not come near unto Corsica,
Moine de Sardaigne tu t'en repentiras,	Much less to Sardinia, thou shalt repent it.
Trestous mourrez frustres de l'Aide grogne,	All of you shall die frustrated of the help of the great ships,
Sang nagera captif ne me Croiras.	Blood shall swim, being captive thou shalt not believe me.

The French are warned to steer clear of Corsica, the birthplace of Napoleon.

88

De Barcelone par mer si grande armee,	From Barcelona, shall come by sea, so great an army,
Toute Marseille de frayeur tremblera,	That Marseilles shall quake for fear,
Isles saisies, de mer aide fermes,	The Islands shall be seized, help by sea shut up
Ton traditeur en terre nagera.	Thy traitor shall swim to land.

The victory of a force coming from Barcelona is predicted.

89

En ce temps la sera frustre Cypres,	At the time Cyprus shall be frustrated,
De son secours de ceux de Mer Aegee,	Of its help, those of the Aegean Sea,
Vieux trucidez, mais par Mesles & Lipre,	Old ones shall be killed, but by Mesles and Lipre,
Seduict leur Roy, Royne plus outragee.	Their King shall be seduced, and the Queen more wronged.

The island of Cyprus will be besieged and a constant source of conflict between the Turks and Greeks. In 1944 the (US) ambassador was killed on Cyprus.

90

Le grand Satyre & Tygre d'Hycarnie,	The great Satyr and Tiger of Hirca-
Don presente a ceux de l'Ocean,	nia,
Un chef de classe iastra de Carmanie,	Shall be a gift presented to those of
Que prendra terre au Tyrran Pho-	the Ocean,
cean.	An admiral of a fleet shall come out
	of Carmania,
	Who shall land in the Thyrren Pho-
	cean.

Hercynia, in ancient geography, is the mountain region of Germany. The Tiger will be taken prisoner and turned over to a maritime people. Carmania (now called Kerman) is in Persia, and the Thyrren Phocean is Marseilles.

91

L'arbre qu'estoit nar si long temps	The tree that has been long dead
seche,	and withered,
Dans une nuict viendra a reverdir;	In one night shall grow green again,
Son Roy malade, prince pied estache,	His king shall be sick, the prince
Craint d'ennemis fera voiles bondir.	shall have his foot tied,
	Being feared by his enemies, he
	shall make his sail rebound.

A metaphorical description of a renaissance of human understanding to take place in the future.

92

Le monde proche du dernier periode,	The world being near its last
Saturne encor tard sera de retour;	period,
Translat empier devers nation	Saturn shall come yet late to his
Brodde,	return,
L'oeil arrache a Narbon par autour.	The empire shall be changed into
	black nations,
	Narbonne shall have her eye picked
	out by a hawk.

Along towards the end of the world, the dark nations shall reign supreme. This presages the rise of the black (African) and third world nations.

93

Dans Avignon tout le chef de l'Empire,	In Avignon all the chief of the Empire
Fera appreste, pour Paris desole;	Shall stay, by reason of Paris being desolate,
Tricast tiendra l'Annibalique ire,	Tricast shall stop the Hanniballic anger,
Lion par change sera mal console.	The Lion by change shall be ill-comforted.

Avignon, once the seat of the Papal government (1307–76), shall again have power, after Paris is desolate by reason of an African (Hanniballic) anger, and much to the disappointment of the British Lion.

94

De cinq cens ans plus compte l'on tiendra,	For five hundred years no account shall be made
Celuy qu'estoit l'ornament de son temps,	Of him who was the ornament of his time,
Puis a un coup grande clarte donra,	Then of a sudden he shall give so great a light,
Que par es siecle les rendra tres contens.	That for that age he shall make them to be most contented.

Nostradamus here refers to himself. After 500 years, i.e., in 2055, his predictions will have been shown to bear fruit.

95

La Loy Moricque on verra deffaillir,	We shall see the Moorish Law to decline,
Apres une autre beaucoup plus seductive,	After which another more seducing shall arise,
Boristhenes premier viendra faillir,	Boris Thenes shall be the first that shall fall,
Par dons & langues une plus attractive.	By gifts and tongue that law shall be most seducing.

This forecasts the decline of Islam and the rise of Communism at the basin of the Dnieper (Boristhenes) River. A brilliant prediction in view of recent events in Afghanistan.

96

Chef de Fossan aura gorge couppes,
Par le ducteur du Limier & L'curier,
Le fait patre par ceux du mont Tarpee,
Saturns en Leo treziesme Fevrier.

The chief of Fossan shall have his throat cut,
By the leader of Hunt and Greyhound,
The act committed by those of the Tarpian Rock,
Saturn being in Leo, the Thirteenth of February.

The chief man of Northern Italy shall be hunted down by those of Rome and shall die an infamous death.

97

Nouvelle loy terre neuve occuper,
Vers la Syrie, Judee & Palestine,
Le grand Empire Barbare corruer,
Avant que Phebe son siecle determine.

A new law shall occupy a new country,
Towards Syria, Judea and Palestine,
The great Barbarian Empire shall fall down,
Before Phoebe makes an end of her course.

The Arab Confederacy shall fall of its own weight and a new Judea and Palestine shall occupy the place of Syria. This anticipates the origin of the state of Israel and confusion within the Arab confederacy.

98

Deux Royals Freres si fort guerroyeront,
Qu'entre 'eux sera la guerre si mortelle,
Qu'un chacun places fortes occuperont,
De regne & vie sera leur grand querelle.

Two Royal Brothers shall war so much one against the other,
That the war between them shall be mortal,
Each of them shall seize upon strong places,
Their quarrel shall be concerning kingdom and life.

An incident to occur before the World Organization of Nations outlaws wars for personal aggrandizement.

99

Aux champs herbeux d'Alein & du Varneigne,	In the meadow fields of Alein and Varneigne,
Du Mont Lebron proche de la Durance,	Of the brown mountains near the Durance,
Camp des deux parts conflit sera si aigre,	Armies on both sides, the fight shall be so sharp,
Mesopotamie deffaillira en la France.	That Mesopotamia shall be wanting in France.

France is to be the battleground for contending armies in a decisive engagement involving heavy losses.

100

Entre Gaulois le dernier honore,	He that least honoured among the French,
D'homme ennemy sera victorieux,	Shall be conqueror of the man that was his enemy.
Force & terrior en moment explore,	Strength and terror shall in a moment be tried,
D'un coup de trait quand mourra l'envieux.	When the envious shall be killed with an arrow.

The underprivileged classes of France shall emerge victors after overthrowing a conspirator who will continue to be their greatest enemy. Also forecasts the rise of General de Gaulle and his victory over Hitler and the subsequent assassination of Admiral Darlan in 1942.

CENTURY IV

1

Cela du reste de sang non espande,	There shall be a remnant of blood unspilt,
Venise quiert secours estre donne,	Venice shall seek for succour,
Apres avoir bien long temps attendu,	After having long waited for it,
Cite livree au premier cornet sonne.	The city delivered at the first sound of the trumpet.

This concerns the Siege of Candia which lasted for twenty years. The Venetians fought a losing battle with the Turks, expecting, but never receiving, help from the Christian Princes, until eventually the city was compelled to surrender.

2

Par mort la France prendra voyage a faire,	By reason of a death, France shall undertake a journey,
Classe par mer, marcher monts Pyrenees.	They shall have a fleet at sea, and march towards the Pyrenees,
Espagne en trouble, marcher gent militaire,	Spain shall be in trouble by an army,
Des plus grandes dames en France emmences.	Some of the greatest ladies in France carried away.

Conditions in France and Spain during a revolutionary period are forecast in this verse as it occurred in France in 1789 and in Spain in 1936 after which Franco assumed power in 1939.

3

D'Arras & Bourges de Brodes grands enseignes.	From Arras and Bourges many colours of Dark men shall come.
Unplus grand nombre de Gascons battre a pied,	A great number of Gascons shall go on foot,
Ceus long du Rhosne saigneront les Espagnes,	Those along the Rhone shall let Spain blood,
Proche du mont ou Sagonte s'assied.	Near the mountain where Saguntus is seated.

Saguntus, a city in Spain destroyed by the Romans, is here used symbolically. Men of the dark Mediterranean races shall roam widespread over Spain, to her detriment.

4

L'impotent prince fasche, plainte & querelles,	The impotent prince angry complains and quarrels,
De raps & pilles par coqs & par Lybiques,	Concerning rapes and plunderings done by the cocks and Libiques,
Grand est par terre, par mer infinies voilles,	Great trouble by land, by sea infinite sails,
Seule Italie sera chassant Celtiques.	Italy alone shall drive away the French.

Referring to France and Italy's African colonizing exploits; France in the northwest (Algeria and the Sahara) and Italy in Ethiopia and Somaliland.

5

Croix paix soubs un, accomply divin verbe,	The cross shall have peace, under an accomplished divine word,
Espaigne & Gaule seront unis ensemble,	Spain and France shall be united together,
Grand clad proche, & combat tresacerbe,	A great battle near hand and a most sharp fight,
Coeur si hardy ne sera qui ne tremble.	No heart so stout but shall tremble.

A bold prophecy. Spain remained neutral in World War II and later was unallied to East and West in the political struggle in the latter half of the twentieth century, but is here visualized as joining with France and NATO (North Atlantic Treaty Organization). Spain and France shall have military, political, and eventually economic ties, i.e., the Common Market.

6

D'habits nouveaux apres fait la treuve,	After the new clothes shall be found out,
Malice tramme & machination;	There shall be malice, plotting and machination,
Premier mourra qui en sera la preuve,	He shall die the first, that shall make trial of it.
Couleur Venise insidiation.	Under the cover of Venice, shall be a conspiracy.

A new form of government, by conspirators cast out by the Italians, shall destroy the innovators.

7

Le mineur fils du grand & hay prince,	The younger of the great and hated prince,
De lepre aura a vingt ans grande tache;	Being twenty years old shall have a great touch of leprosy,
De dueil sa mere mourra bien trist & mince,	His mother shall die of grief, very sad and lean,
Et il mourra la ou tombe chef lasche.	And he shall die of the disease loose flesh.

The King of Rome, Napoleon II, son of Napoleon and the ill-fated Marie Louise, died in 1832 after a wasting sickness lasting a year, at the age of twenty.

8

La grand cite d'assault pront & repentin,	The great city shall be taken by a sudden assault,
Surprins de nuict, gardes interrompus,	Being surprised by night, the watch being beaten,
Les excubies & veilles saint Quintin,	The court of guard and watch of St Quentin,
Trucidez gardes & les portails rompus.	Shall be killed, and the gate broken.

The battle of St Quentin was one of the decisive fights in World War I. The Germans almost broke the Allied lines at this point in a surprise attack.

9

Le chef du camp au milieu de la presse,	The chief of the camp in the middle of the crowd,
D'un coup de flesche blesse aux cuisses.	Shall be wounded with an arrow through both his thighs,
Lors que Geneve en larmes & en detresse	When Geneva being in tears and distress,
Sera trahy par Lozan & Souysses.	Shall be betrayed by Lausanne and the Swiss.

The Treaty of Lausanne completely sabotaged the work of the League of Nations.

10

Le jeune Prince accuse feucement,	The young prince being falsely accused,
Mettra en trouble le camp & en querelles;	Shall put the camp in trouble and in quarrels,
Meurtry le chef pour le sous Levement,	The chief shall be murdered by the tumult,
Scepter appraiser, puis guerir escrouelles.	The sceptre shall be appeased and later cure the king's evil.

Edward, Prince of Wales, was accused of being a Nazi sympathizer. He was feted by the Germans in the 1930s and later became an apologist for their aggressive behaviour. His reign as King Edward VIII did not last very long.

11

Celuy qu'aura couvert de la grand cappe,	He that shall be covered with a great cloak
Sera induit a quelque cas patrer;	Shall be induced to commit some great act,
Le douze rouges viendront souiller la nape,	The twelve red ones shall soil the table cloth,
Soubs meutre, meurtre se viendra perpetrer.	Under murder, murder shall be committed.

Evidently a phase of the activities of the Roman Catholic Church – the Twelve Red Ones, being Cardinals, and the Great Cloak, the Pope.

12

Le camp plus grand de route mis en suit,	The greatest camp being in disorder shall be routed,
Geures plus outre ne sera pourchasse;	And shall be pursued not much after,
Ost recampe & region reduicte	The army shall encamp again, and the troops set in order,
Puis hors de Gaule du tout sera chasse.	Then afterwards, they shall be wholly driven out of France.

The invasions of France by the Germans are here predicted. Nostradamus forecasts the eventual, and complete, victory of France.

13

De plus grand perte nouvelles rapportees,	News being brought of a great loss,
Le rapport fait le camp s'eslongnera,	The report divulged, the camp shall be astonished,
Bendes unies encontre revoltes,	Troops being united and revolted,
Double phalange, grand abandonnera.	The falange shall forsake the great one.

The revolt of the Spanish Army and Falangists against Franco's dictatorial power is predicted. The founder and chief Falangist spokesman, Jose Antonio Primo de Rivera, finally forsook Franco and was executed in November 1936.

14

La mort subiette du premier personnage,	The sudden death of the chief man,
Aura change & mis un autre au regne,	Shall cause a change, and put another in the reign soon,
Tost, tard venu a si haut & bas age,	Late come to so high a degree in a low age,
Que terre & mer faudra qu'on le craingne.	So that by land and sea he must be feared.

The sudden death of the president is here predicted with his successor being a young vice-president. The assassination attempt on President Reagan in 1981 very closely approaches this forecast.

15

D'ou pensera faire venir famine,	Whence one thought to make famine to come,
De la viendra le rassassiement;	Thence shall come the fullness,
L'oeil de la mer par avare canine,	The eye of the sea through a doggish covetousness,
Pour de l'un l'autre donra huille froment.	Shall give to both, oil and wheat.

Nostradamus here anticipated off-shore drilling and recovery of huge oil reserves from the 'eye of the sea.' Further, the sea provides many food products in the form of fish, vegetables, and minerals, but oil is the key to this quatrain.

16

La cite franche de liberte fait serue,	The free city from a free one shall become slave,
Des profligez & resueurs fait azyle;	And of the banished and dreamers shall be a retreat,
Le Roy change a eux non si proterue,	The King changed in mind shall not be so unfavourable to them,
De cent seront devenus plus de mille.	Of one hundred, they shall become more than a thousand.

The Free City of Danzig, enslaved by the Nazis, was nevertheless highly favoured by them, even to the point of expansion.

17

Changer a Beaune, Nuis, Chalons, Dijon,	There shall be a change at Beaune, Nuis, Chalons, Dijon,
Le Duc voulant amender la barree,	The Duke going about to raise taxes,
Marchant pres fleuve, poisson bec de Plongeon,	The Merchant near the river shall see the tail,
Verra la queue port sera serree.	Of a fish, having the bill of a loon, the door shall be shut.

A submarine shall be seen by a merchant, in a river near the above-mentioned French towns.

18

Des plus lettrez dessus les faits celestes,	The most learned in the celestial sciences,
Seront par princes ignorans reprouvez,	Shall be found fault with by ignorant princes,
Punis d'edit, chassez comme celestes,	Punished by a proclamation, chased away as wicked,
Et mis a mort la ou seront trouvez.	And put to death where they shall be found.

The warnings of learned scientists shall be scoffed at by ignorant persons in power, even to the point of persecution.

Nostradamus explicitly charges mankind to heed the warnings of science and take atomic power under international control.

19

Devant Rouan d'insubres mis le siege,	Before Rouen, a siege shall be laid by the Italians,
Par terre & mer enfermez les passages,	By sea and land the passages shall be shut up.
D'Haynaut, & Flandres de Gand & ceux de Liege,	Those of Hainaut, Flanders, Ghent and Liege,
Par dons levees raviront les rivages.	With them troops shall plunder the sea shore.

An incident in the many wars among the European nations is here forecast.

20

Paix ubertre long temps Dieu louera,	Peace and plenty shall be not long praised,
Par tout son regne desert la fleur de lis	All the time of his reign the Fleur de Lys shall be deserted,
Corps morts d'eau, terre la l'on apportera,	Bodies shall die by water, earth shall be bought,
Aperant vain heur d'estre la ensevelis.	Hoping vainly to be there buried.

This predicts a great famine and flood in France, here signified by the Fleur de Lys.

21

Le changement sera fort difficile,	The change shall be very hard,
Cite province au change gain sera,	The city and country shall gain by
Coeur haut, prudent mis, chasse luy	the change,
habile,	A high prudent heart shall be put
Mer, terre, peuple, son estat changera.	in, the unworthy expelled,
	Sea, land, people, its state shall
	change.

This is the forecast of a revolution that will bring great and good changes to all.

22

La grand copie que sera dechassee,	The great army that shall be rejec-
Dans un moment fera besoin au Roy,	ted,
La foy promise de loing sera faussee,	In a moment shall be wanted by the
Nud se verra en piteux desarroy.	King,
	The faith promised afar off shall be
	broken,
	So that he shall be left naked in a
	pitiful case.

A continuation of the preceding stanza, this tells of the disintegration of the royal army and their desertion from the King to the cause of revolution. Note the changes in Iran.

23

La Legion dans la Marine classe,	The Legion in the Maritime Fleet,
Calcine, Magne, souphre & poix	Calcining greatly, shall burn brim-
bruslera,	stone and pitch,
Le long repos de l'asseuree place,	After a long rest in the secure place,
Port Selyn chercher feu les consumera.	They shall seek Port Selyn, but fire
	shall consume them.

A terrific assault by a great fleet equipped with weapons employing potent chemical agents, shall attack a country which has long enjoyed peace and security. They shall attack the great Port of LES N. Y. but will be repulsed by weapons even more terrible.

24

Ouy sous terre saincts d'ame voix fainte,	Underground shall be heard the feigned voice of a holy dame,
Humains flamme pour divin voir luire,	A human flame to see a divine one
Fera des seuls de leur sang terre tainte,	Shall cause the ground to be dyed with their own blood,
Et les saincts temples pour les impure destruire.	And the holy temples to be destroyed by the wicked.

Under the guise of a so-called reform movement, humanity shall suffer much and the holy temples shall be destroyed.

25

Corps sublimes san fin a l'oeil visibles,	The celestial bodies that are always visible to the eye,
Obnubiler viendra par ses raisons,	Shall be darkened for these reasons,
Corps, front comprins, sense, chef & invisibles,	The body with the forehead, sense and head invisible,
Dimineant les sacrees oraisons.	Diminishing the sacred prayers.

The occult knowledge of 'prophets' shall flourish during this period, keeping alive the hope of the world.

26

Lou grand cyssame le levera d'al-belhos,	The great swarm of bees shall rise, And it shall not be known whence they come,
Que non sauran don, te signen ven guddos,	Towards the ambush, the jay shall be under a trellis,
Denech l'embousq, sou gach sous las treilhos,	A city shall be betrayed by five tongues not naked.
Cuitad trahido per cinq lengos non nudos.	

'Bees' refers to the emblem Napoleon used for his dynasty, and the 'five' relates to the Directory which gave way to Napoleon's Consulate.

27

Salon, Mansol, Tarascon de Sex l'arc,	Salon, Mansol, Tarascon of six arches
Ou est debout encor la pyramide;	Where is still standing the pyramids,
Viendront livrer le prince d'Denemark,	Shall come to deliver the Prince of Denmark,
Rachapt honny au temple d'Artemide.	A shameful ransom shall be paid into the temple of Artemis.

Provincial towns are named here and the arches mentioned are the ruins of ancient triumphal monuments erected by the Romans. Artemis is another name for Diana.

28

Lors que Venus du Sol sera couvert;	When Venus shall be covered by the Sun,
Soubs l'esplendeur sera forme occulte;	Under the splendour it shall be an occult form,
Mercure au feu les aura descouvert,	Mercury in the fire shall discover them,
Par bruit bellique sera mis a l'insulte.	And by a warlike rumour shall be provoked.

An allegorical stanza, wherein is expressed a hidden formula, having to do with the preparation of the elixir to make the hermetic Philosopher's Stone. The same occult directions are given also in the three stanzas following.

29

Le Sol cache eclipse par Mercure,	The Sun shall be hid and eclipsed by Mercury,
Ne sera mis que pour le ciel second;	And shall not be set but for the second heaven,
De Vulcan Hermes sera faite pasture,	Hermes shall be made a prey to Vulcan,
Sol sera veu pur rutilant & blond.	And after that the Sun shall be seen pure, shining and yellow.

The Sun refers to gold, the second heaven means a furnace. 'Hermes a prey to Vulcan' indicates the elixir to be put upon the fire in a furnace.

30

Plus onze fois Lune Sol ne voudre,	The Moon will not have the Sun
Tous augmentez & baissez de degree;	above eleven times,
Et si bas mis que peu d'or le secret,	Then both shall be increased and
Qu'apres faim, peste, decouvert le	lessened in degree,
secret.	And put so low, that a little gold
	shall be sewed up,
	So that after hunger and plague, the
	secret shall be discovered.

Alchemical formulae and processes are clearly expressed for the adept, but are most confusing for the uninitiated.

31

Le lune au plain de nuict sur le haut	The moon at full by night upon the
mont	high mount,
Le nouveau sophe d'un seul cerveau	The new Sophe with only one brain
l'a veu,	has seen it,
Par ses disciples estre immortel	Invited by his disciples to become
semond,	immortal,
Yeux au midy, en sens mains corps au	His eyes to the south, his hands and
feu.	body to the fire.

The Sophe, or wise man, has mastered the secret. Invited to reveal the secret to the world, by his disciples, he refuses, and does not become immortal.

32

Es lieux & temps chair au poisson	In places and times, flesh shall give
dorna lieu.	way to flesh,
La loy commune sera faite au con-	The common law shall be made
traire,	against it;
Vieux tiendra fort, puis este du milieu,	The old man shall stand fast, then
Le Panta, Choina Philon, mis fort	being taken away,
arriere.	Then all things common among
	friends, shall be set aside.

Panta, Choina Philon are Greek words expressed best in English as 'All things are common among friends.'

33

Jupiter joint plus Venus qu'a la Lune,	Jupiter being more joined to Venus
Apparoissant de plentitude blanche;	than to the Moon,
Venus cachee sous la blancheur Neptune,	Appearing in a full whiteness,
De Mars frappee par la grande branche.	Venus being hid under the whiteness of Neptune,
	Stricken by Mars through the engraved branch.

Those in power shall give more time to the pleasures of Venus than to other activities, until the sudden onslaught of a war.

34

Le grand mene captif d'estrange terre,	The great one brought prisoner from a far country,
D'or enchaine au Roy Chyren offert;	And chained with gold, shall be presented to Henry, the ruler,
Qui dans Ausonne, Milan perdra la guerre,	Being then at Ausonne, Milan shall lose the war,
Et tout son ost mis a feu & a fer.	And all its host put to fire and sword.

Nostradamus interprets this literally, thus: When a great one from a far country shall be brought prisoner chained with gold, and presented to a King called Henry (for Chyren by transposition of letters is Henryc) who then shall be at Bordeaux (Ausonne), Milan shall lose a great army.

35

Le feu estaint les vierges trahyront,	The fire being put out, the virgins shall betray,
La plus grand part de la bande nouvelle;	The greatest part of the new troupe,
Poudre a fer, lance les seule Roy garderont,	Gunpowder, lance, shall keep only the King,
Etrusque & Corse de nuict gorge allumelle.	In Etruria and Corsica by night, throats shall be cut.

An insurrection in Italy (Etruria) is predicted, which shall take place at night and be betrayed by Virgins.

36

Les jeux nouveaux en Gaule redres-sez,	The new plays shall be set up again in France,
Apres victoire de l'Insubre campagne,	After the victory obtained in Piedmont,
Monts d'Esperie, les grands liez trous-sez,	Mountains of Spain, the great ones tied and carried away,
De peur trembler la Romaine & Espagne.	Romania and Spain shall quake for fear.

France again will be triumphant after a victory over the Italians. Over the mountains of Spain the great ones will be carried away, and Romania and Spain shall be in terror.

37

Gaulois par sauts, monts viendra penetrer.	The French by leaping shall go over the mountains,
Occupera le grand lieu de l'Insubre;	And shall seize the great mount of the Savoyard,
Au plus profond son ost fera entrer,	He shall cause his army to go to the furthermost,
Gennes, Monech pousseront classe rubre.	Genoa, and Monaco shall set out their red fleet.

This prophecy concerns Henry IV, King of France, who went over the Alps and conquered the dukedom of Savoy.

38

Pendant que Duc, Roy, Roynes oc-cupera,	While the Duke shall keep the King and Queen busy,
Chef Bizantin captif en Samothrace;	A great man of Constantinople shall be prisoner in Greece;
Avant l'assaut l'un l'autre mangera,	Before the assault one shall eat up the other,
Rebours ferre suyura de sang la trace.	Rebours armoured shall trace one by the blood.

A great tumult and riot will occur before the city is captured by the heavily armoured enemy.

39

Les Rodiens demanderont secours,	The Rhodians shall ask for aid,
Par le neglet de ses hoirs delaisses,	Being forsaken by the neglect of her heirs,
L'empire Arabe revalera son cours,	The Arabian Empire shall slack his course,
Par Hesperies la cause redressee.	By means of Spain the care shall be mended.

The current dominance of Saudi Arabia in the world of petro-dollars is seen to decline.

40

Les forteresses des assiegez ferrez,	The strong places of the besieged shall be pressed,
Par poudre a feu profondes en abysme;	By gunpowder they shall be plunged into a pit,
Les prodireurs seront tous vifs serrez,	The traitors shall be shut up alive,
Onc aux Sacristes n'advint si piteux scisme.	Never did happen so pitiful a schism to the Sacristes.

By *Sacristes*, the author means that part of the Roman Catholic Church that is in charge of the books and property. There seems to be a warning implicit in this quatrain – probably slanted against those whom Nostradamus considered heretics.

41

Cynique sexe captive hostage,	Cynical sex being captive by hostage,
Viendra de nuict custodes decevoir;	Shall come by night to deceive her keepers,
Le chef du camp deceu par son lignage,	The chief of the camp being deceived by her language,
Liarra le genre, fera piteux avoir.	Shall keep her folks, a thing pitiful to behold.

Clearly foretells the trials and tribulations of Patti Hearst in America in 1974–1975. Ransom and gifts in millions were provided before this radical group was disbanded.

42

Geneve & Langres par ceux de Char- *tre & Dole*	Geneva and Langres by those of Chartres and Dole,
Et par Grenoble captif au Montlimar,	And by one of Grenoble captive at
Seysset, Losanne par fraudulente *dole,*	Montelimar,
Les trahyront par or soixante marc.	Seisset, Lausanne by a fraudulent deceit,
	Shall betray them for thirty pounds weight of gold.

The sense is plain, and this apparently refers to struggles among various towns in France.

43

Seront ouys au ceil les armes battre,	There shall be heard in the air the
Celuy an mesme les divins ennemis,	noise of weapons,
Voudront Loix Sainctes injustement *debatre,*	And in that same year, the divines shall be enemies,
Par foudre & guerre bien croyants a *mort mis.*	They shall unjustly put down the Holy Laws,
	And by thunder and the war, true believers shall die.

A religious war shall break out, during which many true believers will suffer again. Also, once again, Nostradamus forecasts aerial warfare.

44

Deux gros de Mende de Rhodes & *Millaud,*	Two great ones of Mendes, of Rhodes and Millaud,
Cahors, Limoges, Castre malo sep- *mano,*	Cahors, Limoges, Castres, an evil week,
De nuech l'intrado, de Bordeaux an *cailhau,*	By night the entry shall be from Bordeaux one cailhau,
Par Perigort au toc de la Campano.	Through Perigort at the ringing of the bell.

Towns near the home of Nostradamus are spoken of here, and a rising against tax collectors is indicated.

45

Par conflit Roy Regne abandonnera,
Le plus grand chef faillira au besoing,
Morts profligez, peu en rechappera,
Tous destranchez, un en sera tesmoin.

By a battle the King shall forsake his kingdom,
The great commander shall fail in time of need,
They shall be killed and routed, few shall escape,
They shall be cut off, one only shall be left for a witness.

The Battle of Waterloo is prognosticated. His defeat in this battle, due to the failure of Marshal De Grouchy, caused Napoleon to lose his Empire.

46

Bien deffendu le fait par excellence,
Garde toy Tours de ta proche ruyne;
Londres & Nantes par Reims fera deffence
Ne passez outre au temps de la bruyne.

The fact shall be defended excellently well,
Tours beware of thy approaching ruin,
London and Nantes by Rheims shall stand upon their defence,
Do not go further in foggy weather.

Tours, a city in France, is warned of a fog, and told to beware of her approaching ruin.

47

Le noir farouche quand aura essaye,
Sa main sanguine par feu, fer arcs, tendus,
Trestout le peuple sera tant effraye,
Voir les plus grands par col & pieds pendus.

The wild black one, after he shall have tried,
His bloody hand by fire, sword, bended bows,
All the people shall be so frightened,
To see the greatest hanged by neck and feet.

Astonishingly accurate prophecy of the fate of Mussolini, Leader of the Black Shirts. After his death, he was hung by his feet for the mob to spit upon.

48

Plannure, Ausonne fertille, spacieuse,	The plain about Bordeaux fruitful and spacious,
Produira tahons si tant de sauterelles,	Shall produce so many hornets and so many grasshoppers,
Clarte solaire viendra nubileuse,	That the light of the sun shall be darkened,
Ronger le tout, grand peste venir d'elles.	They shall fly so low, a great plague shall come from them.

The prediction here is of the D-Day invasion of France by the Allies in World War II; at that time the sky was darkened by the tremendous concentration of Air Power.

49

Devant le peuple sang sera respandu,	Before the people, blood shall be spilt,
Que du haut ciel ne viendra eslongner;	Who shall not come far from high heaven,
Mais d'un long temps ne sera entendu,	But it shall not be heard of for a great while,
L'esprit d'un seul le viendra tesmoigner.	The spirit of one shall come to witness it.

Foretells the assassination of a great leader, John F. Kennedy, later followed by his alter ego (spirit) brother, Robert Kennedy. The 'great while' implies some passage of time between the death of Robert Kennedy and the attempt on the life of the last brother, Edward Kennedy.

50

Libra verra regner les Hesperies,	Libra shall see Spain to reign,
De Ciel and Terra tenir la monarchie,	And have the monarchy of Heaven and Earth,
D'Asie forces nul ne verra peries,	Nobody shall see the forces of Asia to perish,
Que sept ne tiennent par rang la Hierarchie.	Till seven have kept the Hierarchy successively.

A Spaniard shall attain to the office of Pope, Monarch of Heaven and Earth, and after seven of the Spanish faction have reigned successively then the Asiatic forces will be overcome.

51

Un Duc cupide son ennemy ensuyvre,
Dans entrera empeschant la phal-
lange,
Hastez a pied si pres viendront pour-
suyvre,
Que la journee conflit pres de Gange.

A Duke being earnest in the pursuit
of his enemy,
Shall come in, hindering the fa-
lange,
Hastened on foot shall follow them
so close,
That the day of the battle shall be
near Ganges.

Lord Louis Mountbatten was appointed Viceroy of India in 1947. Later
strife between India and Pakistan is predicted as well as the murder of
Mountbatten. His yacht was blown up by terrorists.

52

En cite obsessee aux murs hommes &
femmes,
Ennemys hors le chef prest a soy
rendre,
Vent sera fort encontre les
gens-d'armes,
Chassez seront par chaux, poussiere &
cendre.

In a besieged city, men and women
being upon the walls,
The enemy without, the governor
ready to surrender,
The wind shall be strong against
the soldiers,
They shall be driven away by lime,
dust and cinders.

Urban America has become a series of besieged cities whose militia is
under constant harassment by urban guerrillas fighting with stones, debris,
etc.

53

Les fugitifs & bannis revoquez,
Peres & fils grand garnissant les haut
poits;
Le cruel pere & les siens suffoquez,
Son fils plus pire submerge dans le
puis.

The fugitive and banished men
being rescued,
Fathers and sons garnishing the
high walls,
The cruel father and his retinue
shall be suffocated,
His son, being worse, shall be
drowned in the well.

The reappearance of evil men, banished because of their part in the
making of war, once again shall usher in a period of destruction.

54

Du nom qui onc ne fut au Roy Gaulois,	Of a name that a French King never was,
Jamais ne fut un foudre si craintif,	There was never a lightning so much feared,
Tremblant l'Italie l'Espagne & les Anglois,	Italy shall tremble, Spain and the English
De femme estrangers grandement attentif.	He shall be much taken with women strangers.

This concerns Napoleon Bonaparte, even to his many amours.

55

Quand la Corneille sur tour de brique jointe,	When the Crow on a tower made of brick
Durant sept heures ne fera que crier,	For seven hours shall do nothing but cry,
Mort presagee de sang statue tainte,	Death shall be foretold and the statue dyed with blood,
Tyran meurtry, aux Dieux peuple prier.	Tyrant shall be murdered and the people pray to the Gods.

A tyrant will be murdered after a 'crow on a tower of brick' (broadcast studio?) shall cry out the news.

56

Apres victoire de raibeuse langue,	After victory over a raging tongue,
L'esprit tempte en tranquil & repos;	The mind that was tempted shall be in tranquillity and rest,
Victeur sanguin par conflit fait harangue,	The bloody emperor by battle shall make a speech,
Rostir la langue, & la chair & les os.	And roast the tongue, the flesh and the bones.

Adolf Hitler was known to have had a raging tongue. Line 4 predicts the extermination ovens of Nazi Germany. A grim but true prediction.

57

Ignare envie du grand Roy supportee,	Ignorant envy being supported by the great King
Tiendra propos deffendre les escrits;	Shall talk of prohibiting the writings,
Sa femme non femme par un autre tentee,	His wife no wife, being tempted by another,
Plus double deux ne feront ne cris.	Shall no more than they two prevail by crying.

Envious persons, in favour with the King, shall attempt to suppress learning. But the King's mistress shall persuade him to the contrary, and shall prevail.

58

Soleil ardant dans le gosier coller,	Burning sun shall pour into the throat,
De sang humain arroser terre Etrusque;	This human blood shall wet the Etruscan ground,
Chef seille d'eau mener son fils filer,	The chief pail of water shall lead his son to spin,
Captive dame conduite en terre Turque.	A captive lady shall be carried into the Turkish country.

Molten gold shall be poured into a throat and human blood shall flow. Because of this, a great water carrier shall make his son effeminate, and a captive lady shall be exiled.

59

Deux assiegez en ardante fureur,	Two besieged, being in a burning heat,
De soif estaints pour deux plaines tasses,	Shall die for thirst, want of two cups full,
Le fort limen & un vieillard resueur,	The fort being filed, an old doting man,
Aux Genois de Nizza monstrera trasse.	Shall show to the Genoese the way to Nice.

Nice shall be taken by the Italians through the help of an old dotard.

60

Les sept enfans en hostage laissez,
Le tiers viendra son enfant trucider;
Deux par son fils seront d'estoc percez,
Gennes, Florence, lors viendra encon-
der.

The seven children being left in hostage,

The third shall come to kill his child,

Two of their sons shall be run through,

Genoa and Florence shall second them.

Evidently this indicates an event which occurred during the time of Nostradamus, and according to him should be understood by all.

61

Le vieux mocque, & prive de sa place,
Par l'estranger qui le subornera;
Mains de son fils mangees devant sa
face
Les freres a Chartres, Orleans, Rouen
trahyra.

The old man shall be baffled and deprived of his place,

By the stranger that shall have instigated him,

But his sons shall be eaten before his face,

The brothers at Chartres, Orleans shall betray Rouen.

Foretells the downfall and disgrace of President Nixon. His 'sons' refers to his party colleagues who were soundly defeated after the Watergate scandal.

62

Un coronel machine ambition,
Se saisira de la plus grande armee;
Contree son prince fainte invention,
Et descouvert sera sous sa ramee.

A colonel intrigues a plot by his ambition,

He shall seize upon the best part of the army,

Against the prince he shall have a feigned invention,

And shall be discovered under the harbour of the vine.

Nostradamus here predicts the downfall of the dictator of Libya, Col. Muammar el-Qaddafi. His rivalry with the Saudi princes shall remain fierce until his demise.

63

L'armee Celtique contre les Montag-nars,	The Celtic army shall go against the Highlanders,
Qui seront sceus & prins a la pipee;	Who shall stand upon their guard, and being taken with trickery,
Paysans irez pouseront tost faugnars,	The peasant being angry, shall roll down the stones,
Precipitez tous au fil de l'espee.	They shall be all put to the edge of the sword.

The heroic peasant rebellion of the Austrian Tyrol, under Andreas Hofer, against the French Republican Army, is here prophesied by our author.

64

Le deffaillant en habit de bourgeois,	The guilty, in a citizen's habit,
Viendra le Roy tempter de son offense,	Shall come to tempt the King concerning his offence,
Quinze soldats la plus part ostagois,	Fifteen soldiers the most part hostages,
Vie derniere & chef de sa chevance.	Last shall be his life and the best part of his estate.

Note the Iranian crisis with the United States in 1979–1980. The King (Shah) had to abdicate under the pressure of the citizenry and the American hostages were taken and eventually freed.

65

Au deserteur de la grand forteresse,	To the deserter of the great fortress,
Apres qu'aura son lieu abandonne;	After having forsaken his place,
Son adversaire fera si grand provesse,	His adversary shall do great feats,
L'Empereur tost mort sera condamne.	That the Emperor shall soon be condemned to death.

Treachery shall play a prominent part in the destruction of a future emperor who will be condemned to a living death.

66

Soubs couleur fainte de sept'testes rasees,	Under the feigned colour of seven shaven heads,
Seront semez divers explorateurs;	Shall divers spies be framed,
Puys & fontaines de poison arrousees,	Wells and fountains shall be sprinkled with poison,
Au fort de Gennes humaine devorateurs.	In the fort of Genoa shall be human devourers.

Seven priests or monks shall poison the well of public opinion, and in Genoa shall be those that live on human flesh.

67

L'an que Saturne & Mars eagaux combust,	In the year that Saturn and Mars shall be fiery,
L'air fort seiche, longue trajection;	The air shall be very dry, in many countries,
Par feux secrets, d'ardeur grand lieu adust	By secret fires, many places shall be burnt with heat,
Peu pluye, vent, chaud, guerres, incursions.	There shall be scarcity of rain, hot winds, wars, wounds.

A prognostication that Saturn (Commerce) and Mars (War) shall have a Roman Holiday.

68

En l'an bien proche eslongue de Venus,	In the year that is to come soon, and not far from Venus,
Les deux plus grands de L'Asie & d'Affrique;	The two greatest ones of Asia and Africa,
De Rhin, & Hyster, qu'on dira sont venus,	Shall be said to come from the Rhine and Ister,
Cris, pleurs a Malte & coste a Lycustique.	Crying and tears shall be at Malta and on the Italian Shore.

From the shores of the Rhine and Danube shall come those who will bring woe on Malta and also to the Italian shores.

69

La cite grande les exilez tiendront,	The banished shall keep the great city,
Les citadins morts meurtris & chassez;	
Ceux d'Aquilee a Parmee promet-tront,	The citizens being dead, murdered and expelled,
Monstrer l'entree par les lieux non trassez.	Those of Aquelia shall promise to Parma,
	To show the entrance by unknown paths.

Aquelia and Parma are Italian cities and, according to Nostradamus, they will be involved in inter-city warfare.

70

Bien contigue des grands monts Pyrenees,	Near the great Pyrenees Mountains,
Un contre l'Aigle grand copie addres-ser;	One shall raise a great army against the Eagle,
Ouvertes vaines, forces exterminees,	Veins shall be opened, forces driven out,
Que jusque a Pau, le chef viendra chasser.	So that the chief shall be driven as far as the Po.

Near the Spanish border one shall raise an army against an Emperor, whose emblem is the Eagle, but to no avail, as the chief of the army will flee and his forces will be scattered.

71

En lieu d'espouse les filles trucidees,	Instead of the bride, the maid shall be killed,
Meurtre a grand faute ne sera super-stile;	The murder shall be a great fault, none shall be surviving,
Dedans le puys vestuies inondees,	In the well they shall be drowned with their clothes,
L'espouse estaint par haute d'Aco-nite.	The bride shall be disposed of by high Aconite.

This tells of the tragic aftermath of a marriage, in which the bridesmaids shall be drowned in their wedding finery and the bride poisoned by Aconite.

72

Les Artomiques par Agen & Lectoure,	The Artomiques, through Agen and Lectoure,
A saint Felix feront leur parlement,	Shall keep their parliament at Saint Felix,
Ceux de Basas viendront a la malheure,	These of Bazan shall come in an unhappy hour,
Saisir Condon & Marsan promptement.	To seize Condon and Marsan speedily.

By Artomiques, our author means the Protestants, who take the Communion with leavened bread, called in Greek, *Artos.* The towns mentioned are all in Gascony.

73

Le nepveu grand par forces prouvera,	The great nephew by force shall provoke,
Le peche fait du coeur pusillanime;	The sin committed by a pusillanimous heart,
Ferrare & Ast le Duc esprouvera,	Ferrari and Asti shall make a trial of the Duke,
Par lors qu'au soir fera la pantomime.	When the pantomime shall be in the evening.

While the performance of a comedy is being enacted, a cowardly person, provoked by his nephew, shall go on a rampage.

74

Du Lac Leman & ceux de Brannonices,	From Lake Geneva and to Verona,
Tous assemblez contre ceux d'Aquitaine,	They shall be gathered against those of England,
Germains beaucoup encor plus souisses,	Great many Germans and many more mercenaries,
Seront defaicts avec ceux d'Humaine.	Shall be routed together with many people.

The Germans and their allies shall be decisively beaten by the English-speaking allies during a great campaign in Italy.

75

Prest a combattre fera defection,	One being ready to fight shall faint,
Chef adversaire obtiendra la victoire,	The chief of the adverse party shall obtain the victory,
L'arriere garde fera defension,	The rear guard shall fight it out,
Les deffaillans mort au blanc terri- *toire.*	Those that fall away shall die in the white country.

A prediction of the conflict in the Pacific between the US and Japan. After the original naval feint at islands other than Pearl Harbor, Japan made its attack on the American Fleet. Later, American victories developed from rearguard actions against Japanese resistance on many islands.

76

Les Nictobriges par ceux de Perigort,	The Nictobriges by those of Perigort,
Seront vexez tenant jusques au *Rhosne,*	Shall be vexed as far as the Rhone,
L'associe de Gascons & Bigorre,	The associate of the Gascons and Bigorre,
Trahir le temple, le prestre estant au *prosne.*	Shall betray the church while the priest is in his pulpit.

Nictobriges, in Greek, signifies a people of a dark and moist country. – Perigort and Bigorre are towns in France.

77

Selyn monarque, L'Italie pacificque,	Selyn being monarch, Italy shall be in peace,
Regnes unis Roy Chrestien du monde;	Kingdoms shall be united, a Christian King of the world,
Mourant voudra coucher en terre bel- *sique,*	Dying, shall desire to be buried in Europe.
Apres pyrates avoir chasse de l'onde.	After he shall have driven the pirates from the sea.

During a time of peace, all the world will be united under a great and noble king who will be a Christian.

78

La grand armee de la pugnee civille,	The great army belonging to the civil war,
Pour de nuict Parme a l'estrange trouvee	Having found by night Parma possessed by strangers,
Septante neuf meurtris dedans la ville,	Shall kill seventy-nine in the town
Les estrangers passez tous a l'espee.	And put all the strangers to the sword.

Great civil wars are promised for Parma and other Italian cities.

79

Sang Royal fuis, Monheurt, Mas, Aiguillon,	Royal Blood run away from Monheurt, Marsan, Aiguillon,
Remplis seront de Bourdelois les Landes,	The Landes shall be full of Bourdelois,
Navarre, Bigorre, pointes & eguillons,	Navarre, Bigorre, shall have points and pricks,
Profonds de faim, vorer de liege, glandes.	Being deep in hunger, they shall devour the cork and acorns.

Bourdelois refers to the people of Bordeaux. Landes is a desert region in France near the towns of Navarre and Bigorre. As in quatrain 76, there seems to be no deeper significance beyond Nostradamus's concern with these French towns and their current troubles.

80

Pres du grand fleuve grand fosse terre egeste	Near the great river, a great pit, earth dug out,
En quinze part sera l'eau divisee,	In fifteen parts, the water shall be divided,
La cite prinse, feu, sang, cris, conflit mestre,	The city taken, fire, sword, blood, cries, fighting,
Et la plus part concerne au collisee.	The greatest part concerns the Colosseum.

In Rome there shall be a great tumult and fighting, concerning in most part a revival of ancient ideas.

81

Pont on fera promptement de nacelles,
Passer l'armee du grand prince Belgique;
Dans profondrees & non loing de Bruxelles,
Outre passez, destrenchex sept a picque.

A bridge of boats shall suddenly be made,
To pass over the army of the great Belgian Prince.
In deep places, and not far from Brussels,
Being gone over, there shall be seven cut with a pike.

A prophecy of the Siege of Antwerp by the Spanish under the Prince of Parma, who eventually erected a pontoon bridge over the River Schelde and captured the city.

82

Amas s'approche venant d'Esclavonie,
L'Olestant vieux cite ruynera;
Fort desclee vera sa Romaine,
Puis la grand flamme estaindre ne scaura.

A great troop gathered shall come from Russia,
The old Olestant shall ruin a city,
He shall see his Romania very desolate,
And after that, shall not be able to quench that great flame.

Russia will dominate a bloc of neighbouring countries but the flame of freedom shall not be extinguished. After uprising after uprising, Russia shall be in big trouble – see Yugoslavia, Poland, Czechoslovakia, Romania, East Germany.

83

Combat nocturne le vaillant capitaine,
Vaincu fuyra, peu de gens profligee;
Son peuple esmeu, sedition non vaine,
Son propre fils le tiendra assiege.

In a fight by night, the valiant captain
Being vanquished shall run away, overcome by few.
His people being moved, shall make no small mutiny,
His own son shall besiege him.

An event in Nostradamus's time which he felt needed no explanation.

84

Un grand d'Auxerre mourra bien mis-
erable,
Chasse de ceux qui soubs luy ont este,
Serre de chaisnes, apres d'un rude
cable,
En l'an que Mars, Venus, Sol mis en
este.

A great man of Auxerre shall die
very miserably,
Being expelled by those who have
been under him,
Bound with chains, and after that,
with a strong cable,
In the year that Mars, Venus, and
Sol shall be in conjunction.

Auxerre is a city in France about fifty miles from Paris. And this stanza merely concerns the unhappy fate of one of its chief men – many, many years ago.

85

Le charbon blanc du noir sera chasse,
Prisonnier fait mene au tumbereau,
More chameau sur pied estrelassez,
Lors le puisne fillera l'aubereau.

The white coal shall be expelled by
the black one,
He shall be made prisoner carried
in a dung cart,
His feet twisted on a black camel,
Then the youngest, shall suffer the
falcon to have more freedom.

A white prince shall be overcome by a black one, and carried to his execution in a dung cart. According to Nostradamus, this is both 'allegorical and metaphorical, and the judgment must be left to the reader.'

86

L'an que Saturne en eau sera con-
joinct,
Avec Sol, le Roy fort & puissant,
A Reims & Aix sera receu & oingt,
Apres conquestes meurtrura innocens.

In the year that Saturn in Aquarius
shall be in conjunction
With Sol, the King being strong
and powerful,
Shall be received and anointed at
Rheims and Aix,
After conquest he shall murder in-
nocent persons.

Rheims, a city in France, and Aix, a city in Germany, shall both be the scene of the coronation of a common ruler. Afterwards his actions shall be ominous.

87

Un fils du Roy tent de langues aprins,	A son of a King having learned divers languages
A son sisne au regne different,	
Son pere beau au plus beau fisz comprins,	Shall fall out with his elder brother for the kingdom,
Fera perir principe adherent.	His father-in-law being more concerned with his elder son,
	Shall cause the principal adherent to perish.

A King having two sons, the elder shall succeed him. The younger, being well educated, shall rebel against the King, his father, but shall be slain by his own father-in-law.

88

Le grand Anthoine du moindre fait sordide,	The great Anthony by name, but in effect sordid,
De Phytriase a son dernier ronge,	By lice, shall at last be eaten up,
Un qui de plomb voudra estre cupide,	One that shall be covetous of lead,
Passant le Port d'Esleu sera plonge.	Passing the Port Esleu shall fall into the water.

One who pretends to greatness shall at last realize his failure. He shall commit suicide by drowning himself.

89

Trente de Londres secret conjureront,	Thirty of London shall secretly conspire,
Contre leur Roy, sur le pont l'entreprinse,	Against the King, upon the bridge the plot shall be made,
Les satalites la mort degousteront,	These satellites shall taste of death,
Un Roy esleu blond, natif de Frize.	A King shall be elected, fair, and born in the low countries.

The Guy Fawkes gunpowder plot against the British Throne is clearly outlined here.

90

Les deux copie aux murs ne pourront joindre,	The two armies shall not be able to join by the walls,
Dans cest instant trembler Milan Ticin,	At the instant Milan and Ticin shall tremble
Faim, soif, doutance si fort les viendra poindre,	Hunger, thirst, and fear shall so seize upon them
Chair, pain, ne vivres, n'auront un seul bouncin.	They shall not have a bit of meat, bread nor victuals.

A description of conditions in Italy during a war is here given, referring specifically to the city of Milan.

91

Au Duc Gaulois constranet battre au duelle,	A French Duke compelled to fight a duel,
La nef Mole Monech n'approchera,	The ship of Mole shall not approach Monaco,
Tort accuse prison perpetuelle,	Wrongfully accused, shall be perpetually imprisoned,
Son fils regner auant mort taschera.	His son shall endeavour to reign before his death.

Publication of the private papers of Louis XIV revealed that the 'Man in the Iron Mask' was Count Girolamo Mattioli. In 1678 he had acted treacherously against Louis XIV and was subsequently imprisoned and masked.

92

Teste trenchee du vaillant Capitaine,	The head cut off of the valiant Captain,
Sera jette devant son adversaire,	Shall be thrown down before his adversary,
Son corps pendu de sa classe a l'antenne,	His body hanged from the ship's antenna,
Confus furia par rames a vent contraire.	Confused, they shall fly with oars against the wind.

This quatrain caused confusion in the mind of Nostradamus. To us, there is an obvious reference to radio in it – but the event itself remains obscure.

93

Un serpent veu proche du lit Royal,	A serpent shall be seen near the Royal bed,
Sera par dame, nuict chiens n'ab-beyeront;	By a lady of the night, the dogs shall not bark,
Lors naistre en France un Prince tant Royal	Then shall be born in France a Prince so much royal,
Du ciel venu tous les Princes verront.	Come from heaven all the Princes shall see it.

All the princes of the world will acknowledge a French Prince as the greatest of them all. The serpent is an allusion to his greatness, as when Alexander was born, a serpent was seen near his mother's bed.

94

Deux grands freres seront chassez d'Espaigne,	Two great brothers shall be driven from Spain,
Laisne vaineu soubs les monts Pyrenees;	The elder of them shall be over-come under the Pyrenean Moun-tains,
Rougir mer, Rhosne sang Leman d'Alemagne,	Bloody sea, Rhone, bloody Geneva of Germany,
Narbon, Blyterres, d'Agath, conta-minees.	Narbonne, the Land of Agath con-taminated.

The two great brothers in crime, Nazism and Fascism, will be driven from Spain, but not before a great struggle takes place near the border of France.

95

Le regne a deux laisse bien peu tien-dront,	The reign left to two they shall not keep it long,
Trois ans sept mois passez feront la guerre;	Three years and seven months being past,
Les deux vestales contre rebelleront,	The vestals shall rebel against them,
Victor puis nay en Armorique terre.	The youngest shall be the con-queror of the Armorick country.

This signifies a Kingdom that shall be left to two, who shall keep it but a short while. Their title will be challenged by two Nuns.

96

La soeur aisnee de l'Isle Britannique,	The eldest sister of the Britannic Island
Quinze ans devant le frere aura naissance,	Shall be born fifteen years before her brother,
Par son promis moyennant verrifique,	By what is promised her and by help of truth,
Succedera au regne de Balance.	She shall succeed in the Kingdom of Libra.

The eldest sister of Britain, the USA, was born in 1776. Fifteen years later, 1791, the Republic of France (brother) came into being.

97

L'an que Mercure, Mars, Venus retrograde,	When Mercury, Mars and Venus shall retrograde
Du grand Monarque la ligne ne faillir,	The line of the great Monarch shall be wanting,
Esleu du peuple lusitant pres de Pactole,	He shall be elected by the Portuguese near Pactole,
Que'n paix & regne viendra fort envillir.	And shall reign in peace a good while.

This signifies the change of state in Portugal, when they threw off the yoke of Spain, and chose their own King.

98

Les Albanois passeront dedans Rome,	The Albanians shall pass through Rome,
Moyennant Langres dimiples affublez,	By means of Langres covered with half helmets,
Marquis & Duc ne pardonner a homme,	Marquis and Duke shall spare no man,
Feu, sang, morbile, point d'eau, faillir les bleds.	Fire, blood, smallpox, water shall fail us, also corn.

The Albanians shall conquer a large territory and take Rome, and desolation shall follow in their wake.

99

L'aisne vailland de la fille du Roy,
Repoussera si avant les Celtique,
Qu'il mettra foudres, combien en tell
arroy,
Peu, & loing puis profondes Hesper-
ique.

The valiant eldest son of the daugh-
ter of the King,
Shall beat back so far, those of
Flanders,
That he shall employ lightnings,
how many in such order,
Little and far, after shall go deep in
Spain.

An able leader of noble birth shall show great skill in employing the
forces of nature in conquering Flanders and Spain.

100

De feu celeste au Royal edifice,
Quand la lumiere du Mars deffaillira,
Sept mois grand' Guerre, mort gent de
malefice,
Rouen Eureux, au Roy ne faillira.

Fire shall fall from the skies on the
King's palace
When Mars' light shall be eclipsed,
Great war shall be for seven
months, people shall die by
witchcraft,
Rouen and Eureux shall not fail the
King.

A seven months' war, of tremendous destructive force such as the world
has never seen before, shall terrify mankind.

CENTURY V

1

Avant venus du ruyne Celtique,
Dedans le temple deux parlemente-
ront,
Poignart coeur, d'un monte au cour-
sier & pique,
Sans faire bruit le grand enterreront.

Before the coming of the ruin of the
Celts,
Two shall discourse together in the
church,
Dagger in the heart of one, on
horseback and spurring,
Without noise they shall bury the
great one.

Nostradamus accurately predicts the conflict in Northern Ireland between the Catholics and the Protestants. As an aside, the British ambassador to Ireland was assassinated in 1976.

2

Sept conjurez au banquet feront luyre,
Contre les trois le fer hors de navire,
L'un les deux classes au grand fera
conduire,
Quand par le mail denier au front luy
tire.

Seven conspirators at a banquet
shall make their iron glisten
Against three, out of a ship,
One shall carry the two fleets to the
great one,
When in the promenade, the last
one shall shoot him in the forehead.

At a banquet a conspiracy of seven shall succeed against three. A naval
officer shall deliver two fleets to a great one, and for his treachery shall be
shot in the forehead.

3

Le successeur de la Duche viendra,
Beaucoup plus outre que la mer de
Toscanne,
Gauloise branche la Florence tiendra,
Dans son giron d'accord nautique
Rane.

The successor to the Dukedom
shall come
Far beyond the Tuscan sea,
A French branch shall hold Florence,
In its lap, to which the Sea Frog
shall agree.

Il Duce, after his fall, shall be succeeded by a non-Italian. Florence will be under French influence.

4

Le gros mastin de cite dechasse,
Sera fasche de l'estrange alliance,
Apres aux champs avoir le chef
chasse,
Le loup & l'ours se donneront
defiance.

The great mastiff being driven from
the city,
Shall be angry at the strange alliance,
After he shall have hunted the hart
in the fields,
The wolf and the bear shall defy
one another.

England shall be angry at a strange alliance, whereby the helpless are hunted down. The Italian Wolf and the Russian Bear shall defy one another.

5

Sous ombre saincte d'oster de servi-
tude,
Peuple & cite l'usurpera luy-mesmes,
Pire fera par faux de jeune pute,
Libre au champ lisant le faux
poesme.

Under the feigned shadow of free-
ing people from slavery,
He shall usurp the people and city
for himself,
He shall do worse by the deceit of a
young whore,
For he shall be betrayed in the field
reading a false poem.

This prognosticates the 'final' days and actions of Hitler, his false marriage to the actress Eva Braun, and his spurious will at his supposed death.

6

Au Roy l'augure sur le chef la main mettre,	The augur shall come to put his hand on the King's head,
Viendra prier pour la paix Italique,	And pray for the peace of Italy,
A la main gauche viendra changer le sceptre,	In the left hand he shall change the sceptre,
De Roy viendra Empereur pacifique.	From a King he shall become a pacific Emperor.

The Latin word *augur* may mean one who foretells events, or may also be taken for a clergyman. Here the significance is, that a priest shall put his hand upon a King's head (Napoleon) and, praying for the peace of Italy, shall place a sceptre in his hand, and install him as Emperor.

7

Du triumvir seront trouvez les os,	The bones of the triumvirate shall be found out,
Cherchant profond tresor enigmatique,	When they shall seek for a deep and enigmatical treasure,
Ceux d'alentour ne seront en repos,	Those there about shall not be in rest,
De concaver marbre & plomb metalique.	This concavity shall be of marble and metallic lead.

This delves into Roman history, and tells of the plot of Octavius Caesar, Marcus Antonius and Lepidus to make themselves masters of the Roman Empire and to divide the spoils among the three of them.

8

Sera laisse le feu mort vif cache,	The fire shall be left burning, the dead shall be hid,
Dedans les globes horribles espouventable	Within the globes terrible and fearful,
De nuict a classe cite en poudre lache,	By night the fleet shall shoot against the city,
La cite a feu, l'ennemy favorable.	The city shall be on fire, the enemy shall be favourable to it.

Terrible new weapons launched from ships shall create fearful destruction and cause unquenchable fires; and so complete will be the havoc, it will be impossible to count the dead. Between the US and Japan at Pearl Harbor at the outset of World War II and Hiroshima and Nagasaki at the end. Foretells a nuclear holocaust.

9

Jusques au fond la grand arq de malve	At the bottom of the great evil arch,
Par chef captif l'amy anticipe,	By a chief that is a captive, the
Naistra de dame front face chevelue,	friend shall be anticipated,
Lors par astuce Duc a mort attrappe.	One shall be born of a lady with
	hairy face and forehead,
	Then by craft shall a duke be put to
	death.

These words are too veiled in obscurity for either Nostradamus or myself to render a clear interpretation.

10

Un chef Celtique dans le conflit	A Celtic leader wounded in battle,
blesse,	Near a cellar, seeing death about to
Aupres de cave vouant siens mort	overthrow his people,
abbatre,	Being much oppressed with blood,
De sang & playes & d'ennemis presse,	wounds and enemies,
Et securs par incogneuz de quatre.	Is succoured by four unknown.

A European leader seriously wounded, and his country severely pressed, will be helped by his allies.

11

Mer par solaires seure ne passera,	Sea by solars, she shall pass safely,
Ceux de Venus tiendront toute l'Affri-	Those of Venus shall hold all
que;	Africa,
Leur regne plus Sol, Saturne n'oc-	Saturn shall hold their kingdom no
cupera,	longer,
Et changera la mort Asiatique.	And shall change the Asiatic port.

Those of Venus, born to the sea, are the English; as a maritime nation they shall hold great colonial possessions.

12

Aupres de Lac Leman sera conduite,	Near Lake Geneva shall be a plot,
Par garse estrange cite voulant trahir,	By a strange whore to betray a city,
Avant sen meurtre a Auspourg la grand suitte,	Before she be killed, her great retinue will come to Augsburg,
Et ceux du Rhin la viendront envahir.	And those of the Rhine shall come to invade her.

The corrupting influence of Fascism had its inception in northern Italy, close to Lake Geneva. Before it ran its mad course it also ruined the Germans.

13

Par grand fureur le Roy Roman Belgique,	By great fury, the Roman-Belgic Kingdom,
Vexer voudra par phalange barbare,	Shall come to vex, by their barbarian falange,
Fureur grincent chassera gent Lybique,	Gnashing fury shall pursue the Savage people,
Depuis Pannons jusques Hercules la Bare.	From Hungary as far as the Straits of Gibraltar.

The shaky peace between the Warsaw Pact nations and NATO will be tested. The alignment of nations dividing Europe into two camps will not hold, to the vexation of both sides.

14

Saturne & Mars en Leo Espagne captive,	Saturn and Mars being in Leo, Spain shall be captive,
Par chef Libique au conflit attrape;	By an African general taken in battle,
Proche de Malte, heredde Prinse vive,	Near Malta, a hereditary Prince shall be taken alive,
Et Romain sceptre sera par coq frappe.	And the Roman sceptre shall be struck by the cock.

Under the joint influence of Saturn (commerce) and Mars (war) Spain shall suffer great defeat. France (the cock) shall contribute to her downfall.

15

En navigant captif prins grand pontife;	In sailing a pope shall be taken captive,
Grands apprestez saillir les clercs tumultuez,	After which, shall be a great uproar amongst the clergy,
Second esleu absent son bien debise,	A second absent elected, consumed his goods,
Son favory bastard a mort tue.	His favourite bastard shall be killed.

A controversy shall arise in the Catholic Church, caused by the election of a Pope who is in disfavour with the clergy.

16

A son haut prix la lerme Sabee,	The Sabean tear shall be no more at its high price,
D'humains chair pour mort en cendre mettre,	To turn human flesh by death into ashes,
A l'isle Pharos par croisars perturbee,	The island Pharos shall be troubled by croisars,
Alors qu'a Rhodes paroistra dure espectre.	When at Rhodes shall a hard phantom appear.

Sabean tear, a term used to describe frankincense, was a vegetable product extensively used in embalming. Pharos, an island opposite Alexandria, shall be troubled by Christians (croisars) when a vision appears in Rhodes.

17

De nuict passant le Roy pres d'une Andronne	The King going by night near an Andronne,
Celuy de Cypres & principal guerre,	He of Cyprus and chief of war,
Le Roy failly la main fuit long du Rhosne,	The King having missed the hand, along by the Rhone,
Les conjurez l'iront a mort mettre.	The conspirators shall put him to death there.

A noted military figure shall conspire against France, but in southern France he shall meet his just fate.

18

De dueil mourra l'infelix proflige,
Celebrera son vitrix l'heccatombe;
Pristine loy, franc edit redige,
Le mur & Prince au septiesme jour
    tombe.

The unhappy one, being overcome,
  shall die of grief,
His victrix shall celebrate the hecatomb,
The former law and free edict shall
  be brought again,
The wall and seventh Prince shall
  go to the grave.

Victrix is a Latin word, the feminine gender of the word victor; Hecatomb was a Grecian sacrifice whereby 100 oxen were killed.

19

Le grand Royal d'or, d'airain aug-
    mente,
Rompu la pache, par ieune ouverte
    guerre,
Peuple afflige par unchef lamente,
De sang barbare sera couvert de terre.

The great golden Royal, being increased with copper,
The agreement being broken by a
  young man, there shall be open
  war,
People afflicted by the loss of a
  chief lamented,
The ground shall be covered with
  barbarous blood.

An alliance between a rich nation with one of little wealth shall result in an open warfare, in which the chief will lose his life.

20

De la les Alpes grande armee passera,
Un peu devant naistra monstre vapin;
Prodigieux & subit tournera,
Le grand Toscan a son lie plus propin.

Beyond the Alps shall a great army
  go,
And a little while before shall be
  born a vapin monster,
Prodigious and suddenly the great
  Tuscan,
Shall return to his own nearest
  place.

Napoleon shall cross the Alps with a great army, and Nostradamus also forecasts his exile to Elba with his return to 'his own nearest place,' i.e., Corsica.

21

Par les trespas du Monarque Latin,	By the death of the Latin Monarch,
Ceux qu'il aura par regne secourus;	Those that he shall have succoured in his reign,
Le feu livra divuse le butin,	The fire shall shine, the booty shall be divided,
La mort publique au hardis incorus.	The bold comers in, shall be put to public death.

A people shall be pillaged after the death of a monarch of Latin origin. However, the persecutors will eventually be publicly executed.

22

Avant qu'a Rome grand aye rendu l'ame,	Before a great man renders up his soul at Rome,
Effrayeur grand a l'armee estrangere;	The army of strangers shall put into a great fright,
Par escadrons l'embusche pres de Parme,	By squadrons the ambush shall be near Parma,
Puis des deux rouges ensemble feront chere.	After that, the two red ones shall make good cheer together.

Most likely the 'two red ones' represent Communist leaders rejoicing at the death of the Pope.

23

Les deux contents seront unis ensemble,	The two contested shall be united together,
Quand la pluspart a Mars sera conjonct,	When the most part shall be joined to Mars,
Le grand d'Affrique en effrayeur & tremble,	The great one of Africa shall be in fear and terror,
Duumvirat par la classe des joints.	Duumvirat shall by the pursuit be disjointed.

The alliance between Israel and Egypt shall not last long. The alliance (duumvirat) will be disrupted by Saudi Arabia, Libya, Syria, and the PLO

24

Le Kegne & Roy soubs Venus esleve,	The Kingdom and King being joined under Venus,
Saturne aura sur jupiter empire,	Saturn shall have power over Jupiter,
La loy & regne par le Soleil leve,	The law and reign raised by the Sun,
Par Saturnius endurera le pire.	Shall be put to the worse by the Saturnians.

The frivolous court of Louis XV, led by Madame Du Barry, made a farce of law and order, by their Saturnalian revels.

25

Le prince Arabs, Mars, Sol, Venus, Lyon,	The Arab Prince, Mars, Sol, Venus, Leo,
Regne d'Eglise par mer succombera,	The Kingdoms of the Church shall be overcome by the sea,
Devers la Perse bien pres d'un million,	Towards Persia very near a million,
Bisance, Egypte, Ver. Serp. invadera.	Turkey, Egypt, Ver. Serp. shall invade.

Christian ideals will be overcome by Oriental ideology (Ver. Serp. meaning true serpents).

26

La gent esclave par un heur martiel,	The Slavic Nation shall by martial luck,
Viendra en haut degre tant esleve,	Be raised to so high a degree,
Changeront prince, naistra un provincial,	That they shall change their Prince and elect one among themselves,
Passer la mer, copie aux monte leve.	They shall cross the sea with an army raised in the mountains.

Russians, by a military revolution, shall change their form of government and they will grow to be a great power and invade many countries.

27

Par feu & armes non loing de la Mer Negro,	By fire and sword not far from the Black Sea,
Viendra de Perse occuper Trebisonde;	They shall come from Persia to seize upon Trebisonde,
Trembler Pharos Methelin, Sol allegro,	Pharos and Methelin shall quake, Sun be Merry,
De sang Arabe d'Adrie covert l'onde.	The sea of Adria shall be covered with Oriental blood.

A Russian invasion, coming through Iran, shall seize Mediterranean ports. In the Adriatic Sea they shall be driven back with great losses.

28

Le bras pendu & la jambe liee,	The arm hanging and the leg bound,
Visage pasle, au sein poignard cache;	With a pale face, a dagger in the bosom,
Trois qui seront jurez de la meslee,	Three shall be sworn to the fray,
Au grand de Gennes sera le Fer lasche.	To the great one of Genoa the Iron shall be darted.

In July 1944, an assassination of Hitler was attempted but this only resulted in arm and leg injuries to him. Thereafter he walked with a limp, and his arm was in a sling. By this time in Italy, Mussolini was already captured.

29

La liberte ne sera recouvres,	Liberty shall not be recovered,
L'occupera noir, fier, vilain inique;	It shall be occupied by a black, fierce and wicked villain,
Quand la matiere du pont sera ouvree,	When the work of the Danube bridge shall be ended,
D'Hister, Venise faschee la republique.	The Italian commonwealth shall be angry.

The black-shirted villain shall destroy Italian liberty. When the wreck of the German alliance is complete, then Italy will really show her anger.

30

Tout a l'entour de la grande cite,	Round about the great city,
Seront soldats logez par champs &	Soldiers shall be in fields and
villes,	towns,
Donner l'assaut Paris, Rome incite,	Paris shall give the assault, Rome
Sur le pont lors sera faite grand pille.	shall be incited,
	Then upon the bridge shall be great
	plunderings.

The capture and sacking of Rome by the French Duke of Bourbon is here described.

31

Par terre Attique chef de la sapience,	In the country of Attica which is
Qui de present est la Rose du Monde;	the head of wisdom
Pont ruyne & sa grand pre-eminence,	And now is the Rose of the World,
Sera subdite & naufrage de undes.	A bridge shall be in ruins with its
	great pre-eminence,
	It shall be subdued and made a
	wreck by the waves.

The country of Attica, or Greece, famed for its wisdom, shall be corrupted by the usages of mankind.

32

Ou tout bon est, tout bien Soleil &	Where all well is, are good Sun and
Lune,	Moon,
Est abondent, sa ruyne s'approche,	Is existent, its ruin approaches
Du ciel s'advance vaner ta fortune,	near,
En mesme estat que la septiesme roch.	The heaven is making haste to
	change thy fortune,
	Into the same state as the seventh
	rock.

This dark stanza seems to predict the bad times that shall exist during a civil war between the Catholics and Protestants.

33

Des principaux de cite rebellee,
Qui tiendront fort pour liberte r'avoir,
Detrencher masses infelice meslee,
Cris hurlemens a Nante; piteux voir.

Of the principal men in a rebelled city,
Who shall stand out to recover their liberty,
The males shall be cut in pieces, O unhappy quarrels!
Cries and howlings, it shall be pity to see at Nantes.

Nantes, in France, shall be the seat of a rebellion against the rest of France. Tremendous massacres of the natives shall follow. And so it was in Nantes, 250 years after Nostradamus wrote this quatrain. Males were guillotined; women, children, and priests were drowned in the Loire in 1793.

34

Du plus profond de l'occident Anglois,
Ou est le chef de l'isle Britannique;
Entrera classe dans Garonne par Blois,
Pa vin & sel, feux cachez aux barriques.

From the most westerly part of England,
Where the chief of the British Island is,
A fleet shall come into the Garonne by Blois,
By wine and salt, fire shall be hidden in barrels.

A British Fleet shall plant mines (barrels) in French waters.

35

Par cite franche de la grand Mer Seline,
Qui porte encore a l'estomach la pierre;
Angloise classe viendra sous la bruine,
Un rameau prendre du grand ouverte guerre.

By a free city of the Mediterranean Sea,
Which carries yet the stone in the stomach,
An English Fleet shall come under a fog,
To take a branch of great open war.

The Free City of Venice in the Mediterranean shall be invaded by an English Fleet under cover of a fog.

36

De soeur le frere par simulte faintise,
Viendra mesler rosee en mineral;
Sur la placente donne a vieille tar-
dive,
Meurt le goustant sera simple & rural.

The brother of the sister, by feigned simulation,
Shall mix dew with mineral;
The aftermath being given to a slow
old woman,
She died tasting, the deed shall be
simple, and rural.

A brother shall poison his sister during childbirth.

37

Trois sens seront d'un vouloir &
accord,
Qui pour venir au bout de leur at-
tainte,
Vingt mois apres tous & records,
Leur Roy trahir simulant haine,
fainte.

Three hundred shall be of one mind
and agreement,
That they may attain their ends.
Twenty months after by all of them
and their partners,
Their King shall be betrayed by
simulating a feigned hatred.

The Legislative Assembly after a period of deliberation finally ordered
King Louis XVI to stand trial for treason.

38

Ce grand monarque qu'an mort suc-
cedera,
Donnera vie illicite & lubrique;
Par nonchalance a tous concedera,
Qu'a la parfin faudra la loy Salique.

The great monarch that shall succeed to the great one,
Shall lead a life unlawful and
lecherous,
By carelessness he shall give to all,
So that in conclusion, the Salic law
shall fail.

The Salic law, most famous for its chapter on succession to private
property, which declares that daughters cannot inherit land, is here
referred to in an incident which seems to indicate the degeneracy of the
males of a royal line, which eventually led to the enthroning of a woman.

39

Du vray rameau des fleurs de lys issu,	Issued out of the true branch of the city,
Mis & loge heritier d'Hetrurie;	He shall be set for heir of Etruria;
Son sang antique de longue main tissu,	His ancient blood weaned by a long while,
Fera Florence florir en l'Armoirie.	Shall cause Florence to flourish in the coats of arms.

A reference to the Medici family and their alliance with the Crown of France – Catherine de Medici, wife of Henry II, was Queen of France when Nostradamus lived.

40

Le sang Royal sera si tresmesle,	The Royal blood shall be so much mixed,
Contrainct seront Gaulois de l'Hes-perie;	The French shall be constrained by the Spaniards,
On attendra que terme soit coule,	They shall stay till the term is past,
Et que memoire de la voix soit perie.	And the remembrance of the voice is over.

This merely signifies the alliance between France and Spain by reason of royal intermarriages.

41

Nay sous les umbres & journee nocturne,	Being born in the shadows and nocturnal time,
Sera en regne & bonte souveraine,	He shall be a sovereign in kingdom and bounty,
Fera renaistre son sang de l'antique urne,	He shall cause his blood to be born again from the antique urn,
Renouvellant siecle d'or pour l'airain.	Renewing a golden age instead of a brass one.

A great king, born in a time of darkness, shall reign with a bountiful sceptre and lead the land to a golden age.

42

Mars esleve en son plus haut beffroy,	Mars being raised in its highest watch tower,
Fera retraire les Allobrox de France,	Shall cause the Allobrox to retreat from France,
La gent Lombarde fera si grand effroy,	The people of Lombardy shall be in so great fear
A ceux de l'aigle compris sous la Balance.	Of those of the eagle, comprehended under Libra.

The Allobrox are those of Savoy, or Italians; retreating from France, they shall cause great havoc.

43

La grand ruyne des sacrees ne s'eslongne,	The great ruin of the sacred things is not far off,
Provence, Naples, Sicile, Sez & Ponce,	Provence, Naples, Sicily, Sez and Ponce,
En Germanie, au Rhin & la Cologne,	In Germany towards the Rhine and Cologne,
Vexez a mort par tous ceux de Mogonce.	They shall be vexed to death by those of Moguntia.

Great damage to sacred monuments of art and religion is predicted. There will be religious troubles in the regions mentioned. Here is forewarning of what became an early one-thousand-plane bombing of Cologne with great destruction by the Allies in World War II.

44

Par mer le rouge sera prins des pyrates,	By sea the red one shall be taken by pirates,
La paix sera par son moyen troublee;	The peace by that means shall be troubled,
L'ire & l'aure commettra par sainct acte,	He shall commit anger by a feigned act,
Au grand pontife sera l'armee doublee.	The high priest shall have a double army.

Very clearly, Nostradamus predicts the threat to Joseph Cardinal Mindszenty in 1956 during the Hungarian uprising, at which time he sought and received asylum in the US legation.

154   *The Complete Prophecies of Nostradamus*

45

Le grand Empire sera tost desole,
Et translate pres d'Arduenne silve;
Les deux bastards pres l'aisne decolle,
Et regnera Aeneodarb, nes de milve.

The great Empire shall soon be made desolate,
And shall be transplanted near the Forest of Arden,
The two bastards shall have their heads cut off by the eldest son,
And he that shall reign shall have a reddish beard and a hawk's nose.

The great Empire of Germany shall be broken up and its lands, especially near the borders of France, will be divided and ruled by many strangers.

46

Par chappeaux rouges querelles &
nouveaux scismes,
Quand on aura esleu le Sabinois,
On produira contre luy grands
sophismes,
Et sera Rome lesee par Albanois.

By red hats, quarrels and new schisms,
When the Sabine shall be elected,
Great sophisms shall be produced against him,
And Rome shall be damaged by the Albanians.

The cardinals of Rome shall raise great quarrels and schisms when a man of Sabine (a region near Rome) is chosen Pope. Rome will further be endangered by the war-like advances of the Albanians.

47

Le grand Arabe marchera bien avant,
Trahy sera par les Bisantinoise,
L'antique Rhodes luy viendra au
devant,
Et plus grand mal par austre Panno-
nois.

The great Arab shall proceed a great way,
He shall be betrayed by the Turks,
Ancient Rhodes shall come to meet him,
Great evil by a south wind from Hungary.

The latter half of the twentieth century has Turkey with NATO on one side and the Arab League with Syria, Jordan, Saudi Arabia, Lebanon, and the PLO on the other.

48

Apres la grande affliction du sceptre,	After the great afflictions of the sceptre,
Deux ennemis par eux seront defaits,	Two enemies shall be overcome by themselves,
Classe d'Affrique aux Pannonois viedra naistre,	A fleet of Africa shall go towards the Hungarians,
Par mer & terre seront horribles faits.	By sea and land shall be horrid facts.

This has relation to the preceding stanza; due to a falling out between two enemies, the Hungarians will be the gainers.

49

Nul de l'Espagne, mais de l'antique France,	None out of Spain, but of the ancient France,
Ne sera esleu pour le tremblant nacelle;	Shall be elected to govern the tottering ship.
A l'ennemy sera faicte fiance,	The enemy shall be trusted,
Qui dans son regne sera peste cruelle.	Who to his kingdom shall be a cruel plague.

Nostradamus predicts that a Frenchman will be chosen Pope. With the selection of John Paul II of Poland in 1978, the first non-Italian Pope since Nostradamus's writing in 1555, the forecast of this quatrain cannot be far distant.

50

L'an d'eux les freres du lys seront en aage,	In the year that the brothers of the lilies shall be of age,
L'un d'eux tiendra la grande Romanis,	One of them shall hold the great Romany,
Trembler les monts, ouvert Latin passage,	The mountains shall tremble, the Latin passage shall be opened,
Pache marcher contre fort d'Armenie.	A Pascha shall march against the fort of Armenia.

One of France's generals will occupy Rome after crossing the Alps with a mighty army. At the same time an Oriental ally will assist the French by marching in from the Near East.

51

La gent de Dace, D'Angleterre &
Polonne,
Et de Bohesme seront nouvelle ligue;
Pour passer outre d'Hercules la Col-
onne,
Barcyns, Thyrrens dresser cruelle
brigue.

The people of Romania, England,
and Poland,
And of Bohemia shall make a new
league,
To go beyond the Pillars of Hercules,
Barcins and Thyrrens shall make a
cruel plot.

Romania, England, Poland and Czechoslovakia shall attempt a united invasion beyond Gibraltar, but will meet with great resistance.

52

Un Roy sera qui donrra l'opposite,
Les exilez eslevez sur le Regne,
De sang nager la gent caste hypolite,
Et florira long temps soubs telle en-
seigne.

A King shall be, who shall be of the
opposite,
To the banished persons raised
upon the Kingdom,
The chaste Hippolite nation shall
swim in blood,
And shall flourish a great while
under such a design.

The recurrent turmoil of the Greek government is forecast here. Recall that from 1832 to 1967, Greece has had four different kings with intermittent bloody strife until Constantine II was removed in 1967.

53

La loy de Sol, & Venus contendans,
Apparopriant l'esprit de prophecie,
Ne l'un ne l'autre ne seront entendans,
Par Sol tiendra la loy du grand
Messie.

The law of the Sun and Venus
contending,
Appropriating   the   spirit   of
prophecy,
Neither one nor the other shall be
heard,
By Sol the law of the great Messiah
shall subsist.

The forces of light and darkness, struggling for domination over the spirit of man, shall both be superseded by the new law of the great Saviour.

54

Du pont Euxine & la grand Tartaric,
Un Roy sera qui viendra voir la
Gaule,
Transpercera Alane & l'Armenie,
Et dans Bisance lairra sanglante
Gaule.

From the Black Sea and great Tartaria,
A King shall come to see France,
He shall go through Alanea and Armenia,
And shall leave a bloody rod in Constantinople.

An Asiatic power shall come to France, by way of Armenia and Turkey. Constantinople will be governed by one of his tools.

55

De la felice Arabie contrade,
Naistra puissant de loy Mahometique,
Vexer l'Espagne, conquester la Grenade,
Et plus par mer a la gent Lygustique.

Out of the country of greater Arabia,
Shall be born a strong master of Mohammedan law,
Who shall vex Spain and conquer Grenada,
And by sea shall come to the Italian nation.

From a country of Mohammedan law (Morocco), shall come one who is a strong master of their law – the sword: Khomeini and the Moslem revolution in Iran.

56

Par le trespas du tres vieillard pontife,
Sera esleu Romain de bon aage;
Qu'il sera dit que le siege debiffe,
Et long tiendra & de picquant courage.

By the death of the very old high priest,
Shall be elected a Roman of good age,
Of whom it shall be said, that he dishonours the seat,
And shall live long, and be of fierce courage.

Always deeply concerned with matters of the Church, Nostradamus here discusses one of the many schisms then current among the clergy.

57

Istra du mont Gaulsier & Aventine,
Qui par le trou advertira l'armee;
Entre deux rocs sera prins le butin,
De Sext. Mansol faillir la renommee.

One shall go out of the mountains
Gaulsier and Aventine,
Who through a hole shall give
notice to the army,
Between two rocks shall be taken
the prize,
And the glory of the Sun shall lose
its renown.

One of Nostradamus's most incredible predictions. Mount Gauffier is really Montgolfier, the inventor of the hot air balloon. Originally used for military reconnaissance with a hole in the bottom of the gondola. Also, 'de Sext' is the only Pope since Nostradamus's time with the number VI after his name; Pius VI reigned during the time of the Montgolfier brothers, 1775–1799.

58

De l'Aqueduct d'Uticense, Gardoing,
Par la forest & mont inaccessible,
Emmy du pont sera tasche ou poing,
Le chef Nemans qui tant sera terrible.

From the Aqueduct of Uticense
and Gardoing,
Through the forest and inaccessible
mountains,
In the middle of the bridge shall be
tied by the wrist,
The chief Nemans, that shall be so
terrible.

An incident in a future war, in France, is here obscurely described. The various places mentioned are probably points of attack.

59

Au chef Anglois a Nimes trop sejour,
Dever l'Espagne au secours Aeno-
    barbe,
Plusieurs mourront par Mars ouvert ce
    jour,
Quand en Artois faillir estoille en
    barbe.

The chief English shall stay too
long at Nismes,
A red-haired man shall go to the
help of Spain,
Many shall die by open war that
day,
When in Artois the star shall fail in
the beard.

A play on words, this appears to have no deep significance, and the only clear reference concerns a bearded comet, or *cometa barbatus* as it is known in Latin.

60

Par teste rase viendra bien mal eslire,	By a shaven head shall be made an ill choice,
Plus que sa charge ne porte passera;	That shall go beyond his commission,
Si grand fureur & rage fera dire,	He shall proceed with so great fury and rage,
Qu'a feu & sang tout sexe tranchera.	That he shall put forth both sexes to fire and sword.

Six years after the death of Nostradamus, on St Bartholomew's Day, August 24, 1572, a massacre of the Huguenots began in Paris. Spurred on by the high clergy of the Catholic Church, it spread to many provinces in France, and before it was checked many, many thousands of people were killed.

61

L'enfant du grand n'estant a sa naissance,	The child of the great one that was not at his birth,
Subjuera les hauts monts Apennins,	Shall subdue the high Apennine Mountains,
Fera trembler tous ceux de la balance,	Shall make all those under Libra to quake,
Et des Monts Feurs jusques a Mont Cenis.	From Mount Feurs, as far as Mount Cenis.

A person, of illegitimate but noble birth, shall attain great heights as a military figure and shall cause havoc in both France and Italy by reason of his conquests.

62

Sur les rochers sang on verra pleuvoir,	It shall rain blood upon the rocks,
Sol Orient, Saturn Occidental,	The sun being in the east, and Saturn in the west,
Pres Orgon guerre, a Rome grand mal voir,	War shall be near Orgon and a great evil at Rome,
Nefs parfondrees & prins le Tridental.	Ships shall be cast away, and the trident be taken.

This quatrain carries on Nostradamus's repeated warnings of a future war between the Orient and Occident, and the horrible consequences thereof.

63

De vaine emprinse l'honneur indeue plainte,	Honour brings a complaint against a vain undertaking,
Gallots errants, par Latins, froid, faim vagues;	Galleys shall wander through the Latin seas, cold, hunger, wars,
Non loing du Tybre de sang terre tainte,	Not far from Tiber, the earth shall be dyed with blood,
Et sur humaine seront diverses plagues.	And upon mankind shall be various plagues.

Tiber is the river on which Rome is situated; and the rest of the verse indicates incidents which shall come to pass.

64

Les assemblez par repos du grand nombre,	The assembly by the rest of the great number
Par terre & mer, conseil contremande;	By land and sea shall recall their council.
Pres de l'Autonne, Gennes, Nue de l'ombre,	Near Autonne, Gennes, Cloud of the shadow,
Par champs & villes le chef contrebande.	In fields and towns, the chief shall be one against another.

Here we have a prognostication of the dissensions among the heads of nations gathered ostensibly for a council of peace.

65

Subit venu l'effrayeur sera grande,	One coming upon a sudden shall cause a great fear,
Des principaux de l'affaire cachez,	To the principals that were hidden and concerned in the business,
Et dame en braise plus ne sera veus,	And the fiery lady shall be seen no more,
Et peu a peu seront les grands fachez.	And little by little the great ones shall be angry.

Consternation shall seize the betrayers of the people when they perceive the growing strength of the masses and their insistence upon a voice in their destiny.

66

Soubs les antiques edifices estaux,
Non eslonguez d'aqueduct ruyne,
De Sol & Luna mont les luysants metaux,
Ardante lampe Trajen d'or burine.

Under the ancient edifices of the vestals,
Not far from a ruined aqueduct,
Are the bright metals of sun and moon,
A burning lamp of Trajan, of engraved gold.

Near a ruined aqueduct will be found ancient articles of gold and silver, including a Roman lamp of gold, inscribed with Trajan's name.

67

Quand chef Perousse n'osera sa tunique,
Sens au couvert tout nud s'expolier,
Seront print sept faict aristocratique,
Le pere & fils morts par points au collier.

When the chief of Perouse shall not dare without a tunic,
To expose himself naked in the dark,
Seven shall be taken for setting up an aristocracy,
The father and son shall die by pricks in the collar.

Perugia is a city in Italy, which will be the seat of an unsuccessful attempt at setting up a revolution.

68

Dans le Danube & du Rhin viendra boire,
Le grand Chameau, ne s'en repentira;
Trembler du Rhosne & plus fort ceux de Loire,
Et pres des Alpes Coq les ruynera.

In the Danube and Rhine shall come to drink,
The great camel and shall not repent,
The Rhone shall tremble and more those of Loire,
And near the Alps the Cock shall ruin him.

A Turkish invasion shall reach Germany as far as the Rhine and Danube. France shall be in danger for a while, but shall finally triumph in a battle near the Alps.

69

Plus ne sera la grand en faux som-meil,	The great one shall be no more in a false sleep,
L'inquietude viendra prendre repos;	The restlessness shall take rest,
Dresser phalange d'or, azur & ver-meil,	He shall raise an army of gold and azure
Subjuger Affrique la ronger jusque aux os.	He shall conquer Africa and gnaw it to the bone.

A great nation shall awake from its false sense of security and isolationism, and raise an immense amount of gold and a great navy. With its newfound strength it will invade the African shore. The isolation and neutrality of the United States prior to World War II is changed (false sleep) into war preparedness (raise an army), subsequently gaining a foothold in North Africa, from which, as Churchill said, to 'attack the soft underbelly of Europe.'

70

Les regions suvjettes a la Balance,	The regions under the sign of Libra,
Feront trembler les monts par grande guerre;	Shall make the mountains quake with great war,
Captif tout sexe deu & toute Bisance,	Slaves of all sexes, with all Constantinople,
Qu'on criera a l'aube terre a terre.	So that in the dawn, they shall cry from land to land.

The European nations shall embark on a universal war, with the complete destruction of Constantinople promised.

71

Par la fureur d'un qui attendra l'eau,	By the fury of one looking forward to the water,
Par la grand rage tout l'exercite esmeu,	By his great rage the whole army shall be troubled,
Charge de nobles a dix-sep022 bat-teaux,	There shall be seventeen boats full of noblemen,
Au long du Rhosne tard messager venu.	Along the Rhone the messenger shall come too late.

The fury and rage of an invader driving his legions towards English shores, shall result in a great destruction of navies.

72

Pour le plaisir d'edict voluptueux,	By the pleasure of a voluptuous edict,
On meslera la poison dans la loy,	The poison shall be mixed with the law,
Venus sera en cours si vertueux,	Venus shall be in so great request,
Qu obsuquera du Soleil tout aloy.	That it shall darken all the alloy of the sun.

Pornography and a liberalization of all moral codes is foreseen here. Nostradamus, however, although he anticipates this, is unhappy with the results it produces.

73

Persecutee de Dieu sera l'Eglise,	The church of God shall be persecuted,
Et les saints temples seront expoliez;	And the holy temples shall be spoiled,
L'enfant la mere mettra nud en chemise,	The child shall turn out his mother nude in her shirt,
Seront Arabes aux Polons railez.	Arabians shall agree with Polonians.

The Catholic Church shall be persecuted and its temples despoiled. Anti-Semitism shall be rampant among the Arabs and Poles.

74

De sang Troy en naistra coeur Germanique,	Of Trojan blood shall be born a German heart,
Qui de viendra en si haute puissance,	Who shall attain to so high a power,
Hors chassera gent estrange Arabique,	That he shall drive away the Eastern people,
Tournant l'Eglise en pristine pre-eminence.	Restoring the church to pristine pre-eminence.

A German of great courage shall attain great eminence by destroying the influence of Oriental power and re-establishing the Church.

75

Montera haut sur le bien plus a dextre,	Mounting high on the good, more to the right,
Demourra assis sur la pierre carree;	He shall remain sitting upon the square stone,
Vers le midy pose a sa fenestre,	Towards the South, being set on the left hand,
Baston tortu en main bouchee serree.	A crooked stick in his hand and his mouth shut.

This predicts and describes the hectic sessions of the National Assembly during the French Revolution, where the parties of the left and the right contended for the power.

76

En lieu libere tendra son pavillon,	He shall pitch his tent in the open air,
Et ne voudra en citez prendre place;	Refusing to lodge in the city,
Aix, Carpen, l'Isle, Volce, Mont Ca-vaillon	Aix, Carpentres, Lille, Volce, Mont Cavaillon,
Par tout les lieux abolira la trasse.	In those places, he shall abolish his trace.

All the places mentioned in this stanza are in Provence. The event referred to has no current interest.

77

Tous les degrez d'honneur Ecclesiasti-que,	All the degrees of Ecclesiastical honour
Seront changez en Dial Quirinal;	Shall be changed into a Quirinal Dial,
En Martial Quirinal flaminique,	Into Martial Quirinal, Flaminus,
Puis un Roy de France le rendra Vulcanal.	After that, a King of France shall make it Vulcanal.

This is another discussion of clerical affairs in the Catholic Church in Nostradamus's time.

78

Les deux unis ne tiendront longuement,	The two united shall not hold long,
Et dans treize ans au Barbare Sattrappe;	Within thirteen years to the Barbarian Satrap,
Aux deux costez feront tel perdement,	They shall cause such loss on both sides,
Qu'un benira la barque & sa cappe.	That one shall bless the boat and its covering.

Adolf Hitler and Von Hindenburg first became associated (historically) in 1920, the year that the Nazi Party was founded. Thirteen years later, just prior to Hindenburg's death, Hitler assumed full power, resulting in the ultimate ruin and destruction of the German State.

79

Le sacree pompe viendra baisse les aisles	The sacred pomp shall bow down her wings,
Par la venue du grand Legislateur;	At the coming of the great law giver,
Humble haussera, vexera les rebelles,	He shall raise the humble and vex the rebellious,
Naistra sur terre aucun semulateur.	No emulator of his shall be born.

The advent of Abraham Lincoln is plainly prophesied here.

80

L'Ogmion grand Bisance approchera,	The Ogmion shall come near great Constantinople,
Chasses sera la Barbarique Ligue,	And shall expel the Barbarian League,
Des deux loix l'une l'unique laschera,	Of the two laws, the wicked one shall yield,
Barbare & France en perpetuelle brigue.	The Barbarian, and the French shall be in perpetual friction.

A King of France shall go to Constantinople, and shall break the Barbarian League; that is, Christian principles shall triumph over the Mohammedan law.

81

L'Oyseau Royal sur la cite Solaire,
Sept mois devant fera nocturne
    augure,
Mur d'Orient cherra tonnerre esclaire,
Sept jours aux portes les ennemis a
    l'heure.

The Royal Bird upon the city of the
    Sun,
Seven months together shall make a
    nocturnal augury,
The Eastern wall shall fall, the
    lightning shall shine,
Then the enemies shall be at the
    gate for seven days.

The Royal Bird (eagle) shall fly for many months over an Eastern city. When it unlooses its most deadly weapon (which shines with the brilliance of lightning) the Eastern wall will crumble.

82

Au conclud pache hors de la forteresse,
Ne sortira celuy en desespoir mis,
Quand ceux d'Arbois, de Langres,
    contre Bresse,
Auront monts Dolle bouscade d'enne-
    mis.

On the conclusion of the pact
    made, out of the fortress,
Shall not come he that was in des-
    pair,
When those of Arbois, of Langres,
    against Brescia,
Shall put in Dolle an ambuscade
    of foes.

During a war a truce will be declared, but the commander of the besieged city shall refuse its terms.

83

Ceux qui auront entrepris subvertir,
Nonpareil regne puissant & invinci-
    ble,
Feront par fraude, nuicts trois adver-
    tis
Quand le plus grand a table lire
    Bible.

Those that shall have undertaken to
    subvert,
The kingdom that has no equal in
    power and victories,
Shall cause by fraud, notice to be
    given for three nights together
When the greatest shall be reading
    a Bible at the table.

A subversive movement within a great nation shall have its inception on a Sunday night.

84

Naistra du gouphre & cite emmesuree,
Nay de parens obscurs & tenebreux;
Quand la puissance du grand Roy
*   reveres,*
Voudre destruire par Rouen &
*   Eureux.*

One shall be born out of the gulf
    and immeasurable city,
Born of parents obscure and dark,
Who, by means of Rouen and
    Eureux,
Will go about to destroy the power
    of the great King.

A person of obscure and dark parentage is predestined to destroy the power of a great King.

85

Par les Sueves & lieux circonvoisins,
Seront en guerre pour cause des neuss.
Gamp marins locustes & cousins,
Du Leman fautes seront bien des-
*   nuees.*

Through Switzerland and the
    neighbouring places,
By reason of the clouds shall fall to
    war,
The lobsters, locusts, and gnats,
The fault of Geneva shall appear
    very naked.

The failure of the League of Nations and the advent of war are prophesied.

86

Par les deux testes & trois bras se-
*   parez,*
La cite grande par eau sera vexes,
Des grandes d'entr'aux par exil es-
*   garez,*
Par teste Perse, Bisance fort pressee.

Divided in two heads and parted in
    three arms,
The great city shall be troubled
    with waters,
Some great ones among them scat-
    tered by banishment,
By a Persian head, Turkey shall be
    much oppressed.

Paris surrenders to Nazi Germany on June 14, 1940, and is overrun (inundated) with Germans. French leaders scatter, and at the same time there is much unrest in the East (Russia) as Hitler attacks the Russians on June 22, 1940.

87

L'an que Saturne sera hors de servage,	In the year that Saturn out of servi-
Au franc terroir sera d'eau inonde;	tude,
De sang Troyen sera son mariage,	In the free country shall be drown-
Et sera seur d'Espagnol circonder.	ed by water,
	With Trojan blood his marriage
	shall be,
	And he surely shall be surrounded
	by Spaniards.

The term 'Trojan blood' refers to the French Nation. The meaning to be gathered from this stanza seems to be that, at the time of a great flood in France, a notable marriage will be made which will endanger French and Spanish relations.

88

Sur le sablon par un hydeux deluge,	Upon the sand through a hideous
Des autres mers trouve monstre marin;	deluge
Proche du lieu sera fait un refuge,	Of other seas, shall be found a sea
Tenant Savone esclave de Turin.	monster,
	Near to that place shall be made a
	sanctuary,
	Which shall make Savoy a slave to
	Turin.

Warfare between two Italian political factions is here predicted.

89

Dedans Hongrie, par Boheme, Na-	In Hungaria, through Bohemia and
varre,	Navarre,
Et par bannieres feintes seditious;	And by banners feigned seditious,
Par fleurs de lys pays portant la barre,	By Fleur de Lys, peace that carries
Contre Orleans fera esmotions.	the bar,
	Against Orleans shall make com-
	motions.

The first two lines of this quatrain foretold the religious troubles that were to happen in Hungaria, Bohemia and Navarre. The last two tell of the Prince of Condé, whose coat of arms bears the flower and the bar, who seized Orleans for the Protestant party.

90

Dans les Cyclades, en Corinthe, &
Larisse,
Dedans Sparte tout le Peloponese;
Si grand famine, peste, par faux con-
nisse,
Neuf mois tiendra & tout le cher-
rouesse.

In the Cyclades, in Corinth and
Larissa,
In Sparta, and all the Peloponne-
sus,
Shall be so great a famine and
plague
To last nine months in the southern
peninsula.

All the Greek regions mentioned shall be afflicted with famine and
plague.

91

Au grand marche qu'on dit des meson-
gers,
De tout torrent & champ Athenien,
Seront surprins par les chevaux legers,
Par Albanois, Mars, Leo, Sat, au
versien.

In the great market called of the
liars,
Which is all torrent and Athenian
field,
They shall be surprised by the light
horses,
Of the Albanese, Mars in Leo,
Saturn in Aquarius.

Athens shall be overrun by the Nordics, here called Albanese by
Nostradamus, after *albus*, Latin for white or blond.

92

Apres le siege tenu dix sept ans,
Cinq changeront en tel revolu terme,
Puis sera l'un esleu de mesme temps,
Qui des Romains ne sera trop con-
forme.

After the seat possessed seventeen
years,
Five shall change in such a space of
time,
After that, one shall be elected at
the same time,
Who shall not be very comformable
to the Romans.

France has had but one ruler who reigned for seventeen years and that
was Louis Philippe (1831–1848) and he had five sons. His successor,
Napoleon III, was 'elected', as forecast by Nostradamus.

93

Sous le terroir de rond globe lunaire,	Under the territory of the round
Lors que sera dominateur Mercure,	lunary globe,
L'isle d'Escosse sera un luminaire,	When Mercury shall be lord of the
Qui les Anglois mettra a deconfiture.	ascendant,

Sous le terroir de rond globe lunaire,
Lors que sera dominateur Mercure,
L'isle d'Escosse sera un luminaire,
Qui les Anglois mettra a deconfiture.

Under the territory of the round lunary globe,
When Mercury shall be lord of the ascendant,
The Island of Scotland shall make a luminary,
That shall put the English to a revolution.

Out of Scotland shall come a great light that will bring about a revolution in England.

94

Translatera en la grand Germanie,
Brabant & Flandres, Gand, Bruges,
* & Bologne;*
La treue sainte le grand duc d'Arme-
* nie,*
Assaillira Vienne & la Cologne.

He shall translate into the Great Germany,
Brabant, Flanders, Gand, Bruges and Boulogne,
The truce feigned, the great Duke of Armenia,
Shall assault Vienna and Cologne.

Germany will attempt to assimilate Belgium and Holland, while a feigned truce with the great Eastern Power will be broken, and the end will be the destruction of Germany itself.

95

Nautique rame invitera les umbres
Du grand Empire, lors viendra conci-
* ter;*
La mer Egee des lignes les encombres,
Empeschant l'onde Tyrrene de floter.

The nautical branch shall invite the shadows,
Of the great Empire, then it shall come to stir,
The Aegean Sea, with lines of encumbers,
Hindering the Thyrrenian Sea to roll.

The navy of a great Empire shall take the lead in a rebellion centering in the Mediterranean.

96

Sur le milieu du grand monde la rose,
Pour nouveaux faits sang public es-
pandu,
A dire vray on aura bouche close,
Lors au besoin viendra tard l'attendu.

In the middle of the great world
shall be the rose,
For new deeds, blood shall be publicly spilt,
To say the truth, every one shall
close his mouth,
Then at the time will be the one
long looked for.

Nostradamus predicts the coming of a great world leader and, by a simple play on words as expressed in the first line, we have his name: rose and world (*welt*, in German) combine to make Roosevelt.

97

Le nay difforme par horreur suffoque,
Dans la cite du grand Roy habitable,
L'edit severe des captifs rovoque,
Gresle & tonnerre Condon inestim-
able.

The deformed shall through horror
be suffocated,
In the habitable city of the great
King.
The severe edict against the ban-
ished shall be revoked,
Hail and thunder shall do inestim-
able harm at Condon.

Condon is a city in old France, the rest is obvious.

98

A quarante-huit degre climatterique,
Afin de Cancer si grande secheresse,
Poisson en mer, fleuve, lac cuit hecti-
que,
Bearn, Bigorre par feu ciel en de-
tresse.

At the climacterical degree of eight
and forty,
At the end of Cancer, shall be such
a drought,
That fish in the sea, river, and lake
shall be boiled hectic,
Bearn and Bigorre by heavenly fire
shall be in distress.

Nostradamus here foretells of a period of great heat and drought, mostly in provinces in France.

99

Milan, Ferrare, Turin & Aquillee,
Capne, Brundis vexez par gent Cel-
  tique,
Par le Lyon a Phalange aquilee,
Quand Rome aura le chef vieux Bri-
  tannique.

Milan, Ferrara, Turin and Aquilia,
Capne, Brundis, shall be vexed by
  the French,
By the Lion and Troop of Aquilia,
When Rome shall have as chief, old
  Britannia.

England shall conquer Italy assisted by the French army, and the military Governor of Rome shall be an Englishman.

100

Le boute-feu par son feu attrape,
De feu du ciel par Tarcas & Cominge,
Foix, Aux, Mazeres, haut vieillard
  eschappe,
Par ceux de Hasse, des Saxons &
  Turinge.

The arsonist shall be overtaken by
  his own fire,
Heavenly fire shall fall at Tartas
  and Cominge,
Foix, Auch, Mazere, a tall old man
  shall escape,
By means of those of Hesse,
  Saxony, and Thuringia.

The ones who set the world on fire, shall be overtaken by stern justice. The Germans shall aid in the escape of one of the guilty ones.

A clear prophecy of the Eichmann trial and indication that Hjalmar Schact the master mind and financial genius who masterminded the Nazi fiasco shall escape the Nuremberg trials.

CENTURY VI

1

Au tour des Monts Pyrenees grand amas,	About the Pyrenean Mountains there shall be a great gathering
De gent estrange, secourir Roy nouveau;	Of strange nations to succour a new King,
Pres de Garonne du grand temple du Mas,	Near Garonne and the great temple of the Maas,
Un Romain chef le craindra dedans l'eau.	A Roman captain shall fear him in the water.

Assistance by a group of nations shall raise a new ruler to power near the Pyrenees Mountains. A Roman leader shall fear this new threat.

2

En l'an cinq cens octante plus & moins,	In the year of five hundred eighty more or less,
On attend le siecle bien estrange;	There shall be a strange age,
En l'an sept cens & trois (cieus en tesmoins)	In the year seven hundred and three (witness heaven)
Que plusieurs regnes un a cinq feront change.	Many kingdoms, one to five shall be changed.

Nostradamus commences his count of time from A.D. 325, the date of the Council of Nicaea. In the above stanza, by using the figure 325 as a key, we find that (1) 589 added to it, gives us the date 1914, one of the most important dates in the history of the world. Similarly, (2) 703 added to 325 gives us 2028, in which year, Nostradamus tells us, there will be a complete change in the lineup of nations.

3

Fleuve qu'esprouve le nouveau nay Celtique,	The river that makes trial of the new-born Celtic,
Sera en grande de l'Empire discorde;	Shall be at great variance with the Empire,
Le jeune prince par gent Ecclesiastique,	The young prince shall be an Ecclesiastical person,
Ostera le sceptre coronal de concorde.	And have his sceptre taken off, and the crown of concord.

The Rhine River shall be the scene of trial for a new Prince of France.

4

Le Celtique fleuve changera de rivage,	The river Rhine shall change her shores,
Plus ne tiendra la cite d'Agripine;	It shall touch no more the city of Cologne,
Tout trasmue ormis le vieil langage,	All shall be transformed, except the language,
Saturne, Leo, Mars, Cancer en rapine.	Saturn, Leo, Mars, Cancer in rapine.

The borders of Germany shall change so as to no longer include Cologne. A complete upheaval will take place in Germany after a period of great unrest.

5

Si grand famine par une pestifere,	So great a famine with a plague,
Par pluye longue le long du Pole Artique;	Through a long rain shall come along the Arctic Pole,
Samarobryn cent lieux de l'hemisphere,	Samarobryn a hundred leagues from the hemisphere,
Vivront sans loy, exempt de politique.	Shall live without law, exempt from politics.

From the northern hemisphere shall come a devastating plague, followed by a period of anarchy throughout the affected countries.

6

Apparoistra vers le Septentrion,	Towards the North shall appear,
Non loing de Cancer l'estoille chevelue;	Not far from Cancer, a blazing star,
Suse, Sienne, Boece, Eretrion,	Suza, Sienna, Boetia, Eretrion,
Mourra de Rome grand, la nuit disperue.	There shall die at Rome a great man, the night being past.

A light in the sky will appear, and a powerful Italian, unable to live in its glare, shall die.

7

Norvege & Dace, & l'isle Britannique,	Norway and Dacia, and the British Island,
Par les unis freres seront vexees;	Shall be vexed by the brothers united,
Le chef Romain issu du sang Gallique,	The Roman Captain issued from French blood,
Et les copis aux forest repoulsees.	His forces shall be beaten back to the forest.

At last, a Pope whose origin is French will be chosen. Here Nostradamus forecasts a retrenchment of Catholicism. The first two lines speak of a conflict between NATO and the Warsaw Pact nations.

8

Ceux qui estoient en regne pour scavoir,	Those that were in esteem for their learning,
Au Royal change deviendront a pouvris,	Upon the change of a King will become poor,
Uns exilez sans appuy, or n'avoir,	Some banished, without help, having no gold,
Lettres & lettres ne seront a grand pris.	Learned and learning shall not be much valued.

A period of oppression against scholars and scientists shall arise.

9

Aux temples saints seront faits grands scandales,	To the holy temples shall be done much scandals,
Comptez seront par honneur & louanges,	That shall be accounted for honours and praises,
D'un que l'on graue d'argent, d'or les medalles,	By one, whose medals are graven in gold and silver,
La fin sera en tourmens bien estranges.	The end of it all shall be in very strange torments.

As an adherent of the Roman Catholic Church, Nostradamus could only look with disapproval on the Protestant party under the leadership of the future Henry IV. As the King of Navarre, he had medals and money stamped with his image for use in the holy temples and cathedrals. The last line proved prophetic, when on St Bartholomew's Day, August 24, 1572, the Protestant Massacre occurred.

10

Un peu de temps les temples de couleurs,	Within a little while the temples of the colours,
De blanc & noir les deux entremeslee;	White and black shall be intermixt,
Rouges & jaunes leur embleront les leurs,	Red and yellow shall take away their colours,
Sang, terre, peste, faim, feu, d'eau affolce.	Blood, earth, plague, famine, fire, water shall destroy them.

After a period of much travail all the races of the world shall lose their prejudices and be as one.

11

Des sept rameaux a trois seront reduits,	The seven branches shall be reduced to three,
Les plus aisnez seront surprins par mort,	The eldest shall be surprised by death,
Fratricider les deux seront seduits,	Two shall be said to kill their brothers,
Les conjures en dormant seront morts.	The conspirators shall be killed being asleep.

Seven brothers shall be reduced to three; of those one shall die suddenly and it will be suspected that he was killed by the other two. And they in turn shall meet violent deaths.

12

Dresser copies pour monter a l'Empire,	To raise an army, to ascend the Empire,
Du Vatican le sang Royal tiendra;	Of the Vatican, the Royal blood shall endeavour,
Flamans, Anglois, Espaigne aspire,	Flemings, English, Spain shall aspire,
Contre l'Italie & France contendre.	And shall contend against Italy and France.

There shall be a great commotion among the nations of Europe over the election of a Pope.

13

Un dubieux ne viendra loing du regne,	A doubtful man shall not come far from the reign,
La plus grand part le voudra soustenir,	The greatest part will uphold him,
Un captiole ne voudra point qu'il regne,	A capitol will not consent that he should reign,
Sa grande chaire ne pourra maintenir.	His great chair he shall not be able to maintain.

Napoleon, after great successes, was finally forced to abdicate.

14

Loing de sa terre roy perdra la bataille,	Far from his country the king shall lose a battle,
Prompt eschappe poursuivy suyuant prins,	Nimble, escaped, followed, following taken,
Ignore prins soubs la doree maille,	Ignorantly taken under the gilded coat of mail,
Soubs faint habit & l'ennemy surprins.	Under a feigned habit the enemy taken.

The Battle of Moscow was the turning point in the career of Napoleon; it was the beginning of the end.

15

Dessous la tombe sera trouve le prince, *Qu'aura le pris par dessus* *Nuremberg;* *L'Espagnol Roy en Capricorn mince,* *Feinct & trahy par le grand* *Vitemberg.*	Under the tomb shall be found the prince, That shall have a price above Nuremberg. That Spanish King in Capricorn shall be thine, Deceived and betrayed by the great Lutheran.

A prince shall commit suicide thus foiling the dictates of the Nuremberg judges. There will be a betrayal of a powerful Spaniard by a German ruler.

16

Ce que ravy sera du jeune Milve, *Par les Normans de France & Picar-* *die;* *Les noirs du temple du lieu Negrisilve,* *Feront aux berg & feu de Lombardie.*	That which shall be taken from the young Kite, By the Normans of France and Picardy, The black ones of the temple of the Black Forest, Shall make a rendezvous and a fire in Lombardy.

The Normans shall succeed in overthrowing a young arrogant Prince, and to celebrate their victory they will build a temple in the Black Forest.

17

Apres les livres bruslez les asiniers, *Constraints seront changer habits* *divers;* *Les Saturnins bruslez par les mus-* *niers,* *Hors la plus part qui ne sera musniers.*	After the books shall be burnt, the asses, Shall be compelled several times to change their clothes, The Saturnins shall be burnt by the millers, Except the greater part, that shall not be discovered.

The millers (unlearned persons) shall attempt to annihilate the culture of the Saturnins (studious people) even to the wholesale burning of books. This prophecy was fulfilled in its entirety when the Nazis publicly banned and burned all books that were against their ideology.

18

Par les physiques le grand Roy de- *laisse,* *Par fort non art ne l'Ebrieu est en vie;* *Luy & son genre au regne haut pousse,* *Grace donne a gent qui Christ envie.*	The great King being forsaken by the physician, Shall be kept alive by power and not by the art of a Hebrew, He, and his kindred shall be put at the top of the kingdom, Grace shall be given to a people that envieth Christ.

A sick King, deserted by his physician, shall be cured by the help of a Jew, and as a token of the King's gratitude, the Jews of that nation will enjoy great privileges.

19

La vray flamme engloutira la dame, *Que voudra mettre les innocens a feu,* *Pres de l'assaut l'excercite s'en-* *flamme,* *Quand dans Seville monstre en boeuf* *sera veu.*	The true flame shall swallow up the lady, That went about to burn the guilt- less, Before the assault the army shall be encouraged, When in Seville, a monster like an ox shall be seen.

A monster shall be seen in Seville, similar to the ancient Minotaur who demanded a tribute of innocent children.

20

L'union feinte sera peu de duree, *Des uns changes reformez la pluspart,* *Dans les caisseaux sera gent endures,* *Lors aura Rome un nouveau leopart.*	The feigned union shall not last long, Some shall be changed, others for the most part reformed, In the ships people shall be penned up, Then shall Rome have a new leopard.

An unstable temporary union between Egypt and Israel. A new leader at Rome will be installed when the union dissolves.

21

Quand ceux de Pole Artique unis ensemble,	When those of the Arctic Pole shall be united together,
En Orient grand effrayeur & crainte,	There shall be in the East, great fear and trembling,
Esleu nouveau soustenu le grand temple,	One shall be newly elected, that shall bear the brunt,
Rhodes, Bisance de sang Barbare taints.	Rhodes, Constantinople, shall be dyed with Barbarian blood.

The people of northern Europe shall unite against those of the East. The actual battle shall take place near Turkey.

22

Dedans la terre du grand temple celique,	Within the ground of the great celestial temple,
Nepueu a Londres par paix faincte meurtry,	A nephew at London by a feigned peace shall be murdered,
La barque alors deviendra scismatique,	The boat at that time shall become schismatical,
Liberte faincte sera au corne & cry.	A feigned liberty shall be with hue and cry.

In St Paul's Cathedral, London, the murdered body of a famous person will be found. It will cause great dissension among the churchmen since one of them will be suspected of the crime.

23

D'esprit de Roy munisememens descriees,	Despite the King, the coin will be brought lower,
Et seront peuples esmeus contre leur Roy,	The people shall rise against their King,
Paix, fait nouveau, sainctes loix empirees,	Peace being made, holy laws made worse,
Paris onc fut en si tresdur arroy.	Paris was never in such a great disorder.

This is a remarkable account of the French Revolution, in proper chronological order – collapse of the financial structure, rising of the people, abandonment of religion and Paris in disorder.

24

Mars & le Sceptre se trouvera conjont,	Mars and the Sceptre, being con-
Dessous Cancer calamiteuse guerre;	joined together,
Un peu apres sera nouveau Roy oingt,	Under Cancer shall be a calamitous
Qui par long temps pacifiera la terre.	war,
	A little while after a new King shall
	be anointed,
	Who, for a long time, shall pacify
	the earth.

Nostradamus here speaks of a constellation called the Sceptre. Looking far into the future, he foretells of a time when this constellation shall be in conjunction with Mars, and the terrible war that will break out under this influence. And out of the debacle there will arise a new world leader and peace will reign for a long time afterward.

25

Par Mars constraire sera la Monar-	By Mars contrary shall the monar-
chie,	chy,
Du grand pescheur en trouble	Of the great fisherman, be brought
ruyneux;	into ruinous trouble,
Jeune, noire, rouge prendra la	A young, black red shall possess
hierarchie,	himself of the hierarchy,
Les prodieurs iront jour bruyneux.	The traitors shall undertake it on a
	misty day.

Nostradamus uses *noire* as an anagram for *roi* (seventeen different times) and here as *roi-N* (for NAPOLEON). The day that Napoleon overthrows the Directory, November 9, 1798, is known as the Eighteenth of Brumaire or 'day of the fog.'

26

Quartre ans le siege quelque peu bien	Four years he shall keep the Papal
tiendra,	seat pretty well,
Un surviendra libidineux de vie,	Then shall succeed one of a libidi-
Ravenne & Pise, Veronne soustien-	nous life,
dront,	Ravenna, Pisa, shall take Verona's
Pour eslever la croix du Pape envie.	part,
	To raise up the Pope's cross to life.

A continuation of the preceding stanza, this predicts that the usurper will reign four years, being then succeeded by a notorious sensualist, whose main support shall come from those in the above-mentioned cities.

27

Dedans les isles de cinq fleuves a un,
Par le croissant du grand Chyren
Selin;
Par les bruynes de l'air fureur de l'un,
Six eschappez, cachez fardeaux de
lyn.

In the islands from five rivers to
one,
By the increase of the great emperor Henry,
By the frost of the air and the fury
of one,
Six shall escape, hidden within
bundles of flax.

Again we have a play on words: *Chyren* meaning Henry, and *Selin* meaning King. Just what king or ruler Nostradamus refers to is not clear, and it is quite possible that he means by this obscurity to indicate some future world leader.

28

Le grand Celtique entrera dedans
Rome,
Menant amas d'exilez & bannis;
Le grand pasteur mettra a mort tout
homme
Qui pour le Coq estoit aux Alpes unis.

The great Celtique shall enter into
Rome,
Leading with him a great number
of banished men,
The great shepherd shall put to
death every man,
That was united for the Cock, near
the Alps.

The campaign of Napoleon, which culminated in the French victory over Italy, is foretold.

29

La vefue saincte entendant les nouvel-
les,
De ses rameaux mis en perplex &
trouble,
Qui sera duict appraiser les querelles,
Par son pourchas des razes fera
comble.

The holy widow hearing the news,
Of her branches put in perplexity
or trouble,
That shall be skilful in appeasing
of quarrels,
By his purchase shall make a heap
of shaven heads.

Nostradamus here discusses a time of *interregnum* – the period after the death of a Pope until a new one is elected – and refers to the various parts of the Church in his usual obscure manner: by 'the holy widow' he means the City of Rome; the 'branches' are the clergymen; and the 'shaven heads' refer to priests.

30

Par l'apparence de faincte sainctete,	By the appearance of a feigned holiness,
Sera trahy aux ennemis le siege,	
Nuict qu'on coidoit dormir en seurete,	The siege shall be betrayed to the enemies,
Pres de Braban marcheront ceux du Liege.	In a night that everyone thought to be secure,
	Near Brabant shall march those of Liege.

This appears to be a description of some trouble which occurred between the two regions mentioned.

31

Roy trouvera ce qu'il desiroit tant,	A King shall find what he so much longed for,
Quand le Prelat sera reprins a tort;	When a Prelate shall be censured wrongfully,
Responce au Duc le rendra mal content,	His answer to the Duke will make him discontented,
Qui dans Milan mettra plusieurs a mort.	Who in Milan shall put many to death.

Nostradamus discusses one of the many involved quarrels between the State and the Church.

32

Par trahisons de verges a mort battu,	By treason one shall be beaten with rods to death,
Puis surmonte sera par son desordre;	Then the traitor shall be overcome by his disorder,
Conseil frivole au grand captif sentu,	The great prisoner shall try a frivolous counsel,
Nez par fureur quand Berich viendra mordre.	When Berich shall bite another's nose through anger.

'When traitors fall out amongst themselves, honest men rejoice.' Such is the sense of this stanza.

33

Sa main derniere par Alus san-
    guinaire,
Ne se pourra plus la mer garentir;
Entre deux fleuves craindre main mi-
    litaire,
Le noir l'ireux le fera repentir.
	His last hand bloody through all US
	Shall not save him by sea,
	Between two rivers he shall fear the
	    military hand,
	The black and wrathful one shall be
	    repentant.

The rise of Black Power and riots in the US.

34

De feu volant la machination,
Viendra troubler au grand chef as-
    siegez;
Dedans sera telle sedition,
Qu'en desespoir seront les profligez.
	The contraption of flying fire,
	Shall trouble so much the captain of
	    the besieged,
	And within shall be so much riot-
	    ing,
	That the besieged shall be in des-
	    pair.

Predicting flame-throwing tanks that besieged the countryside around Paris, leading to its downfall. The 'contraption of flying fire' could be nothing less than a flame-throwing tank.

35

Pres de Rion & proche Blanchelaine,
Aries, Taurus, Cancer, Leo, la
    Viergge,
Mars, Jupiter, les Sol ardra grand
    plaine,
Bois & cites lettres cachez au cierge.
	Near Rion and towards Blanche-
	    laine,
	Aries, Taurus, Cancer, Leo, Virgo,
	Mars, Jupiter, the Sun shall burn a
	    great plain,
	Woods and cities, letters hidden in
	    a wax candle.

The first line of this verse is anagrammatic – the word 'rion,' spelled backwards, becomes *noir*, black; 'blanche' contains the letters *blanc*, meaning white. Therefore, we must surmise that when the above-mentioned constellations are in conjunction there will be a fire of almost worldwide proportions, the aftermath of which will be a definite division in the world of 'black' and 'white.'

36

Ne bien ne mal par bataille terrestre,	Neither good nor evil by a loud fight,
Ne parviendra aux confins de Perouse,	Shall reach to the borders of Perugia,
Rebeller Pise, Florence voir mal estre,	Pisa shall rebel, Florence shall be in a bad way,
Roy nuict blesse sur mulet a noire housse.	A King being on his mule shall be wounded in the darkness.

All the cities named are in Italy; the balance should be easy to decipher.

37

L'oeuvre ancienne se parachevera,	The ancient work shall be finished,
Du toict cherra sur la grand mal ruyne,	From the house tops shall fall great misfortunes,
Innocent faict mort on accusera,	The innocent in fact, shall be accused after his death,
Nocent cache, taillis a la bruyne.	The guilty shall be hidden in a wood in misty weather.

King Louis XVI attempted to escape from the rebels, but was apprehended in a forest hiding-place.

38

Aux profligez de paix les ennemis,	To the vanquished the enemies of peace,
Apres avoir l'Italie supperee;	After they shall have overcome Italy,
Noir sanguinaire, rouge sera commis,	A bloody Black One shall be committed,
Feu sang verser, eau de sang coloree.	Fire and blood shall be discharged, and water coloured with blood.

This is the prognostication of the rape of Italy by the Fascists under the leadership of Mussolini.

39

L'enfant du regne par paternelle prince,	The child of the kingdom through his father's imprisonment,
Expolie sera pour delivrer;	Shall be deprived of his kingdom for the delivering of his father,
Aupres du Lac Trasimen l'azur prinse,	Near the Lake Trasimene shall be taken in a tower,
La trope hostage pour trop fort s'eny-urer.	The troop that was in hostage being drunk.

Lake Trasimene, where Hannibal fought a famous battle with the Romans, is the only clear expression in this otherwise obscurely worded quatrain.

40

Grand de Magonce pour grand soif estaindre,	The great one of Mayence to quench a great thirst,
Sera prive de la grand dignite;	Shall be deprived of his high dignity,
Ceux de Cologne si fort le viendront plaindre,	Those of Cologne shall mourn him so much,
Que le Grand Groppe au Ryn sera jette.	That the Great Groppe shall be thrown into the Rhine.

The German populace shall feel the loss of their great prestige, and shall mourn the loss of their leader, Schickel-GROPPE (Hitler), even to the point of making his name synonymous with the German National Symbol, the River Rhine.

41

Le second chef du regne Dannemarc,	The second head of the Kingdom of Denmark,
Par ceux de Frise & l'isle Britanni-que,	By those of Holland, and the British Isles,
Fera despendre plus de cent mille marc,	Shall cause to be spent over 100 thousand marks,
Vain exploiter voyage en Italique.	Vainly trying to find a way into Italy.

A signification that Danish, Dutch, and English forces will attempt a costly and ultimately futile invasion of Italy.

42

A l'Ogmyon sera laisse le regne,
Du grand Selin qui plus sera de faict,
Par l'Italie estendra son enseigne,
Regne sera par prudent contrefait.

Unto l'Ogmion shall be left the kingdom,
Of great Selyn, who shall do more than the rest,
Through Italy he shall spread his ensigns,
He shall govern by prudent forgeries.

A King of France shall dictate to the Vatican and exert great influence throughout Italy.

43

Long temps sera sans estre habitee,
Ou Seine & Marne autour vient ar-
rouser,
De la Tamise & martiaux tentee,
Deceus les gardes en evidant repous-
ser.

For a long time shall be uninhabited
Where the Seine and Marne come to water about,
From the Thames and martial people, they shall attempt
To deceive the guards into thinking to resist.

Because of traitors within her gates ruin will fall upon Paris, and the flight of the inhabitants will result in an almost deserted city.

44

De nuict par Nantes l'iris apparoistra,
Des Arcs Marins susciteront la pluye,
Arabique Goulfre grand classe par-
fondra,
Un monstre en Saxe naistra d'ours &
truye.

By night in Nantes the rainbow shall appear,
Arches of the Sea shall cause rain,
The Arabian Gulf shall drown a great fleet,
A monster shall be in Saxony from a bear and a sow.

Incendiary bombs shall light up the nights in France; and in Germany, the British shall cause great destruction.

45

Le gouverneur du Regne bien scavant,	The governor of the Kingdom being wise,
Ne consentir voulant au fait Royal,	Shall not consent to the King's will,
Mellile classe par le contraire vent,	He shall ponder setting out a fleet by the contrary wind,
Le remettra a son plus desloyal.	Which he shall put into the hands of the most disloyal.

After the Franco-German armistice in 1940, the French fleet remained in the hands of the Vichy government. By 1942 when the Allies invaded North Africa, the French fleet, stationed at Toulon, was about to be seized by the Germans but was scuttled and sabotaged, thus preventing the Germans from using this valuable asset.

46

Un juste sera en exil anvoye,	A just person shall be banished,
Par pestilence aux confins de Non Seggle,	By plague to the borders of Non-Seggle,
Response au rouge le fera desvoyer,	The answer to the red one shall make him deviate,
Roy retirant a la Rane & l'Aigle.	Retiring himself to the Frog and the Eagle.

Russia, formerly allied against France, shall be privately assured that her best interests lie in deserting her partner and joining France and her allies.

47

Entre deux monts les deux grands assemblees,	Between two mountains the two great ones shall meet,
Delaiseront leur simulte secrette;	They shall forsake their secret enmity,
Bruxelles & Dolle par Langres accablees,	Brussels and Dolle shall be crushed by Langres,
Pour a Malignes executer leur peste.	To put their plague in execution at Maline.

The Mideast is in focus here. Nostradamus correctly anticipates the alliance between Anwar Sadat and Menachem Begin. Meeting in the Sinai ('between two mountains') they forsook their enmity.

48

La sainctete trop saincte & seductive,	The feigned and seducing holiness,
Accompagnee d'une langue diserte;	Accompanied with a fluent tongue,
La cite vieille & Palme trop hastive,	Shall cause the old city and the too
Florence & Sienne rendront plus de-	hasty Parma,
sertes.	Florence and Sienna to be more
	desert.

The sanctimonious mouthings of a fluent demagogue shall influence many people in Rome and other important Italian cities, and cause them to abet him in his nefarious schemes.

49

De la partie de Mammer grand pon-	By the project of Mammon, high
tife,	priest,
Subjuguera les confins du Danube,	They shall subjugate the borders of
Chasser les croix par fer raffe ne riffe,	the Danube,
Captifs, or, bagues, plus de cent mille	They shall pursue crosses of iron,
rubles.	topsy-turvy,
	Slaves, gold, jewels, more than a
	hundred thousand rubles.

The Swastika, crooked-cross emblem of the Nazis, is clearly foreseen by Nostradamus; also the financial origin of their unholy crimes against humanity.

50

Dedans le puits seront trouvez les los,	In the well shall be found the
Sera l'incest commis par la marastre;	bones,
L'estat change, on querre bruit les los,	Incest shall be committed by the
Et aura Mars ascendant pour son	stepmother,
astre.	The state being changed, there
	shall be a great stir about the
	bones,
	And she shall have Mars for her
	ascending planet.

A stepmother shall have a child by her son-in-law, and will commit infanticide, throwing the body in a well. When the bones are discovered a great furore will take place.

51

Peuple assemble voir nouveau specta-cle	People assembled to see a new show.
Princes & Roys par plusieurs assis-tans,	Princes and Kings, with many assistants,
Pilliers faillir, murs, mais comme miracle,	Pillars shall fail, walls also, but as a miracle,
Le Roy sauve & trente des instans.	The King saved, and thirty of the standers-by.

This pertains to the Congress of Vienna, which convened after the defeat of Napoleon and effected many changes among the nations of Europe.

52

En lieu du grand qui sera condamne,	Instead of the great one that shall be condemned,
De prisons hors, son amy en sa place;	And put out of prison, his friend being in his place,
L'espoir Troyen en six mois joint mort nay,	The Trojan hope in six months united, still-born,
Le Sol a l'Vurne seront prins fleuves en glace.	The Sun in Aquarius, then rivers shall be frozen.

Richard Nixon resigns the presidency; his vice-president, Spiro Agnew (Greek descent), had also resigned but was kept out of jail.

53

Le grand Prelat Celtique a Roy sus-pect,	The great Celtic Prelate suspected by his King,
De nuict par cours sortira hors du regne,	Shall in haste by night go out of the government.
Par Duc fertille a son grand Roy Bretagne,	By means of a Duke, fruitful to his King, Great Britain,
Bisance a Cypres & Tunes insuspect.	Turkey to Cyprus, and Tunis shall be unsuspected.

A Prelate of Celtic origin shall be removed from power by his King. Great Britain shall be the gainer.

54

Au poinct du jour second chant du coq,	At the break of day, at the second crowing of the cock,
Ceux de Tunes, de Fez, & le Bugie,	Those of Tunis, and Fez and Bugia,
Par les Arabes captif le Roy Maroq,	By means of the Arabians, shall take prisoner the King of Morocco
L'an mil six cens & sept de Liturgie.	In the year 1607 by liturgy.

Here again we have recourse to Nostradamus's key figure (as noted in quatrain 2, Century VI). By using this number, 325, and adding to it the figure 1607 referred to above, we get 1932. In this instance, the date is approximate, since the inference gathered from the quatrain clearly applies to conditions leading up to the Spanish Civil War which began in 1936.

55

Au Chelme Duc, en arrachant l'esp-once,	The Chelme Duke, on throwing the sponge,
Voille Arabesque voir, subit des-couverte;	Shall see Arabian Sails suddenly discovered,
Tripolis, Chio, & ceux de Trape-sonce,	Tripoli, Chios, and those of Trapesan,
Duc Prins, Marnegro, & sa cite de-serte.	The Duke shall be taken, Marnegro, and the city shall be deserted.

The regions mentioned are near or in Turkey. *Chelme* is a German word signifying a rogue. The meaning here seems to be that there shall be conflict between this wicked Duke and the rulers of these various cities.

56

La crainte armee de l'ennemy Narbon,	The feared army of the enemy Narbonne
Effrayera si fort les Hesperiques;	Shall so much terrify the Spaniards,
Parpignan vuide par L'aveugle d'Arbon,	That Perpignan shall be left empty by the blind d'Arbon,
Lors Barcelon par mer donra les piques.	Then Barcelona by sea shall give the weapons.

Perpignon, a border town between France and Spain, shall be captured by the French. Barcelona shall come to the rescue by way of the sea.

57

Celuy qu'estoit bien avant dans le regne,
Avant chef rouge proche la hierarchie;
Aspre & cruel, & se fera tant craindre,
Succedera a Sacree Monarchie.

He that was a great way in the kingdom,
Having a red head and near the hierarchy,
Harsh and cruel, shall make himself so dreadful,
That he shall succeed to the Sacred Monarchy.

A Cardinal of great power – backed by much influence – shall make himself so indispensable to the Vatican, that he will be awarded the Papacy.

58

Entre les deux monarques eslongnez,
Lors que Sol par Selin cler perdue;
Simulte grande entre deux indignez,
Qu'aux Isles & Sienne la liberte rendue.

Between the two monarchs that live far from each other.
When the Sun shall be eclipsed by Selene,
Great enmity shall be between the two,
So that liberty will be restored to the Isles and Sienna.

When the Sun is eclipsed by the Moon, Sienna shall have its liberty restored.

59

Dame en fureur par rage d'adultere,
Viendra a son prince conjurer non de dire,
Mais bref cogneu sera le vitupere,
Que seront mis dixsept a martyre.

A lady in fury by rage of an adultery,
Shall come to her prince and conjure him to say nothing,
But soon shall the shameful thing be known,
So that seventeen shall be put to death.

An explicit statement that should be clear to all.

60

Le prince hors de son terroir Celtique,	The Prince being out of his Celtic country,
Sera trahy, deceu par interprete;	Shall be betrayed and deceived by an interpreter.
Rouan, Rochelle, par ceux d'Armor-ique,	Rouen, Rochelle, by those of Gascony,
Au Port de Blaye deceus par moine & prestre.	At the Port of Bordeaux shall be deceived by a monk and priest.

A false interpretation of a political message shall cause an uproar throughout France.

61

Le grand tapis plie ne monstrera,	The great carpet folded shall not show,
Fors qu'a demy la pluspart de l'his-torie;	But by half the greatest part of the history,
Chasse du regne loing aspre apparois-tra.	The exiles of the kingdom shall appear sharp afar off.
Qu'au fait bellique chacun le viendra eroire.	In warlike matters everyone shall believe.

The true historical facts concerning an exiled leader, who maintained his powerful influence even during his banishment, shall be forever concealed from posterity.

62

Trop tard tous deux, les fleurs seront perdues,	Both the flowers shall be lost too late,
Contre la loy serpent ne voudra faire;	Against the law the serpent shall do nothing,
Des ligueurs forces par gallops confon-dues,	The forces of the leaguers, by gallops, shall be confounded,
Savone, Albigne, par Monech grand martyre.	Savoy, Albigne, by Monaco shall suffer great martyrdom.

Nostradamus here expresses his hatred for heretics by referring to them as serpents. By 'gallops' he means horsemen, and the meaning to be drawn from this stanza is that the heretics of the above-named towns shall be persecuted and driven out.

63

La dame seule au regne demeuree,	The lady shall be left to reign alone,
L'unique estaint premier au lict d'honneur,	The unique one being extinguished, first in the bed of honour,
Sept ans sera de douleur exploree,	Seven years she shall weep for grief,
Quis longue vie au regne par grand heur.	After that she shall live long in the reign by grandeur.

Catherine de Medici outlived her husband, Henry II of France, by many years. After his death she went into deep mourning for seven years.

64

On ne tiendra pache aucun arreste,	No binding agreement shall be kept,
Tous recevans iront par tromperie;	Those that admit of it deal in trumpery,
De paix & trefue, terre & mer proteste;	There shall be no protestations by land and sea,
Par Barcelone classe prins d'industrie.	Barcelona shall take a fleet by ingenuity.

An armed truce with trickery on all sides shall beset the nations, and Spain shall be the gainer.

65

Gris & bureau, demie ouverte guerre,	Between the grays and the bureaus shall be half open war,
De nuict seront assailliz & pillez;	By night they shall be assaulted and plundered,
Le bureau prins passera par la serre,	The government being taken shall put in custody,
Son temple ouvert, deux aux plastres grillez.	His temple shall be opened, two shall be put in the grate.

Conflict between lower classes and bureaucrats is foreshadowed ending with the overthrow of a government.

66

Au fondement de la nouvelle secte,	At the founding of a new sect,
Seront les os du grand Romain trouvez,	The bones of the great Roman shall be found,
Sepulchre en marbre apparoistra converte.	The Sepulchre shall appear covered with marble,
Terra trembler en Avril, mal enfovez.	The earth shall quake in April, they shall be ill-buried.

The order (sect) founded by St Francis, for whom San Francisco is named. A major earthquake will occur in April as it once already did in 1906.

67

Au grand Empire par viendra tout un autre,	To the great Empire quite another shall come,
Bonte distant plus de felicite;	Being distant from goodness and happiness,
Regi par un issu non loing du peautre,	Governed by one of base parentage,
Corruer Regnes grande infelicite.	The Kingdom shall fall, a great unhappiness.

The rise and dominance of Communism will progress toward the subjugation of the Western democracies and cause great unhappiness.

68

Lors que soldats fureur seditieuse,	When the seditious fury of the soldiers,
Contre leur chef feront de nuict fer livre,	Against their chief shall make the iron shine by night,
Ennemy d'Albe soit par main furieuse,	The enemy d'Albe shall by a furious hand,
Lors vexer Rome & principaux seduire.	Then vex Rome and seduce the principal one.

The Duke of Alba, commander of the Spanish Army in the war against the Roman forces of the Pope, unmercifully forced the war to a successful conclusion for his master, Emperor Charles V.

69

La grand pitie sera sans long tarder,	What a great pity will it be before long,
Ceux qui donoient seront contraints de prendre,	Those that did give, shall be constrained to receive,
Nuds affamez de froid, soif, soy bander,	Naked, famished with cold, to mutiny,
Passer les monts en faisant grand esclandre.	To go over the mountains making great disorders.

A land of plenty shall soon be in want and the people will revolt.

70

Un chef du monde le grand Chyren sera;	A chief of the world, the great Henry shall be,
Plus outre, apres ayme, craint, redoute;	At first, beloved, afterwards feared, dreaded,
Son bruit & los les cieux sur passera,	His fame and praise shall go beyond the heavens,
Et du seul titre Victeur, fort content.	And shall be contented with the title of Victor.

The nations will organize a super-government covering the entire world. The president will be named Henry.

'Chyren' by transposition of letters is an anagram for 'Henryc', the then current form of Henry.

71

Quand on viendra le grand Roy parenter,	When they shall come to celebrate the obsequies of the great King,
Avant qu'il ait du tout l'ame rendue,	A day before he be quite dead,
On le verra bien tost apparenter,	He shall be seen presently to be allied,
D'Aigles, Lions, Crois, Couronne vendue.	With Eagles, Lions, Crosses, Crowns of Rue.

A continuation of the previous stanza; at the end of Henry's reign, he shall be exposed as being allied with predatory interests, bringing much sorrow and suffering to mankind.

72

Par fureur faincte d'esmotion divine,	By a feigned fury of divine inspira-tion,
Sera la femme du grand fort violee;	The wife of the great one shall be ravished,
Judges voulants damner telle doctrine,	Judges willing to condemn such a doctrine
Victime au peuple ignorant immolee.	A victim shall be sacrificed to the ignorant people.

Marie Antoinette, wife of Louis XVI of France, was condemned to death by the judges of the revolution and guillotined in the presence of a howling mob.

73

En cite grand un moyne & artisan,	In a great city a monk and an artisan
Pres de la porte logez & aux murail-les;	Dwelling near the gate and walls,
Contre modene secret, cave disant,	Against woman secrets, beware fur-ther,
Trahis pour faire sous couleur d'es-pousailles.	A treason shall be plotted under pretence of marriage.

The life and history of the Reverend Daniel Berrigan is here portrayed. He leaves the ministry and marries, but not before much protest and plotting.

74

La dechassee au regne tournera,	The expelled shall come again to the kingdom,
Ses ennemis trouvez des conjurez;	Her enemies shall be found to be conspirators,
Plus que jamais son temps triomphera,	More than ever his time shall triumph,
Trois & septante a mort trop asseurez.	Three and seventy appointed by death.

Napoleon I and his Empire were removed but later restored under Napoleon III. He triumphed but eventually met death from surgery in 1873 in England.

75

Le grand Pilot sera par Roy mande	The great Pilot shall be sent for by
Laisser la classe, pour plus haut lieu attaindre;	Royal mandate, To leave the fleet, and be preferred
Sept ans apres sera contrebande,	to a higher place,
Barbare armee viendra Venise craindre.	Seven years after he shall be countermanded,
	A barbarian army shall put Venice to fear.

A great leader, long absent from public life, shall be recalled to pilot his country's destiny during a time of great stress. The latter part of the stanza indicates his final fall from grace in the face of overwhelming public opposition.

76

La cite antique d'Antenoree forge,	The ancient city founded by Antenor,
Plus ne pouvant le tyran supporter;	Not being able to bear the tyrant
Le manche fainct au temple couper gorge,	any longer,
Les siens le peuple a mort viendra bouter.	The feigned handle in the temple cut a throat,
	The people will come to put his servants to death.

The city founded by Antenor, who came to Italy with Aeneas, is Padua. Being a university city, it will not be able to stand the antics of a tyrant any longer. He shall have his throat cut, and his companions will also be put to death.

77

Par la victoire du deceu fraudulente,	By the deceitful victory of the deceived,
Deux classes une, la revolte Germains,	One of the two fleets shall revolt to
Le chef meurtry & son fils dans la tente,	the Germans,
Florence, Imole pourchassez dans Romaine.	The chief and his son murdered in their tent,
	Florence, Imole, persecuted in Romania.

The Germans shall be deceived into thinking that they have won a victory. Trouble in Italy shall hasten their disillusionment and contribute to their final defeat.

78

Crier victoire du grand Selin crois-
sant,
Par les Romains sera l'Aigle clame,
Ticcin, Milan & Gennes ny consent,
Puis par eux mesmes Basil grand
reclame.

They shall cry at the victory of the
great Selin's crescent,
By the Romans the Eagle shall be
claimed,
Ticin, Milan and Genoa consent
not,
Then by themselves the great Basil
shall be claimed.

The Romans, defeated in a battle with the Turks, will request aid from
other Italian cities. Being refused by them, they will then appeal to the
great King (Basil from the Greek word *Basileus*).

79

Pres de Tesin les habitants de Logre,
Garonne & Saone, Siene, Tarn &
Gironde,
Outre les monts dresseront promon-
toire,
Conflit donne, Pau granci, submerge
onde.

Near the Tesin the inhabitants of
Logre,
Garonne and Saone, Siene, Tarn
and Gironde,
Shall erect a promontory beyond
the mountains,
Conflict given, the Po passed over,
some shall be drowned.

The Italians shall attempt to build an empire beyond their own borders.
Eventually they will be defeated in this purpose, and shall suffer great
losses.

80

De Fez le Regne parviendra a ceux
d'Europe,
Feu leur cite, & lame trenchera;
Le grand d'Asie terre & mer a grand
troupe,
Que bleux, pars, croix a mort dechas-
sera.

The Kingdom of Fez shall come to
those of Europe,
Fire and sword shall destroy their
city,
The great one of Asia, by land and
sea with a great army,
So that blues, greens, crosses to
death he shall drive.

'A strange prophecy if it prove true,' said a 17th-century disciple of
Nostradamus. And time so proves it – that this is the prediction of the
Spanish Civil War, of the uprisings which began in Morocco and spread to
Spain; and even indicates the aid that was given the Loyalists by Russia and
Franco by Germany.

81

Pleurs, cris, & plaincts, hurlemens, effrayeurs,	Tears, cries and complaints, howlings, fear,
Coeur inhuman, cruel, noir, & transy.	An inhuman heart, cruel black and astonished,
Leman, les Isles de Gennes les majeurs,	Geneva, the Islands of the great ones of Genoa,
Sang espancher, tochsain, a nul mercy.	Shall spill blood, the bell shall ring and no mercy given.

During the course of a war that shall involve most of the earth's surface, a battle of great importance will be fought with the Dodecanese Islands as the prize.

82

Par les deserts de lieu, libre, & farouche,	Through the deserts of a place free and ragged,
Viendra errer nepveu du grand Pontife;	The nephew of the Pope shall come to wander,
Assomme a sept avec ques lourde souche,	Knocked in the head by seven with a heavy club,
Par ceux qu'apres occuperont le cyphe.	By those who after shall obtain the cipher.

A nephew of the Pope shall be exiled to a desert, where he shall be attacked by seven men, one of which will afterwards gain the Papacy.

83

Celuy qu'aura tant d'honneur & carresses,	He that shall have had so many honours and welcomes,
A son entree en la Gaule Belgique,	At his going into French Belgium,
Un temps apres fera tant de rudesses,	A while after shall commit so many rudenesses,
Et sera contre a la fleur tant bellique.	And shall be against the warlike flower.

This concerns the Duke of Alençon who was sent into the Low Countries as Governor for Henry III, King of France. So entranced was he by the beauty and riches of Antwerp, that he attempted to seize the city, but he was overcome by the citizens and most of his followers were destroyed.

84

Celuy qu'en Sparte Claude ne veut regner,	He that Claudius will not have to reign in Sparta,
Il fera tant par voye seductive;	The same shall do so much by a deceitful way,
Que de court, long, le fera araigner,	That he shall cause him to be arraigned short and long,
Que contre Roy fera sa perspective.	As if he had made his prospect upon the King.

One shall be hindered from reigning, by the machinations of another.

85

La grand cite de Tharse par Gaulois,	The great city of Tharse taken by the French,
Sera destruite, captifs tous a Turban,	All who wore the turban shall be made slaves,
Secours par mer, du grand Portuga-lois,	Help by sea from the great Portuguese,
Premier d'este le jour de sacre Urban.	The first day of summer and the installation of Urban.

What is meant by the taking of Tarsus, the birthplace of the Apostle Paul, is not clear to me. The rest of the stanza refers to the persecution and enslavement of non-Christians during the reigns of various early Popes (indicated by 'Urban,' the name taken by eight different Popes, the last of whom held office from 1623 to 1644).

86

Le grand Prelat un jour apres son songe	The great Prelate the next day after his dream,
Interprete au rebours de son sens;	Interpreted contrary to his sense,
De la Gascongne luy surviendra un monge,	From Gascony shall come to him a monk,
Qui fera eslire le grand Prelat de Sens.	That shall cause the great Prelate of Sens to be elected.

A lowly monk shall come to a princely churchman, and, following his advice, the Prelate will be elected to a high office.

87

L'election faicte dans Francfort,	The election made at Frankfurt,
N'aura nul lieu, Milan s'opposera;	Shall be void, Milan shall oppose it;
Le sien plus proche semblera si grand fort,	He of the Milan party shall be so strong,
Qu'outre le Rhin es mareschs chassera.	As to drive the other beyond the marshes of the Rhine.

At Frankfurt in Germany, the ancient German rulers were elected.
Milan is the place where the Italian Fascist leaders first became powerful.
The rest is plain.

88

Un regne grand demourra desole,	A great king shall be left desolate,
Aupres del Hebrose seront assemblees;	Near the River Hebrus an assembly shall be made,
Monts Pyrenees le rendront console,	The Pyrenean Mountains shall comfort him,
Lors que dans May seront terres tremblees.	When in May shall be an earthquake.

A reference to an ancient incident, this concerns a King who, after
being defeated in a battle near the River Hebrus (the ancient name for the
River Maritza), loses his kingdom and is forced to flee to the shelter of the
Pyrenees Mountains.

89

Entre deux cymbles pieds & mains estachez,	Between two boats one shall be tied hand and foot,
De miel face oingt, & de laict substante;	His face anointed with honey, and be nourished with milk,
Geuspes & mouches seront amour fachez,	Wasps and bees shall make much of him mad,
Poccilateurs faucer, cyphe tente.	For being treacherous cup bearers, and poisoning the cup.

A description of a form of ancient torture meted out to poisoners – put
between two troughs called boats, their bodies were daubed with honey, so
that wasps and bees could torment them to death.

90

L'honnissement puant abominable,
Apres le faict sera felicite;
Grand excuse, pour n'estre favorable,
Qu'a paix Neptune ne sera incite.

The stinking and abominable defiling,
After the deed shall be successful,
The great one excused for not being favourable,
That Neptune might be persuaded to peace.

This refers to an infamous pact, agreed upon by several nations, ostensibly for the preservation of peace. The Munich Pact and the temporary acclamation of the role played by Chamberlain are clearly indicated.

91

Le conducteur de la Guerre Navale,
Rouge effrene, severe, horrible grippe,
Captif eschappe de l'aisne dans la baste;
Quand il naistra du grand un fils Agrippe.

The leader of the Naval War,
Red, rash, severe, horrible executioner.
Being slave, shall escape, hidden among the harness,
When shall be born to the great one, a son named Agrippa.

Cornelius Agrippa, 1486-1535, a German soldier, philosopher and alchemist, is here alluded to.

92

Prince de beaute tant venuste,
Au chef menee, le second faict trahy;
Le cite au glaive de poudre face aduste,
Par trop grand meurtre le chef du Roy hay.

A Prince of an exquisite beauty,
Shall be brought to the chief, the second fact betrayed,
The city shall be given to fire and sword,
By too great a murder, the chief man of the King shall be hated.

Louis XVI, a prince of beauty, was beheaded by the guillotine (*glaive/* single-edged blade).

93

Prelat avare, d'ambition trompe,	A covetous Prelate, deceived by ambition,
Rien ne fera que trop cuider viendra,	Shall do nothing but covet too much,
Ses messagers, & luy bien attrape,	His messengers and he shall be trapped,
Tout au rebours voir qui le bois fendra.	When they shall see one cleave the wood the contrary way.

There will be a counter-religious movement downgrading the radio and video-evangelist preachers.

94

Un Roy ire sera aux sedifragues,	A King shall be irate against the treaty breakers,
Quand interdicts seront hernois de guerre,	When the warlike armour shall be forbidden,
La poison taincte au succre par les fragues,	The poison with sugar shall be put in the strawberries,
Par eaux meurtris, morts disant serre serre.	They shall be killed and die, saying, 'close, close.'

After a trial held against the treaty breakers, they shall be executed saying, 'We came very close.'

95

Par detracteur calomnie a puis nay;	The youngest son shall be slandered by a detractor,
Quand istront faict enormes & martiaux;	When enormous and martial deeds shall be done,
La moindre part dubieuse a l'aisne,	The least part shall be doubtful to the eldest,
Et tost au regne seront faicts partiaux.	And soon after they shall both be equal in the government.

Nostradamus here predicts that Ted Kennedy will become President. He is (1) 'youngest son,' (2) 'martial deeds' have been done (Vietnam), (3) John Kennedy, already assassinated, is, of course, unaware of the new development, and (4) the equality in government reveals that Ted Kennedy will be President.

96

Grand cite a soldats abandonnee,
Onc ny eut mortel tumult si proche,
O qu'elle hideuse calamite s'approche,
Fors une offense n'y sera pardonnee.

A great city shall be abandoned to the soldiers,
There never was a mortal tumult so near,
Oh! what a hideous calamity approaches,
Except one offence, nothing shall be pardoned.

A great city shall be pillaged by a barbarian horde; the only ones spared shall be those of the same race.

97

Cinq & quarante degrez ciel bruslera,
Feu approcher de la grand cite neuve,
Instant grand flamme esparse sautera,
Quand on voudra des Normans faire preuve.

The heaven shall burn at five and forty degrees,
The fire shall come near the great new city,
In an instant a great flame dispersed shall burst out,
When they shall make a trial of the Normans.

A cataclysmic fire shall engulf the greatest and newest of the world's big cities, particularly at the level of the 45th parallel, i.e., New York, Chicago, Minneapolis, San Francisco, Bucharest, Belgrade, Rome, Paris, and Madrid.

98

Ruyne aux Volsques de peur si fort terribles,
Leur grand cite taincte, faict pestilent;
Piller sol, lune, & violer leurs temples;
Et les deux fleuves rougir de sang coulant.

Ruin shall happen to the Vandals that will be terrible,
Their great city shall be tainted, a pestilent deed;
They shall plunder sun and moon, and violate their temples,
And two rivers shall be red with running blood.

The atomic bombing of Hiroshima is foretold by Nostradamus. Its location, between two rivers, is given, as well as the mention of the temples of the Japanese.

99

L'ennemy docte se tournera confus,	The learned enemy shall go back confounded,
Grand camp malade, & de faict par embusches,	A great camp shall be sick and in effect through ambush,
Mont Pyrenees & Pernus luy seront faict refus,	The Pyrenean Mountains shall refuse him,
Proche du fleuve descouvrant antiques ruches.	Near the river discovering the ancient hives.

An educated yet barbarous nation shall be defeated in its attempt to foist its culture on other peoples, and its leaders shall be refused sanctuary wherever they try to flee.

100

Fille de l'Aure, asyle du mal sain,	Daughter of Laura, sanctuary of the sick,
Ou jusqu'au ciel se void l'amphiteatre;	Where to the heavens is seen the amphitheatre;
Prodige veu, ton mal est fort prochain,	A prodigy being seen, the danger is near,
Seras captive, & des fois plus de quatre.	Thou shalt be taken captive above four times.

An ingenious stanza, it contains many things. The reference to 'Daughter of Laura' concerns the city of Nismes in Languedoc, famous for its amphitheatre and for being the birthplace of Laura, mistress of the poet Petrarch. The last two lines contain a warning of approaching civil war in France, clearly an indication of the far-in-the-future French Revolution.

LEGIS CAUTIO CONTRA IN-EPTOS CRITICOS

Qui legent hos versus, mature cen-
sunto;
Prophanum vulgus & inscium ne at-
trectato.
Omnesque Astrologi, Blenni, Barbari
procul sunto,
Qui aliter faxit, is rite sacer esto.

INVOCATION OF THE LAW AGAINST INEPT CRITICS

Those who read these verses, let
them consider with mature
mind,
Let not the profane, vulgar and
ignorant be attracted to their
study.
All Astrologers, Fools and Barbarians draw not near,
He who acts otherwise, is cursed
according to rite.

CENTURY VII

[Various quatrains within the following Century were found to duplicate those occurring in the previous Centuries, and therefore have been deleted. The numbering of the quatrains has been maintained according to the original sequence.]

1

L'arc du thresor par Achilles deceu,
Aux procrees sceu la quadrangulaire;
Au faict Royal le comment sera sceu,
Corps veu pendu au veu du populaire.

The arch of the treasure by Achilles deceived,
Shall show to posterity the quadrangle,
In the royal deed the comment shall be known,
The body seen hung in full view of the people.

Marshal d'Ancre, Treasurer of France, and favourite of the Queen Regent, Marie de Medici, was exposed by Achilles de Harlay, President of Paris, and convicted for the mishandling of funds. By order of Louis XIII, he was killed in the quadrangle of the Louvre and his body was later hanged in a public place.

2

Par Mars ouvert Arles ne donra guerre,
De nuict seront les soldats estonnez;
Noir, blanc, a l'Inde dissimule eu terre,
Sous la saincte ombre traistre verrez & sonnez.

Arles shall not proceed by open war,
By night the soldiers shall be astonished,
Black, white, and blue dissembled on the ground,
Under the feigned shadow will be proclaimed traitors.

Nostradamus anticipates the use of laser beams in warfare. 'Arles' is an anagram of laser, which is particularly useful in night combat. The use of a laser beam focused upon the ground from an orbiting satellite is yet to occur but it is predicted for the near future.

3

Apres de France la victoire navale,	After the naval victory of the French,
Les Barchinons, Sallinons, les Phocens,	Upon those of Tunis, Salle, and the Phocens,
Lierre d'or, l'enclume serre dedans la balle,	Keg of gold, the anvil shut up in a ball,
Ceux de Toulon au fraud seront consents.	Those of Toulon to the fraud shall consent.

A naval victory of the French over those of the Barbary Coast shall be attained by means of a novel weapon, an anvil and a ball, shut up in a keg of gold.

4

Le Duc de Langres assiege dedans Dole,	The Duke of Langres shall be besieged in Dole,
Accompagne d'Ostin & Lyonnois;	Being in company with those of Autun and Lion,
Geneve, Auspourg, joinct ceux de Mirandole,	Geneva, Augsburg, those of Mirandola,
Passer les monts conter les Anconnois.	Shall go over the mountains against those of Ancona.

France, Italy, Switzerland, and Germany shall be involved in a military expedition.

5

Vin sur la table en sera respandu,	Wine shall be spilt upon the table,
Le tiers n'aura celle qu'il pretendoit;	By reason that a third person shall not have her,
Deux fois du noir de Parme descendu,	Twice, the black one, descended from Parma,
Perouse a Pise ce qu'il cuidoit.	Shall do to Perugia and Pisa what he intended.

The all-powerful Black One in Italy shall dominate and ravage Italian centres of culture at will.

6

Naples, Palerme, & tout la Sicile,	Naples, Palermo and all Sicily,
Par main barbare sera inhabitee,	By barbarous hands shall be depopulated,
Corsique, Salerne & de Sardeigne, l'Isle,	Corsica, Salerno and the Island of Sardinia,
Faim, peste, guerre, fin de maux intemptee.	In them shall be famine, plague, war and endless evils.

A picture, as foreseen by Nostradamus, of conditions in Italy in the closing years of World War II.

7

Sur le combat des grands chevaus legers,	At the fight of the great light horsemen,
On criera le grand croissant confond,	They shall cry out, confound the great crescent,
De nuict tuer moutons, habits de bergers,	By night they shall kill sheep dressed as shepherds,
Abismes rouges dans le fosse profond.	Red abysms shall be in the deep ditch.

East-West conflict here. 'Confounding the great crescent' is meant to include the Soviet (sickle). Defeat of the Reds is forecast in line 4.

8

Flora, fuis, fuis le plus proche Romain,	Flora, fly, fly from the nearest Roman,
Au Fesulan sera conflit donne;	In the Fesulan shall be the fight,
Sang espandu, les plus grands prins a main,	Blood shall be spilt, the greatest shall be taken,
Temple ne sexe ne sera pardonne.	Neither temple nor sex shall be spared.

When the Nazis retreated from Florence they blew up the bridges across the Arno. However, rather than destroy the famous Ponte Vecchio, they blew up the buildings on either side of the bridge, thereby making it impassable.

9

Dame a l'abscence de son grand capitaine,	A lady in the absence of her great captain,
Sera priee d'amour du Viceroy,	Shall be entreated of love by the Viceroy,
Faincte promesse & mal'heureuse estraine,	A pretended promise and unhappy New Year's gift,
Entre les mains du grand Prince Barroys.	In the hand of the great Prince of Bar.

Bar was a principality adjoining Lorraine, which Henry IV gave as a marriage gift to his sister Catherine, when she married the Duke of Lorraine's son. The rest of this quatrain indicates some unhappiness connected with this match.

10

Par le grand Prince limitrophe du Mans,	The great Prince dwelling near Le Mans,
Preux & vaillant chef de grand exercite;	Stout and valiant, general of a great army,
Par mer & terre de Gallois & Normans,	Of Britons and Normans by sea and land,
Caspre passer Barcelonne pille Isle.	Ravaging Cape Barcelona and plunder the Island.

Charles de Gaulle epitomized the gallantry of French royalty with his military bearing and statesmanlike posture.

11

L'enfant Royal contemnera la mere,	The Royal Infant shall despise his mother,
Oeil, pieds blessez, rude, inobeissant,	Eye, feet wounded, rude, disobedient,
Nouvelle a dame estrange & bien amere,	News to a lady very strange and bitter,
Seront tuez des siens plus de cinq cens.	There shall be killed about five hundred.

In 1615, when Louis XIII, King of France, was about fifteen years of age, he was persuaded to make war against his own mother, Marie de Medici, then Regent of the Kingdom. In the ensuing battle about five hundred of the Queen's soldiers were slain.

12

Le grand puisnay fera fin de guerre,	The great young brother shall make an end of the war,
Aux dieux assemble les excusez,	In two places he shall gather the excused,
Cahors, Moissac iront long de la serre,	Cahors, Moissac, shall go out of his clutches,
Rusec, Lectore, les Agenoise rasez.	Russec, Lectore and those of Agen shall be cut off.

When Ted Kennedy is president ('the great young brother') he shall end a war the United States is engaged in. The two places where he shall gather the excused will be revealed later.

13

De la cite marine & tributaire,	Of the maritime city and tributary,
La teste raze prendra la satrapie;	The shaven head shall take the government,
Chasser sordide qui puis sera contraire,	He shall turn out a vile man who shall oppose him,
Par quatorze ans tiendra la tyrannie.	During fourteen years he will keep away the tyranny.

Napoleon was known to his soldiers as 'le petit tondu' (the little crophead). He made his mark early in the siege of the maritime city of Toulon and enjoyed absolute power for fourteen years, from 1799 to 1814.

14

Faux exposer viendra topographie,	They shall show topography falsely,
Seront les cruches des monuments ouvertes;	The urns of the monuments shall be open,
Pulluler secte, sainte philosophie,	Sects shall multiply and holy philosophy,
Pour blanches, noires, & pour antiques vertes.	Shall give black for white, and green for gold.

A corrupt period in history is foretold, when too many sects will spring up, creating great conflict in the Church.

15

Devant cite de l'insubre countree,	Before a city of the lower country,
Sept ans sera le siege devant mis;	Seven years of siege shall be laid,
Le tres grand Roy y fera son entree,	The most great King shall make his entry into it,
Cite puis libre hors de ses ennemis.	Then the city shall be full being out of the enemies' hands.

A city in the Low Country will be under siege for seven years, after which it will be liberated and the former inhabitants, who had fled from their enemy, will return to enjoy the new freedom.

16

Entree profonde par la grand Royne faicte;	The deep trench made by the Queen,
Rendra le lieu puissant inaccessible;	Shall make the place powerful and inaccessible,
L'armee des trois Lyons sera deffaicte,	The army of the three lions shall be defeated,
Faisant dedans cas hideux & terrible.	Doing within a hideous and terrible thing.

An army, owing allegiance to an alliance of three predatory monarchs, shall be defeated but not before committing hideous crimes against captured civilians.

17

Le Prince rare en pitie & clemence,	The Prince, rare in pity and clemency,
Apres avoir la paix aux siens baille,	After he shall have given peace to his subjects,
Viendra changer par mort grand cognoissance,	Shall by death change his great knowledge,
Par grand repos le regne travaille.	After great rest the kingdom shall be troubled.

This concerns Henry IV, peace-loving King of France, who was assassinated on May 14, 1610, by Ravaillac. After his death there was much trouble in the Kingdom caused by the dissension among the Princes.

18

Les assiegez couleront leurs paches,	The besieged shall colour their
Sept jours apres feront cruelle issue,	articles,
Dans repoulez, feu sang, sept mis a	Seven days after they shall make a
l'hache,	cruel issue,
Dame captive qu'avoit la paix issue.	They shall be beaten back, fire,
	blood, seven put to the axe,
	The lady shall be prisoner who
	tried to make peace.

The political dissidents, later known as the 'Chicago Seven,' tried to upset a Democratic National Convention and were eventually brought to trial.

19

Le fort Nicene ne sera combatu,	The Nicene fort shall not be fought
Vaincu sera par rutilant metal,	against,
Son faict sera un long temps debatu,	By shining metal it shall be over-
Au citadins estrange espouvantal.	come,
	The doing of it shall a long time be
	debated,
	It shall be a strange fearful thing to
	the citizens.

Monte Carlo (Monaco) is adjacent to Nice and has long dominated it through its revenues from gambling ('shining metal' – gold!).

20

Ambassadeurs de la Toscane langue,	The ambassadors of the Tuscan
Avril & May Alpes & mer passer,	tongue,
Celuy de veau exposera l'harangue,	In April and May, shall go over the
Vie Gauloise en voulant effacer.	Alps and the sea,
	One like a calf, shall make a speech,
	Attempting to defame French cus-
	toms.

On May 7, 1938, Mussolini, in a mutual admiration session with the Fuehrer, in Berlin, flamboyantly stated, 'Germany and Italy have left behind them the Utopias to which Europe has entrusted her destiny. It is this law which Nazi Germany and Fascist Italy has obeyed, obeys, and will obey.'

21

Par pestilente inimitie Volsique,	By a pestilent Italian enmity,
Dissimulee chassera le tyran;	The dissembler shall expel the tyrant,
Au pont de Sorgues se fera la traf-	The bargains shall be made at Sor-
fique,	gues bridge,
De mettre a mort luy & son adherent.	To put him and his adherent to death.

Premier Pierre Laval, cohort of Mussolini, was eventually expelled, captured and executed, thus fulfilling the prophecy.

22

Les Citoyens de Mesopotamie,	The citizens of Mesopotamia,
Irez encontre amis de Tarraconne,	Being angry with the friends of Tarrogona,
Jeux, Ris, banquets, toute gent endor-	Sport, laughter, banquets, every-
mie,	body being asleep,
Vicaire au Rhosne, prins cite, ceux	The vicar being in Rhone, the city
d'Ausonne.	taken by those of Bordeaux.

This concerns a region of France which lies between two rivers, and its long since forgotten quarrel with the citizens of Bordeaux.

23

Le Royal Sceptre sera contrainct de	The Royal Sceptre shall be con-
prendre,	strained to take
Ce que ses predecesseurs voint engage;	What his predecessors had mort-
Puis que l'aigneau on fera mal enten-	gaged,
dre,	After that they shall misinform the
Lors qu'on viendra le palais saccager.	lamb,
	When they shall come to plunder the palace.

Clearly, this refers to the plunder of the royal palace in Iran when the Shah abdicated in 1979. The assets of the Pahlavi dynasty were mortgaged for armaments, planes, and sophisticated military hardware.

24

L'ensevely sortira du tombeau,	The buried shall come out of his
Fera de chaines lier le fort du pont,	grave,
Empoisonne avec oeufs de Barbeau,	The fort of the bridge shall be tied
Grand de Lorraine par le Marquis du	with chains,
Pont.	Poisoned with the roe of a Barbel,
	Shall a great one of Lorraine be, by
	the Marquis Dupont.

The first part of this verse has no importance or relationship to the prophecy, which concerns the poisoning of the Duke of Lorraine by the Marquis Du Pont.

25

Par guerre longue tout l'exercite es-	By a long war, all the army drained
puiser,	dry,
Que pour soldats ne trouveront	So that to raise soldiers, they shall
pecune,	find no money,
Lieu d'or, d'argent, cuir on viendra	Instead of gold and silver, they
cuser,	shall stamp leather,
Gaulois aerain, signe croissant de	The French copper, marked with
Lune.	the signs of the crescent moon.

Before the discovery of the West Indies, and the consequent expansion and exploitation of the colonies, many European countries were forced to use substitutes for the usual gold and silver coins.

26

Fustes galees autour de sept navires,	Flying boats and galleys round
Sera livree une mortelle guerre;	about seven ships,
Chef de Madrid, recevra coup de	Shall be in the livery of deadly war,
vires,	The chief of Madrid shall receive
Deux eschapees, & cinq menees a	blows of oars,
terre.	Two shall escape, and five carried
	to land.

The concept of 'flying boats' could forecast the original Howard Hughes 'Spruce Goose' and the initial Pan American Airways Clipper which landed on water. And further, the multiple nuclear warheads of the Trident missile class fired from underwater by submarines is foretold in lines 1 and 2.

27

Au coin de vast la grand cavalerie,
Proche a Ferrare empesche au
    bagage,
Pompe a Turin feront tel volerie,
Que dans le fort raviront leur hostage.

In a corner of the wasted, the great
    cavalry,
Near Ferrara, shall be busy about
    the baggage,
Pomp at Turin, they shall make
    such a robbery,
That in the fort they shall ravish
    their hostage.

During a war the people of the country will sustain great losses and suffer greatly, while their leaders will lead lives of luxury in a fortified city.

28

Le captaine conduira grande proye,
Sur la montagne des ennemis plus
    proche,
Environne, par feu fera telle voye,
Tous eschappez, or trente mis en
    broche.

The captain shall lead a great prey,
Upon the mountain, that shall be
    nearest to the enemies,
Being encompassed with fire, he
    shall make such a way,
All shall escape, except thirty that
    shall be spitted.

A leader, surrounded by enemy soldiers, shall contrive to lead his men out of danger, except thirty who will be taken and tortured by their captors.

29

Le grand duc d'Albe se viendra rebel-
    ler,
A ses grands peres fera le tradiment;
Le grand de Guise le viendra debeller,
Captif mene & dresse monument.

The great Duke of Alba shall rebel,
To his grandfathers he shall make
    the plot,
The great Guise shall vanquish
    him,
Led prisoner, and a monument
    erected.

The Duke of Alba was sent to Rome by Charles V of Spain, to lend his aid to others of the Spanish Party in that city.

30

Le sac s'approche, feu, grand sang espandu,	The sack draws near, fire, abundance of blood spilt,
Pau, grand fleuve, aux bouvirs l'entreprinse,	Pau, a great river, an enterprise by churls,
De Gennes, Nice, apres long attendu,	Of Genoa, Nice after they shall have stayed long,
Foussan, Turin, a Savillan la prinse.	Fossan, Turin, the prize shall be at Savillan.

For four years, 1555–59, there was constant fighting among various cities in Italy, especially those near the River Pau (Po).

31

De Languedoc, & Guienne plus de dix,	From Languedoc and Guienne more than 10,000
Mille voudront les Alpes repasser;	Would be glad to repass the Alps,
Grans Allobroges marcher contre Brundis,	Great Allobroges shall march against Brundis,
Aquin & Bresse les viendront recasser.	Aquin and Bresse shall beat them back.

A French army passing over the Alps into Italy will regret this manoeuvre.

32

Du Mont Royal naistra d'une casane,	Out of Montreal shall be born in a cottage,
Qui duc, & compte viendra tyranniser,	One that shall tyrannize over duke and earl,
Dresser copie de la marche Millane,	He shall raise an army in the land of the rebellion,
Favence, Florence d'or & gens espuiser.	He shall empty Favence and Florence of their gold.

Pierre Elliot Trudeau was born in Montreal in 1919 and served as the Canadian Prime Minister from 1968–1979 and again in 1981. The rebellion referred to is between the French- and English-speaking Canadians.

33

Par fraude, regne, forces expolier,	By fraud a kingdom and army shall be despoiled,
La classe obsesse, passages a l'espie;	The fleet shall be possessed, passages shall be made to spies,
Deux faincts amis se viendront t'allier,	Two feigned friends shall agree together,
Esueiller haine de long temps assoupie.	They shall raise up a hatred that had long been dormant.

The alliance between Hitler and Mussolini is predicted. The infiltration by propaganda, the rousing of Anti-Semitism and their 'divide and conquer' technique are described.

34

En grand regret sera la gent Gauloise,	In great regret shall the French nation be,
Coeur vain, leger croira temerite;	Their vain and light heart shall believe rashly,
Pain, sel, ne vin, eau, venin ne cervoise,	They shall have neither bread, salt, wine nor beer,
Plus grand captif, faim, froid, necessite.	Moreover, they shall be prisoners and shall suffer hunger, cold and need.

This continuation of the preceding stanza tells of conditions in France under the heel of the Axis invader.

35

Le grand poche viendra plaindre, pleurer,	The great pouch shall bewail and bemoan,
D'avoir esleu, trompez seront en l'aage,	Having elected one, they shall be deceived,
Guiere avec eux ne voudra demeurer;	His age shall not stay long with them,
Deceu sera par ceux de son langage.	He shall be deceived by those of his own language.

This continues the previous prediction of conditions in France, under Hitlerism; and goes on to outline the sabotaging, by the French underground movement, of the Vichy regime under Marshal Pétain.

36

Dieu, le ciel tout le divin verbe a l'onde,
Porte par rouges sept razes a Bizance,
Contre les oingts trois cens de Trebisonde,
Deux loix mettront, & horreur, pluis credence.

God, Heaven all the divine world in water,
Carried by red ones, seven shaved heads at Stamboul,
Against the anointed, three hundred of Trebizond,
They shall put two laws, and horror, and afterwards believe.

A great disputation is to take place in Constantinople, seven priests against three hundred unbelievers.

37

Dix envoyez, chef de nef mettre a mort,
D'un adverty, en classe guerre ouverte;
Confusion chef, l'un se picque & mord,
Le ryn, stecades nefs, cap dedans la nerte.

Ten shall be sent to put the captain of the ship to death,
He shall have notice by one, the fleet shall be in open war,
Great confusion shall be, by pricks and bites,
The Rhine, dung boats, within the north cape.

A mutiny shall take place within the German Navy.

38

L'aisne Royal sur coursier voltigeant,
Picquer viendra si rudement courir;
Cueulle, lipee, pied dans l'estrain pliegnant,
Traine, tire, horriblement mourir.

The eldest Royal, prancing upon a horse,
Shall spur, and run fiercely,
Open mouth, the foot in stirrup, complaining,
Drawn, pulled, die horribly.

The eldest son of a King shall die a horrible death as the result of being thrown from a horse.

39

Le conducteur de l'armee Francoise,	The leader of the French army,
Cuidant perdre le principale pha-	Hoping to rout the principal pha-
lange;	lanx,
Par sur pave de l'Avaigne & d'ar-	Upon the pavement of Avaigne and
doise,	slate,
Soy parfondra par Gennes gent es-	Shall sink in the ground by Genoa,
trange.	a strange nation.

A French General shall meet with disaster in his attempt to attack the strongest flank of the enemy. The land being strange to him, he shall lead his men into swampy territory and they shall flounder and sink into the ground, and thus be routed.

40

Dedans tonneaux hors oingts d'huile	In empty tuns slippery with oil and
& gresse,	grease,
Seront vingt un devant le port fermez,	Before the harbour, one and twenty
Au second guet par mort feront	shall be shut,
prouesse,	At the second watch by death they
Gaigner les portes, & du guet assom-	shall do great feats of arms,
mez.	To win the gates, and be killed by
	the watch.

By a stratagem, twenty-one men shall attempt to sneak through the gates of an enemy harbour but shall fail and be killed.

41

Les os des pieds & des mains enserrez,	The bones of the feet and hands in
Par bruit maison long temps inha-	shackles,
bitee,	By a noise a house shall be a long
Seront par songes concavant deterrez,	time deserted,
Maison salubre & sans bruit habitee.	By a dream the buried shall be
	taken out of the ground,
	The house shall be salubrious, and
	inhabited without noise.

A ghost shall inhabit a house, wherein a skeleton is shackled. After decent burial of the remains the house shall again be at rest.

42

Quand Innocent tiendra le lieu de Pierre,	When Innocent shall hold the place of Peter,
Le Nizaram Sicilian se verra,	The Sicilian Nizaram shall see himself,
En grands honneurs, mais apres il cherra,	In great honours, but after that he shall fall,
Dans le bourbier d'une civil guerre.	Into the dirt of a civil war.

This prognostication is remarkable for its clarity of wording and the exactness of its fulfilment. Setting the period of time, our first reference is to Innocent X who was elected Pope in 1644. His noted contemporary, the French Cardinal Mazarin (anagrammatically referred to here as Nizaram) was of Italian origin. Under the sponsorship of Richelieu he became a citizen of France and eventually the successor of the great Cardinal. He was one of the most powerful figures of his time and led the fortunes of France during the closing years of the Thirty Years' War.

43

Lutece en Mars, Senateurs en credit,	Lutetia in Mars, Senators shall be in credit,
Par une nuit Gaule sera troublee,	In a night France shall be troubled,
Du grand Croesus l'Horoscope predit,	The Horoscope of the Great Croesus predicts,
Par Saturnus, sa puissance exilee.	That by Saturn his power shall be put down.

Lutetia is the Latin word for Paris. After the death of Henry IV, King of France, the Parliament of Paris began to check on the activities of various noblemen, among them the Marquis d'Ancre. His fate is described in Quatrain 1, Century VII.

44

Deux de poison saisis nouveaux Venus,	Two by poison provided by the new Venus,
Dans la cuisine du grand Prince verser;	To pour in the kitchen of the great Prince,
Par le souillard tous deux au faict cogneus,	By the scullion the fact shall be known,
Prins qui cuidoit de mort l'aisne vexer.	And be taken, that thought by death to vex the elder.

A woman shall provide poison, in a plot to do away with a great Prince. A cook's boy shall discover the plot when tasting the King's dish.

73

Renfort de sieges manubis & man-iples,	Recruit of sieges, spoils and prizes,
Changez le sacre & passe sur le Pronsne,	Holy day shall be changed and passed over the Pronsne,
Prins & captifs n'arreste les priz triples,	Taken, made captive and not held in the triple field,
Plus par fonds mis, esleve, mis au trosne.	Moreover, one from the bottom shall be raised to the throne.

A period of military unrest will take place, resulting in the raising of a little Corporal to the throne.

80

L'Occident libres les Isles Britanni-ques,	The West shall be free, and the British Isles,
Le recogneu passer le bas, puis haut,	The discovered shall pass low, then high,
Ne content trist Rebel, corff, Escoti-ques,	Scotch Pirates shall be, who shall rebel,
Puis rebeller par plui & par nuict chaud.	In a rainy and hot night.

John Paul Jones, called by the British 'the Scotch Pirate and Rebel,' is here referred to by Nostradamus, as is the fact that the West (America) shall be free.

82

La stratageme simulte sera rare,	The simulated stratagem shall be scarce,
La mort en voye rebelle par contree,	Death shall be in a rebellious way through the country,
Par le retour du voyage Barbare,	By the return from the Barbarian voyage,
Exalteront la protestante entree.	They shall exalt the Protestant entrance.

A political stratagem shall result in the triumph of the Protestants.

83

Vent chaud, conseil, pleurs, timidite,	Hot wind, counsel, tears, fearful-ness,
De nuict au lit assailly sans les armes,	He shall be assaulted in his bed by night without arms,
D'oppression grand calamite,	From that oppression shall be raised a great calamity,
L'Epithalame converty pleurs &	The Epithalamium shall be conver-ted into tears.
larmes.	

The Epithalamium, a nuptial song or poem in praise of the bride or bridegroom, is referred to here. The connected event can be gathered from the text of the stanza.

Epistle to Henry II

To the most invincible, most high and most Christian King of France, Henry the Second: Michael Nostradamus, his most obedient servant and subject, wishes victory and happiness.

By reason of that singular observation, O most Christian and victorious King, my face, which had been cloudy a great while, did present itself before your immeasurable Majesty. I have been ever since perpetually dazzled, continually honouring and worshipping that day, in which I presented myself before it, as before a singular and humane Majesty. Now seeking after some occasion whereby I might make appear the goodness and sincerity of my heart and extend my acquaintance toward your most excellent Majesty, and seeing that it was impossible for me to declare it by effects, as well as because of the darkness and obscurity of my mind, even for the enlightening it did receive from the face of the greatest Monarch in the world. It was a great while before I could resolve to whom I should dedicate these three last Centuries of my Prophecies, which make the complete thousand. After I had a long time considered, I have with a great temerity made my address to your Majesty, being no way daunted by it, as the great author Plutarch related in the Life of Lycurgus, that, seeing the offerings and gifts that were

---

This dedicatory letter was used by Nostradamus as the preface to his second edition which contained new prophecies.

The following notation appeared, on the page preceding the above epistle, in the 1672 edition of *The Prophecies or Prognostications of Michael Nostradamus*, translated and annotated by Theophilus de Garencieres.

Friendly Reader,

Before you read the following epistle, I would have you be warned of a few things: One is, that according to my opinion, it is very obscure and intelligible (*sic*) in most places, being without any just connection, and besides the obscurity of the sense, the crabbedness of the expression is such, that had not the importunity of the Bookseller prevailed, I would have left it out, but considering the respect due to Antiquity, the satisfaction we owe to curious persons, who would perhaps have thought the Book imperfect without it, we let it go, trusting to your candour and ingenuity.

sacrificed in the temples of their heathen gods, many came no more, lest the people should wonder at the expense.

Notwithstanding, seeing your royal splendour joined with an incomparable humanity, I have made my address to it, not as to the Kings of Persia, of whom to come near it was forbidden, but as to a most prudent and wise prince. I have dedicated my nocturnal and prophetical calculations, written rather by a natural instinct and poetical furor than by any rules of poetry; and the most part of it written and agreeing with the years, months and weeks, of the regions, countries and most of the towns and cities in Europe; touching also something of Africa, and of a part of Asia, by the change of regions that come near to those climates, and compounded in a natural fashion. But some may answer (who hath need to blow his nose) that the rhyme is as easy to be understood, as the sense is hard to get at. Therefore, O most humane King, most of the prophetical stanzas are so difficult, that there is no way to be found for the interpretation of them. Nevertheless, being in hope of setting down the towns, cities, and regions, wherein most of those shall happen, especially in the year 1585, and in the year 1606, beginning from this present time, which is the 14th of March, 1557.

Going further to the fulfilling of those things, which shall be in the beginning of the seventh millenary, according to my astronomical calculation and other learning which I could reach (at which time the adversaries of Christ and of His Church shall begin to multiply), all has been composed and calculated in days and hours of election, and well disposed, and all as accurately as was possible for me to do. And the whole '*Minerva libera et non invita,*'* calculating almost as much of the time that is come, as of that which is past, comprehending it in the present time, and what by the course of the said time shall be known to happen in all regions punctually as it is here written, adding nothing superfluous, although it be said '*Quod de futuris non est determinata omnino veritas.*'† It is very true, Sir, that by my natural instinct given me by my progenitors, I did think I could foretell anything; but having made an agreement between this said instinct of mine, and a long calculation of art, and by a great tranquillity and repose of mind, by emptying my soul of all care, I have foretold most part of these *ex tripode æneo* (by the brass tripod), though there be many

* 'When Minerva was free and favourable.'

† 'There can be no truth entirely determined for certain which concerns the future.'

who attribute to me some things that are no more mine than what is nothing at all. Only the eternal God, who is the searcher of men's hearts, being pious, just, and merciful, is the true Judge of it; Him I beseech to defend me from the calumny of wicked men, who would as willingly question how all your ancient progenitors, the Kings of France, have healed the disease called the Kings'-evil; how some other nations have cured the bitings of venomous beasts, others have had a certain instinct to foretell things that are to come, and of others too tedious to be here inserted. Notwithstanding those in whom the malignancy of the wicked spirit shall not be suppressed by length of time, I hope that after my decease my work shall be in more esteem than when I was alive.

However, if I should fail in the calculation of times, or should not please some, may it please your most imperial Majesty to forgive me, protesting before God and His Saints, that I do not intend to insert anything in writing in this present Epistle that may be contrary to the true Catholic faith, while consulting the astronomical calculations, according to my learning. For the space of times of our fathers that have been before us are such, submitting myself to the correction of the most learned, that the first man Adam was before Noah, about one thousand two hundred and forty-two years, not computing the time according to the Gentile records, as Varro did, but only according to the Sacred Scriptures, taking them as a guide to my astronomical calculations, and to the best of my understanding. After Noah and the universal flood, about a thousand and fourscore years, came Abraham, who was a supreme astrologer, according to most men's opinion, and did first invent the Chaldean letters; after that came Moses, some five hundred and fifteen or sixteen years after. And between the time of David and Moses there passed about five hundred and seventy years. After which, between the time of David and that of our Saviour and Redeemer Jesus Christ, born of the Virgin Mary, there passed (according to some chronographers) a thousand three hundred and fifty years.

Some may object, that this calculation is not true; because it differs from that of Eusebius. And from the time of human redemption, to that of the execrable seduction of the Saracens, have passed six hundred and four and twenty years or thereabouts. From that time hitherto, it is easy to gather what times are past. If my computations be not good among all nations, however, all has been calculated by the course of the celestial bodies joined with emotion infused in me at certain loose hours, the emotion which has been handed down to me by my ancient progenitors. But the danger at this time (most excellent King) requires that such secret events should not be manifested except by an enigmatical sentence, having but one sense and only one intelligence, without having mixed with it any ambiguous or amphibological calculation. But rather under a cloudy obscurity, through a natural infusion, coming near to the sentence of one of the thousand and two Prophets, that have been since the Creation of the world, according to the calculation and Punic Chronicle of Joel: *'Effundum spiritum meum super omnem carnem, et prophetabunt filii vestri, et filiae vestrae.'** But such a prophecy did proceed from the mouth of the Holy Spirit, who was the supreme and eternal power, which being come with that of the celestial bodies, has caused some of them to predict great and wonderful things.

For my part I challenge no such things in this place, God forbid. I confess truly, that all comes from God, for which I give Him thanks, honour, and praise, without having mixed anything of that divination which proceeds *à fato*, but *à Deo, à natura* (which proceeds from fate, but from God, and nature). And most of it is joined with the motion and course of the celestial bodies, much as if seeing in a lens, and through a cloudy vision, the great and sad events, the prodigious and calamitous accidents that shall befall the worshippers. First upon the temples of God, and secondly upon those who draw their support from earth, this draws near, with a thousand other calamitous accidents, which shall be known in the course of time.

For God will take notice of the long barrenness of the great Dame, who afterwards shall conceive two principal children. But, being in danger she will give birth with risk at her age of death in the eighteenth year, and not able to go beyond thirty-six, shall leave behind her three males and one female, and he will have two who never had any of the same father. The differences between the three brothers shall be such, though united and agreed, that the three and four parts of Europe will tremble. By the lesser in years shall the Christian monarchy be upheld and augmented; sects shall rise and presently be put down again; the Arabians shall be put back; kingdoms shall be united and new laws made. Concerning the other children, the first shall possess the furious crowned Lions, holding their paws upon the escutcheons. The second, well attended by the Latins, will go so deep among the Lions, that a second trembling and furious descent will be made, to get upon the Pyrenees Mountains. The ancient monarchy shall not be

* See Joel ii.28.

transferred, and the third inundation of human blood shall happen; also for a good while Mars shall not be in Lent.

The daughter shall be given for the preservation of the Church, the dominator of it falling into the Pagan sect of the new unbelievers, and she will have two children, one from faithfulness, and the other from unfaithfulness, by the confirmation of the Catholic Church. The other, who to his confusion and late repentance, shall go about to ruin her, shall have three regions over a wide extent of leagues, that is to say, the Roman, the German, and the Spanish, and it will take a military hand to adequately take care of the area stretching from the 50th to the 52nd degree of latitude. And all those remote regions north above the 48th degree, who by vain fright shall quake, and then those of the west, south and east shall tremble because of their power, and the power of that what shall be done cannot be undone by warlike power. They shall be equal in nature, but much different in faith.

After this the barren Dame, of a greater power than the second, shall be admitted by two people, by the first made obstinate by him that had power over the others; by the second, and by the third, that shall extend his circuit to the east of Europe; there his forces will stop and be overcome, but by sea he will make his excursions into Trinacria and the Adriatic with his myrmidons. Germany shall fall, and the Barbarian Sect shall be wholly driven from among the Latins. Then the great Empire of Antichrist shall begin in the Attila, and Xerxes come down with an innumerable multitude of people, so that the coming of the Holy Ghost, proceeding from the 48th degree, shall transmigrate, driving away the abomination of the Antichrist, who made war against the royal person of the great vicar of Jesus Christ and against His Church, and His Kingdom, and reign *per tempus, et in occasione temporis* (for a time, and to the end of time). And before this shall precede a solar eclipse, the most dark and obscure that was since the creation of the world, till the death and passion of Jesus Christ, and from Him until now. There shall be in the month of October, a great revolution made, such that everybody will think that the earth has lost its natural motion and has gone down into perpetual darkness. In the spring before and after this, shall happen extraordinary changes, reversals of kingdoms, and great earthquakes; all this accompanied with the procreation of the New Babylon, a miserable prostitute large with the abomination of the first holocaust. And this shall last only seventy-three years and seven months.

Then from that stock that has been so long time barren,

proceeding from the 50th degree, one will issue who will renovate all the Christian Church. Then shall be a great peace, union and concord, between some of the children of races long wandering and separated by diverse kingdoms; and such peace shall be made that the instigator and the promoter of military function by diversity of religions, shall be tied to the bottom of the deep, and united to the kingdom of the furious who shall counterfeit the wise. The countries, towns, cities and provinces that had deserted their first ways to free themselves, captivating themselves more deeply, shall be secretly angry at their liberty and religion lost, and shall begin to strike from the left, to return once more to the right.

Then restoring the holiness, so long beaten down with their former writings, afterwards will come the great dog, the irresistible mastiff (war) who shall destroy all that was done before. Churches shall be built up again as before, the clergy shall be restored to its former state, until it falls back again into whoredom and luxury, and commits a thousand crimes. And being near to another desolation, when she shall be in her higher and more sublime dignity, there shall rise powers and military hands, who shall take away from her the two swords, and leave only the resemblance, after which, tired of the crookedness that is about them, the people will cause these things to straighten. Not willing to submit unto them by the end opposite to the sharp hand that touches the ground they shall provoke. To the branch long barren, will proceed one who shall deliver the people of the world from that meek and voluntary slavery; putting themselves under the protection of Mars, depriving Jupiter of all his honours and dignities, for the free city established and seated in another little Mesopotamia. And the chief governor shall be thrust out of the middle, and set in the high place of the air, being ignorant of the conspiracy of the conspirators, with the second Thrasibulus, who long before did prepare for this thing. Then shall the impurities and abominations be objected with great shame, and made manifest to the darkness of the veiled light, and shall cease toward the end of the change of his kingdom, and the chief men of the Church shall be put back from the love of God and many of them shall apostatize from the true faith.

Of the three sects (Lutheran, Catholic, and Mahometan), that which is middlemost, by the actions of its worshippers, shall be thrown into ruins. The first, wholly in all Europe, and the most part of Africa undone by the third, by means of the poor in spirit, who by madness elevated shall, through libidinous luxury, commit adultery. The people will rise and maintain it, and shall drive away those that did adhere to the legislators, and it shall seem, from the kingdoms spoiled by the Eastern men, that God the Creator has loosed Satan from his infernal prison, to cause to be born the great Dog and Dohan (Gog and Magog), who shall make so great and abominable a breach in the Churches, that neither the reds nor the whites, who are without eyes and without arms, shall not judge of it, and their power shall be taken away from them.

Then shall there be a greater persecution against the Church than ever was, and in the meantime shall be so great a plague, that two parts of three in the world shall fail, so much so that no one shall be able to know the true owners of fields and houses, and there shall happen a total desolation to the clergy, and martial men shall usurp what shall come from the City of the Sun, and from Malta, and from the Islands of Hières, and the great chain of the port shall be open which takes its name from a sea ox (Bosphorus).

A new incursion shall be made from the sea coasts, willing to deliver the Castulan Leap from the first Mahometan taking, and the assaulting shall not altogether be in vain, and that place where the habitation of Abraham was, shall be assaulted by those who shall have reverence for the Jovials. The great eastern city of Achem shall be encompassed and assaulted on all sides by a great power of armed men. Their sea forces shall be weakened by the western men, and to that kingdom shall happen great desolation, and the great cities shall be depopulated, and those that shall come in shall be comprehended within the vengeance of the wrath of God. The Holy Sepulchre, held in great veneration for so long a time, shall remain a great while open to the universal aspect of the heavens, sun and moon. The sacred place shall be converted into a stable for cattle small and large, and put to profane uses. O what a calamitous time shall be then for women with child! For then the principal Eastern Ruler, being for the most part moved by the Northern and Western men, shall be vanquished and put to death, beaten, and all the rest put to flight, and the children he had by many women put in prison. Then shall be fulfilled the prophecy of the Royal Prophet: '*Ut audiret gemitus compeditorum, et solveret filios interemptorum.*'*

What great oppression shall be made then upon the princes and governors of kingdoms, and especially on those that shall live eastward and near the sea, their languages intermixed with all nations. The language of the Latin nations mixed with Arabic and

* 'Let the sighing of the prisoner come before thee, to release the children of death.' (Ps. lxxviii. 11).

North African communication. All the Eastern kings shall be driven away, beaten and brought to nothing, not altogether by means of the strength of the kings of the North, and the drawing near of our age, but by means of three secretly united, seeking for death by ambushes one against another. The renewing of the triumvirate shall last seven years, while the fame of such a sect shall be spread all the world over, and the sacrifice of the holy and immaculate host shall be upheld. And then shall the lords be two in number, victorious in the North against the Eastern ones, and there shall be such a great noise and warlike tumult that all the East shall quake for fear of those two brothers of the North who are yet not brothers. And because, Sir, by this discourse, I put all things confusedly in these predictions as to the time concerning the event of them; for the account of the time which follows, very little is conformable, if at all, to that I have done before, being by astronomic rule and according to the Sacred Scriptures, in which I cannot err.

I could have set down in every quatrain the exact time in which they shall happen, but it would not please everybody, and much less the interpretation of them, till, Sir, your Majesty has granted me full power so to do, that my calumniators may have nothing to say against me. Nevertheless, reckoning the years since the creation of the world to the birth of Noah, there passed 1506 years, and from the birth of Noah to the building of the ark at the time of the universal flood, 600 years passed (whether solar years, or lunar, or mixed), for my part according to the Scriptures, I hold that they were solar. And at the end of those 600 years Noah entered into the ark to save himself from the flood, which flood was universal upon the earth and lasted a year and two months; and from the end of the flood to the birth of Abraham did pass 295 years; and from the birth of Abraham to that of Isaac did pass 100 years; from Isaac to Jacob, sixty years; and from the time he went into Egypt until he came out of it, did pass 130 years; and from the time that Jacob went into Egypt until his posterity came out of it did pass 430 years; and from the coming out of Egypt to the building of Solomon's Temple in the fortieth year of his reign did pass 480 years; and from the building of the Temple to Jesus Christ, according to the computations of the chronographers, did pass 490 years. And thus by this calculation, which I have gathered out of the Holy Scriptures, the whole comes to about 4173 years and eight months more or less. But since the time of Jesus Christ hitherto, I leave it because of the diversity of opinion. Having calculated these present prophecies in accordance to the order of the chain which contains the revolution, and all by astronomical rule, and according to my natural instinct; after some time, and including in it the time Saturn takes to turn to come in on the 7th of the month of April until the 25th of August; Jupiter from the 14th of June to the 7th of October; Mars from the 27th of April till the 22nd of June; Venus from the 9th of April to the 22nd of May; Mercury from the 3rd of February to the 24th of the same; afterwards from the 1st of June to the 24th of the same; and from the 25th of September to the 16th of October, Saturn in Capricorn, Jupiter in Aquarius, Mars in Scorpio, Venus in Pisces, Mercury within a month in Capricorn, Aquarius in Pisces, the moon in Aquarius, the Dragon's head in Libra, the tail opposite to her sign. Following a conjunction of Jupiter and Mercury, with a quadrin aspect of Mars to Mercury, and the head of the Dragon shall be with a conjunction of Sol and Jupiter; the year shall be peaceful without eclipse.

Then the beginning of that year shall see a greater persecution against the Christian Church than ever was in Africa, and it shall be in the year 1792,[*] at which time everyone will think it a renovation of the age. After that the Roman people shall begin to stand upright again, and to put away the obscure darkness, receiving some of its former light, but now without great divisions and continual changes. Venice, after that, with great strength and power will lift up her wings so high that she will not be much inferior to the strength of ancient Rome. And at that time great Byzantine sails, joined with the Italians by the help and power of the North, shall hinder them so that those of Crete shall not keep their faith. The ships built by the ancient martial men will keep company with them under the waves of Neptune. In the Adriatic there shall be a great discord, what was united shall be put asunder, and what was before a great city shall become a house, including the Pampotan and Mesopotamia of Europe, in (19)45, and others to 41, 42, and 47. And in that time and those countries the infernal power shall rise against the Church of Jesus Christ. This shall be the second Antichrist, which shall persecute the said church and its true vicar by the means of the power of temporal kings, who through their ignorance shall be seduced by tongues more sharp than any sword in the hands of a madman.

The said reign of Antichrist shall not last but till the ending of him who was born of Age, and of the other in the city of Plancus (Lyons), accompanied by the elect of Modena, Fulcy by Ferrara,

---

[*] Date of French Revolution.

maintained by the Adriatic, Liguriens, and the proximity of the great Trinacria (Sicily). Afterwards the Gallic Ogmion shall pass the Mount Jovis (Barcelona), followed with such a number that even from afar off the Empire shall be presented with its grand law, and then and for some time after, shall be profusely spilled the blood of the innocents by the guilty raised on high. Then by great floods the memory of those things contained in such instruments, shall receive incalculable loss, even to the letters themselves. This will happen to the Northerns. By the Divine Will Satan will be bound once more, and universal peace shall be among men, and the Church of Jesus Christ shall be free from all tribulation, although the Azostains (debauchees) would desire to mix with the honey their pestilent seduction. This shall happen about the seventh millenary, when the sanctuary of Jesus Christ shall no more be trodden down by the unbelievers that shall come from the North. The world will then be near its great conflagration, although by the calculations of my prophecies, the course of time goes much further.

In the epistle that some years ago I dedicated to my son Caesar Nostradamus, I have openly enough declared some things without prognosticating. But here, Sir, are comprehended many great and wonderful events, which those that come after us shall see. And during the said astrological computation, in harmony with the Sacred Scriptures, the persecution of the clergy shall have its beginning in the power of the Northern Kings joined by the Eastern ones. And that persecution shall last eleven years, or a little less, at which time the chief Northern king shall fail, which years being ended, shall come in his stead a united Southern one, who shall yet more violently persecute the clergy of the Church for the space of three years by the apostolical seduction of one that shall have absolute power over the militant Church of God. The holy people of God and keepers of His law, and all order of religion, shall be grievously persecuted and afflicted, so much that the blood of the true ecclesiastical men shall flow all over. One of these horrid kings shall be praised by his followers for having spilt more human blood of the innocent clergymen than anybody has done to wine. The said king shall commit incredible crimes against the Church; human blood shall run through public streets and Churches, as water coming from an impetuous rain. Next, rivers shall be red with blood. In a sea fight the sea shall be red, so that one king will say to another, '*Bellis rubuit navalibus aequor*'.* After

* 'The sea blushed red with the blood of naval fights.'

that in the same year, and those following, shall happen the most horrible pestilence, caused by the famine preceding, and so great tribulations as ever did happen since the first foundation of the Christian Church throughout all the Latin regions, some marks remaining in some countries under Spain.

Then the third Northern king (Russia?), hearing the complaint of the people of his principal title, shall raise up so great an army, shall go through the limits of his last ancestors and progenitors, that they will all be set up again in their first state. The great Vicar of the Cope shall be restored in his former estate, but desolate and altogether forsaken, shall then go back to the sanctuary that was destroyed by Paganism, when the Old and New Testament will be thrust out and burnt. After that shall the Antichrist be the infernal prince. And in this last era all the kingdoms of Christianity and also of the unbelievers shall quake for the space of years, and there shall be more grievous wars and battles; towns, cities, castles and other buildings shall be burnt, desolated and destroyed with a great effusion of vestal blood, married women and widows ravished, sucking children dashed against the walls of towns, and so many evils shall be committed by the means of the infernal prince, Satan, that almost the entire world shall be undone and desolate.

Before these events many unusual birds shall cry through the air, crying, 'Huy, huy.' ('Now, now.') A little while after they shall vanish. After this shall have lasted a good while, there shall be renewed a reign of Saturn and a golden age. God the Creator shall say, hearing the affliction of His people, Satan shall be put and tied in the bottom of the deep, and there shall begin an age of universal peace between God and man. The ecclesiastical power shall return in force and Satan shall be bound for the space of a thousand years, and then shall be loosed again.

All these figures are justly fitted by the Sacred Scriptures to the celestial things, that is to say, Saturn, Jupiter and Mars, and others joined with them, as may be seen more at large in some of my quatrains. I would have calculated it more deeply, and coordinated one with the other, but seeing, O most excellent King, that some stand ready to censure me, I shall now withdraw my pen to its nocturnal repose.

'*Multa etiam, O Rex potentissime proeclara, et sane in brevi ventura sed omnia in hac tua Epistola, innectere non possumus, nec volumus, sed ad intellegenda quoedam facta, horrida fata pauca libanda sunt, quamvis tanta sit in omnes tua amplitudo et humanitas homines, deosque pietas, ut solos amplissimo et Christianissimo Regis nomine, et ad quem summa totius religionis auctoritas deferatur dignus esse videare.'** But I shall only beseech you, O most merciful King, by your singular and prudent goodness, to understand rather the desire of my heart, and the earnest desire I have to obey your most excellent Majesty, ever since my eyes were so near to your royal splendour, than the greatness of my word can attain to or deserve.

Faciebat Michael Nostradamus
Solonoe Petrae Provincae

From Salon this 27th June, 1558

---

* 'So many things, O most potent King of all, of the most remarkable kind are to happen soon, that I neither would nor could incorporate them all into this epistle; but in order to intelligently comprehend certain facts, a few horrible fated events must be set down in extract, although your amplitude and humanity towards mankind is so great, as is your piety to God, that you alone seem worthy of the great title of the most Christian King, and to whom the highest authority in all religion should be deferred.'

CENTURY VIII

1

Pau, nay, loron plus feu qu'a sang
  sera,
Laude nager, fuir grand aux surrez,
Les aggassas entree refusera,
Pampon, Durance, les tiendra enser-
  rez.

Pau, nay, loron, more in fire their
  blood shall be,
Seen to swim, great ones shall run
  to their surreys,
The aggassas shall refuse the entry,
Pampon, Durance shall keep them
  enclosed.

This seemingly obscure and unintelligible quatrain conceals a complex play on words by means of which Nostradamus predicts the advent of Napoleon, viz. nay-pau-loron, a man of fire (gunfire?). Also the dispatch of the pre-French-Revolution nobility in flight in their surreys. *Aggassas* in French is magpie or pie or pius, whom Napoleon held hostage (Pius VI and Pius VII).

2

Condon & Aux & autour de Mir-
  ande,
Je voy du ciel feu qui les environne,
Sol, Mars, conjoint au Lion, puis
  Marmande,
Foudre, grand guerre, mur tombe
  dans Garonne.

Condon and Aux, and about Mir-
  ande,
I see a fire from heaven that sur-
  rounds them,
Sol, Mars, in conjunction with the
  lion, and then Marmande
Lightning, great war, wall falls into
  the Garonne.

Fire from heaven suggests extra-terrestrial spacecraft landing amid a great war on earth.

3

Au fort chasteau de Vigilanne & Res-viers,	In the strong castle of Vigilanne and Resviers,
Sere serre le puisnay de Nancy;	Shall be kept close the youngest son of Nancy,
Dedans Turin seront ards les premiers,	Within Turin, the first shall be burnt up,
Lors que de dueil Lyon sera transy.	When Lyons shall be overwhelmed with sorrow.

Contemporary politics, that loomed large at the time but which have since lost their significance, are here recorded.

4

Dedans Monech le Coq sera receu,	Within Monaco the Cock shall be received.
Le Cardinal de France apparoistra,	The Cardinal of France shall appear,
Par Logarion Romain sera deceu,	By Logarion Roman shall be deceived,
Foiblesse a l'Aigle, & force au Coq naistra.	Weakness to the Eagle, and strength to the Cock shall grow.

Monaco, then an Italian possession, admitted the French for the first time, persuaded by the policy of Cardinal Richelieu, the Gallic Cock being the gainer thereby.

5

Apparoistra temple luisant orne,	A brilliantly adorned temple shall appear,
La lampe & cierge a Borne & Bre-tueil,	The lamp and wax candle of Borne and Bretueil,
Pour la Lucerne le canton destorne,	For Lucerne the canton is turned,
Quand on verra le grand Coq cercueil.	When the great Cock shall be seen in his coffin.

After the death of a French King the glory of France will be at its zenith.

6

Charte fulgure a Lyon apparente	A thundering light at Lyons ap-
Luysant, print Malte, subit sera es-	pearing,
trainte,	Brightly, Malta instantly shall be
Sardon, Mauris traitera decevante,	put out,
Geneve a Londres a Coq trahison	Sardon shall treat Mauris deceit-
feinte.	fully,
	From Geneva to London, the Cock
	a pretended treason.

Tremendous aerial bombardments shall devastate France and extend even to Malta and Sardinia. The French shall pretend to be unfaithful to Geneva and London.

7

Verceil, Milan donra intelligence,	Verceil, Milan shall give intelli-
Dedans Tycin sera fait la paye,	gence,
Courir par Seine eau, sang feu par	In the Ticin shall the peace be
Florence,	made,
Unique choir d'haut en bas faisant	Run through Seine water, blood,
maye.	fire through Florence,
	Only one shall fall from top to
	bottom making friends.

Italian cities in northern Italy shall make peace with the French; only one person shall suffer by this act.

8

Pres de Linterne dans de tonnes	Near Linterne, enclosed within the
fermez,	farms,
Chivaz fera pour l'Aigle la menee,	Chivas shall drive the plot for the
L'esleu casse, luy ses gens enfermez,	Eagle,
Dedans Turin rapt espouse emmenee.	The elect dismissed, he and his
	men shut up,
	Within Turin, the bride raped and
	carried away.

Linterne and Chivas are small towns in Italy. In a plot to gain power, the local government will be overcome and the prize seized.

9

Pendant que l'Aigle & le Coq a Savone	While the Eagle and Cock at Savonna
Seront unis, Mer, Levant & Hongrie,	Shall be united, Sea, Levant and Hungary,
L'armee a Naples, Palerme, Marque d'Ancone,	The army at Naples, Palermo, Mark of Ancona,
Rome, Venise, par barbe horrible crie.	Rome, Venice, cry because of a horrid barb.

The American Eagle and the French Cock shall be in a united campaign against the Italians, Hungarians, etc., and the Italian armies shall be in great distress because of a new and punishing weapon used against them.

10

Puanteur grande sortira de Lausanne,	A great stink shall come forth from Lausanne,
Qu'on ne scaura l'origine du fait,	So that no one shall know the origin of it,
L'on mettra hors tout la gent loingtaine,	They shall put out all the foreigners,
Feu veu au ciel, peuple estranger deffait.	Fire seen in heaven, a strange people defeated.

The presages contained in this quatrain are now *faits accomplis*, written with a bloody pen on the pages of History. The Conference of Lausanne is predicted and the signing of many diplomatic instruments, including the Treaty of Peace itself. Cynically Nostradamus refers to the 'stink that shall come forth from Lausanne,' indicating the cynicism of the participants; he even shows the blind faith with which these documents were accepted by the people of the world. He foretells that the 'peace' shall be short-lived; that minorities shall be persecuted; that the fires of war shall be rekindled and again sweep over the earth.

11

Peuple infiny paroistra a Vicence,	Infinite number of people shall appear at Vincenza,
Sans force feu brusler la basilique,	Without force, fire shall burn in the basilick,
Pres de Lunage deffait grande de Valence,	Near Lunage the great one of Valencia shall be defeated,
Lors que Venise par mort prendra pique.	When Venice by death shall be piqued.

Basilick is the name of an old Italian fort which was heavily fortified by cannon. The sense of this verse then is that Italy will be engaged in a war.

12

Apparoistra aupres de Buffalore	Near the Bufalore shall appear
L'haut & procere entre dedans Milan,	The high and tall, come into Milan,
L'Abbe de Foix avec ceux de Sainct Maure,	The Abbot of Foix with those of Saint Maure,
Feront la forbe habillez en vilain.	Shall make the deceit, being clothed like a villain.

Foix and St Maure are towns in France. This concerns a debate among the clergymen of these communities.

13

Le croise frere par amour effrenee,	The crossed brother through unbridled love,
Fera par Praytus Bellerophon mourir,	Shall cause Bellerophon to be killed by Praytus,
Classe a mil ans la femme forcenee,	Fleet to thousand years, the women frantic,
Beu le bruvage, tous deux apres perrir.	The drink being drunk, both after that shall perish.

Bellerophon was a hero of Greek mythology. He fell from his steed Pegasus and perished, while attempting to fly to heaven.

14

Le grand credit, d'or, d'argent, l'abundance,	The great credit, of gold, of silver, great abundance,
Aveuglera par libide l'honneur;	Shall blind honour by lust,
Cogneu sera d'adultere l'offense,	The offence of the adulterer shall be known,
Qui parviendra a son grand deshonneur.	Which shall come to his great dishonour.

Most appropriately, the economic plight of the twentieth century includes soaring inflation and currency devaluation, alongside universal laxity in morals and lust rampant with little social restraint.

15

Vers Aquilon grands efforts par hommasse	Towards the North great endeavours by a masculine woman,
Presque l'Europe & l'univers vexer,	To trouble Europe, and almost all the world,
Les deux eclipses mettre en telle chasse,	The two eclipses shall be put to flight,
Et aux Pannons vie & mort renforcer.	And shall reinforce life, and death to the Poles.

Catherine the Great, 1729–96, Empress of Russia, is here indicated. She was a disciple and friend of the Encyclopaedists, especially of Voltaire, and although she started out with the intention of following their principles in the matters of domestic reform, it was short-lived and completely shattered by the advent of the French Revolution. During her reign she engineered the shameless partitions of Poland, to the great detriment of that nation.

16

Au lieu que Jieson feit sa nef fabriquer,	In the place where Jason carried his ship to be built,
Si grand deluge sera & si subite,	So great a flood shall be and so sudden,
Qu'on n'aura lieu ne terres s'ataquer,	That there shall be neither place nor land to save themselves,
L'onde monter Fesulan Olympique.	The waves shall climb upon the Olympic Fesulan.

Mount Olympus, the mythical home of the gods, is where Jason built his ship, for the Argonauts' voyage. The sense of this stanza is that an inexorable movement shall engulf all those in authority and a new order be created.

17

Les bien aisez subit seront desmis,	Those that were at ease shall be put down,
Le monde mis par les trois freres en trouble,	The world shall be put in trouble by three brothers,
Cite marine saisiront ennemis,	The maritime city shall be seized by its enemies,
Faim, feu, sang, peste, & de tous maux le double.	Hunger, fire, blood, plague, and double of all evils.

Social conditions are to change; world wide repercussions with an abundance of misfortunes shall beset all, due to the machinations of three brothers.

18

De Flore issue de sa mort sera cause,	Issued from Flora, shall be the cause of her death,
Un temps devant par jeusne & vieille bueyre,	A time before, by fasting and stale drink,
Car les trois lys luy feront telle pause,	For the three lilies, shall make her such a pause,
Par son fruit sauve comme chair crue meuyre.	Saved by her fruit, as raw flesh dead.

The three lilies represent the Fleur de Lys, symbol of France. After a period of want and suffering France will be succoured by the sacrifices of her patriots.

19

A soustenir la grand cappe troublee,	To maintain up the great troubled cloak,
Pour l'esclaireir les rouges marcheront,	The red ones shall march to clear it,
De mort famille sera presque accablee,	A family shall be almost crushed to death,
Les rouges rouges, le rouge assommeront.	The red reds, shall knock down the red one.

Nostradamus predicts great peril for the Pope. The red ones (cardinals) surround and protect him from the red reds (Communists, terrorists), who in their turn do kill a cardinal and simultaneously, in a crowd panic, almost crush a family of observers.

20

Le faux message par election feinte,	The false message, by a fraudulent election,
Courir par urban rompue pache arreste,	Shall be stopped from going about the town,
Voix acceptees, de sang chapelle tainte,	Voices shall be bought, and a chapel tinted with blood,
Et a un autre l'empire contraincte.	By another, who contests the rule.

By bribery a fraudulent rumour shall be perpetrated, and a bloody struggle will arise in the church.

21

Au port de Agde trois fustes entreront,	In the Port of Agda, three ships shall enter,
Portant infection avec foy & pestilence,	Carrying with them infection and pestilence,
Passant le pont mil milles embleront,	Going beyond the bridge, they shall carry away thousands,
Et le pont rompre a tierce resistance.	At the third resistance the bridge shall be broken.

Agda, a city in France, shall be the entering point for foreign propaganda, eventually conquering the country thereby.

22

Gorsan, Narbonne, par le sel advertir,	Gorsan, Narbonne, by the salt shall give notice,
Tucham, la grace Parpignan trahie,	To Tucham, the grace Perpignan betrayed,
La ville rouge n'y voudra consentir,	The red city will not give consent to it,
Par haulte Voldrap gris vie faillie.	By high Voldrap, gray life ended.

French cities are named; by an edict from the 'red city' (Rome) help will be given to their inhabitants.

23

Lettres trouvees de la Royne les coffres,	Letters found in the Queen's coffers,
Point de subscrit sans aucun nom d'autheur,	No superscription, no name of author,
Par la police seront cachez les offres,	By the police shall be concealed the offers,
Qu'on ne scaura qui sera l'amateur.	So that no one shall know who shall be the lover.

The affair of The Diamond Necklace, involving Cagliostro, the master swindler, Cardinal Rohan, and the Queen of France, is here indicated.

24

Lieutenant a l'entree de l'huys	The lieutenant shall at the entrance of the door,
Assommera la grand de Perpignan,	Knock down the great one of Perpignan,
En se cuidant sauver a Montpertuis,	Thinking to save himself at the mountain straits,
Sera deceu bastard de Lusignan.	And the bastard of Lusignan shall be deceived.

Perpignon, at the frontier between Spain and France, shall be the scene of many disgraceful events.

25

Coeur de l'amant ouvert d'amour furtive,	The lover's heart, being by a furtive love
Dans le ruisseau fera ravir la Dame,	Shall cause the lady to be ravished in the brook,
Le demy mal contrefera lascive,	The lascivious shall counterfeit half a discontent.
Le pere a deux privera corps de l'ame.	The father shall deprive them both of their souls.

A father, discovering his mistress and his son in a compromising situation, shall kill both of them.

26

De Carones trouvez en Barcelonne,	From Carons found in Barcelona,
Mys descouvers, lieu terrouers & ruyne,	Found discovered, in place of soil and ruin,
Le grand qui tient ne voudra Pamplonne,	The great that hold, will not Pampelone,
Par l'abbaye de Montferrat bruyne.	By the abbey of Montserrat, a fine rain.

This evidently refers to the discovery of some sort of plant, which eventually becomes one of the staple foods of the poor people of Europe.

27

La voye Auxelle l'un sur l'autre fornix,	The way Auxelle, one arch upon another,
Du muy de ser hor mis brave & genest,	Being brave and gallant put out the iron vessel,
L'escript d'Empereur le Phoenix,	The writing of the Emperor, the Phoenix,
Veu en celuy ce qu'a nul autre n'est.	In it shall be seen, what nowhere else is.

The return of Napoleon from Elba is here compared to the rising of the phoenix from its ashes.

28

Les simulachres d'or et d'argent enflez,	The idols swollen with gold and silver,
Qu'apres le rapt, lac au feu furent jettez,	Which after the rape were thrown into the lake and fire,
Au descouvert estaincts tous & troublez,	Being discovered after the putting out of the fire,
Au marbre escripts, perscripts interietez.	Shall be written in marble, precepts being inserted.

An incident of antiquity is described here: the stealing of gold and silver idols from a temple, their desecration by fire and water, and the subsequent erection of a marble monument inscribed in their honour.

29

Au quart pilier l'on sacre a Saturne,	At the fourth pillar where they sacrifice to Saturn,
Par tremblant terre & deluge fendu,	Shaken by an earthquake and a flood,
Sous l'edifice Saturnin trouves urne,	A funeral urn shall be found under that Saturnin edifice,
D'or Capion, ravy & puis rendu.	Full of gold, stolen, and then returned.

A funeral urn, in which the ancient Romans kept the ashes of their great ones, shall be uncovered by an upheaval, but gold will be found in it instead.

30

Dedans Tholose non loing de Beluzer,	Within Toulouse not far from Be-
Faisant un puis loing, palais d'espec-	luzer,
tacle	Digging a well, for the palace of
Thresor trouve un chacun ira vexer,	spectacle,
Et en deux locs tout & pres des vesa-	A treasure found that shall vex
cle.	everyone,
	In two parcels and near the Basacle.

In Toulouse, in the industrial part of the city called the Basacle, a Pandora's box will be found.

31

Premier grand fruict le Prince de	The first great fruit the Prince of
Pesquiere;	Pescaire,
Mais puis viendra bien & cruel malin,	But he shall become very cruel and
Dedans Venise perdra sa gloire fiere,	malicious,
Et mis a mal par plus joyue Celin.	He shall lose his fierce pride in
	Venice,
	And shall be put to evil by the young Turks.

Pescaire, a town near Naples, will be the birthplace of a statesman. Rising to power at an early age, he will become arrogant and over-confident. At the height of his career he will be killed in a duel with a Turk.

32

Garde toy roy Gaulois de ton nepveu,	Take heed, O French King, of thy
Qui fera tant que ton unique fils,	nephew,
Sera meurtry a Venus faisant voeu,	Who shall cause that thine only
Accompagne denuict que trois & six.	son,
	Shall be murdered making a vow to Venus,
	Accompanied with three and six.

Napoleon III, nephew of Napoleon Bonaparte, is referred to here; the significance being the complete disintegration of Napoleonic prestige under his reign.

33

Le grand naistra de Veronne & Vincense,	The great one of Verona and Vincenza shall be born,
Qui portera un surnon bien indigne,	Who shall bear a very unworthy name,
Qui a Venise voudra faire vengeance,	Who shall endeavour at Venice to avenge himself,
Luy mesme prins homme du guet & signe.	But he shall be taken by a policeman.

Another reference to Mussolini, this retells the sordid details of his ignoble fate.

34

Apres victoire du Lion au Lion,	After the victory of the Lion against the Lion,
Sur la montagne de Jura Secatombe,	Upon the mountain of Jura, Hecatombe,
Delues, & brodes septiesme million,	Of them decorated, the seventh million,
Lyon, Ulme a Mausol mort & tombe.	Lyons, Ulme fall dead at Mausol.

The mention of places in Switzerland, France, Germany, and the word 'lion' taken as meaning Great Britain, we believe that these things in connection with the phrases 'seventh million' and 'fall dead' refer to the world wars and their casualties.

35

Dedans l'entree de Garonne & Blaye,	Within the entrance of Garonne and Blaye,
Et la forest non loing de Damazan,	And the forest not far from Damazan,
Du Marsaves gelees, puis gresle & bize,	Of Marsaves frosts, then hail and north wind,
Dordonnois gelle par erreur de Mezan.	Dordonois frozen by the error of Mezan.

This describes an unusually bad winter in Europe – rivers frozen solid, terrible winds and hailstorms raging throughout the land.

36

Sera commis contre Oinde a Duche,
Se Saulne, & sainct Aubin & Be-
*   loeuvre,*
Paver de marbre, de tous loing es-
*   pluche,*
Non Bleteran resister & chef
*   d'oeuvre.*

The Duche shall be committed
   against Oinde,
Of Saulne and Saint Aubin and
   Beloeuvre,
To have with marble and of towers
   well picked,
Not Bleteran to resist, and master
   stroke.

In these latter-day prophecies, we find a few obscure and unintelligible
verses. This quite apparently is one of them.

37

Le forteresse aupres de la Thamise,
Cherra par lors, le Roy dedans serre,
Aupres du pont sera veu en chemisee,
Un devant mort, puis dans le fort
*   barre.*

The fortress near the Thames,
Shall fall, then the King that was
   kept within
Shall be seen near the bridge in his
   shirt,
One dead before, then in the fort
   kept close.

Charles was brought to Windsor Castle, overlooking the Thames, after
his defeat on December 23, 1648. On January 30, dressed in a white shirt,
he was taken out and beheaded.

38

Le Roy de Bloys dans Avignon
*   regner,*
Un autre fois le peuple emonopole,
Dedans le Rhosne par murs fera baig-
*   ner,*
Jusques a cinq, le dernier pres de
*   Nolle.*

The King of Blois in Avignon shall
   reign,
Another time the people do
   murmur,
He shall cause in the Rhone to be
   bathed through the walls,
As many as five, the last shall be
   near Nole.

A King of France shall occupy Avignon, a city in France belonging to a
Pope. Some of the inhabitants, objecting to this seizure, shall be thrown
over the city walls into the river.

39

Qu'aura este par prince Bizantin,	What shall have been by a Byzantine prince,
Sera tollu par prince de Tholose,	Shall be taken away by the prince of Toulouse,
Lay foy de Foix, par le chef Tholentin,	The faith of Foix by the chief Tholentin,
Luy faillira ne refusant l'espouse.	Shall fail him, not refusing the spouse.

The French shall occupy territory in the Near East, formerly ruled by the Mohammedans.

40

Le sang du juste par Taur & la Dorade,	The blood of the just by Taur and Dorade,
Pour se venger contre les Saturnins	To avenge themselves against the Saturnins,
Au nouveau lac plongeront la Mainade,	In the new lake shall plunge the Mainade,
Puis marcheront contre les Albanins.	Then shall march against the Albanins.

The Byzantine and Arab influence in Algiers and its civil war with France in the late 1950s, ending in 1961, under Charles de Gaulle's leadership is predicted here. De Gaulle, the 'prince' of Toulouse, grants independence to Algeria.

41

Esleu sera Renard ne sonnant mot,	A fox shall be elected that said nothing,
Faisant le saint public, vivant pain d'orge,	Making a public saint, living with barley bread,
Tyrannizer apres tant a un cop,	Shall tyrannize after upon a sudden
Mettant la pied des plus grands sur la gorge.	And put his foot upon the throat of the greatest.

Nostradamus anticipates the appearance of a puritan ('barley bread') in the guise of a fox. (Robespierre, Napoleon III, or Premier Paul Reynaud, who was elected in 1940 at the time of the Nazi occupation.)

42

Par avarice, par force & violence,	By avarice, and force and violence,
Viendra vexer les siens chefs d'Orleans,	Shall come to vex his own chief of Orleans,
Pres Sainct Memire assault & resistance,	Near St Memire, assault and resistance,
Mort dans sa tente, diront qu'il dort leans.	Dead in his tent, they shall say, he sleepeth there.

At St Memire, a French town, a mutiny against the tyrannical local government chiefs shall result in the murder of one of them. To protect the murderer, the inhabitants shall, for a long time, attempt to conceal the body from the authorities.

43

Par le decide de deux choses bastars,	By the decision of two things, bastards,
Nepveu du sang occupera le regne,	Nephew of the blood shall occupy the government,
Dedans lectoure seront les coups de dards,	Within Lectore shall be blows of darts,
Nepveu par pleira l'enseigne.	Nephew through fear shall fold up his ensigns.

The nephew here foretold is Napoleon III, who became president of France in 1848 and soon began to pursue his absolutist policies as Emperor in 1852. However, he was defeated in the 1870 Franco-Prussian war and folded his insignia. After his release as a prisoner he retired to England to end his days.

44

Le procree naturel l'Ogmion,	The natural begotten of Ogmion,
De sept a neuf du chemin destorner,	From seven to nine shall be put out of the way,
A roy de longue & amy au my hom,	To king of long, and friend to half man,
Doit a Navarre fort de Pau prosterner.	Ought to Navarre prostrate the fort of Pau.

An illegitimate son of a great monarch shall attempt to murder the king.

45

La main escharpe & la jambe bandee,	The hand on a scarf and the leg bandaged,
Louis puisne de palais partira,	The younger Louis shall depart from the palace,
Au mot du guet la mort sera tardee,	At the watchword his death shall be protracted,
Puis dans le temple a Pasques saig- nera.	Then afterwards at Easter he shall bleed in the temple.

A remarkable prediction. The younger Louis here refers to the Dauphin, son of Louis XVI and Marie Antoinette, who died in prison. He had been named Louis XVII by the loyalists.

46

Pol Mensolee mourra trois lieues du Rhosne,	Paul Mensolee shall die leagues from the Rhone,
Fuis les deux prochains Tarare des- trois;	Avoid the two straits near the Tarara,
Car Mars fera le plus horrible throsne,	For Mars shall keep such a horrible throne,
De coq & d'aigle, de France freres trois.	Of cock and eagle, of France three brothers.

Paul Mensolee is warned to avoid the roads to Mt Tarare, as they are infested with thieves and murderers.

47

Lac Trasmenian portera tesmoignage,	Trasmenian Lake shall bear wit- ness,
Des conjurez sarez dedans Perouse,	Of the conspirators shut up in Per- ugia,
Un despolle contrefera le sage,	A Des Polle shall simulate the pru- dent,
Tuant Tedesq de Sterne & Minuse.	Killing Germans of Sterne and Minuse.

A reference to the victory of Hannibal at Lake Trasimenus near the town of Perugia, Italy.

48

Saturne en Cancer, Jupiter avec Mars,	Saturn in Cancer, Jupiter with Mars,
Dedans Fevrier, Caldondon, salvaterre,	In February Caldondon, ground saved,
Sault, Castallon, assailly de trois pars,	The Republic assaulted on three sides,
Pres de Verbiesque, conflit mortelle guerre.	Near Verbiesque, fight and mortal war.

The oft-repeated warning of a great war is here contained.

49

Saturne au beuf, Jove en l'eau, Mars en fleiche,	Saturn in bull, Jupiter in water, Mars in arrow,
Six de Fevrier mortalite donra,	The sixth of February shall give mortality,
Ceux de Tardaigne a Bruge si grand breche,	Those of Tardaigne shall make in Bruges so great a breach,
Qu'a Ponterose chef Barbarin mourra.	That the chief Barbarin shall die at Ponterose.

The event indicated shall occur under the influence of these planets, when Saturn is in Taurus, Jupiter in Aquarius, and Mars in Sagittarius. By the death of the chief Barbarin is meant the death of Pope Urban VIII.

50

La pestilence l'entour de Capadille,	The plague shall be round about Capadillo,
Une aurte faim pres de Sagone s'appreste	Another famine cometh near to that of Sagunce,
Le chevalier bastard de bon senille,	The knight bastard of the good old man,
Au grand de Thunes fera tranche la teste.	Shall cause the great one of Tunis to be beheaded.

Drought, famine, and disease plague West Africa from 1975 on. The great one of Tunis is Habib Bourguiba. He was re-elected to his fourth five-year term in 1974, and then in 1975 was elected president for life. However, Nostradamus predicts his death by violent means.

51

Le Bizantin faisant oblation,	The Byzantin, making an offering,
Apres avoir Cordube a soy reprinse;	After he hath taken Cordova to
Son chemin long, repos pamplation,	himself again,
Mer passant proy par la Cologne	His road long, rest, contemplation,
prinse.	Crossing the sea hath a prey by
	Cologne.

The reference here is to the abdication of Charles V, King of Spain. He retired to a small house in the grounds of a monastery and spent the last years of his life in study and contemplation.

52

Le roy de Bloys Avignon regner,	The King of Blois shall reign in
D'Amboise & Seme viendra le long de	Avignon,
Lyndre,	He shall come from Amboise and
Ongle a Poitiers sainctes aisles ruyner	Seme, along the Linden,
Devant Bony.	A nail at Poitiers shall ruin his holy
	wing,
	Before Bony.

One must delve deeply into this quatrain to gather its full meaning. It depicts the phenomenal rise of Napoleon, and even refers to the unprecedented procedure of the Pope's journey to Paris to crown Napoleon as Emperor.

53

Dedans Bologne voudra laver ses	Within Boulogne, he shall want to
fautes,	wash himself of his faults,
Il ne pourra au temple du soleil,	In the church of the sun, but he
Il volera faisant chose si hautes,	shall not be able,
En hierarchie n'en fut oneq un pareil.	He shall fly, doing things too high,
	That in the hierarchy was never the
	like.

This predicts that Cardinal Richelieu, who attained greater secular heights than any other man of the church, shall wish to go on a holy pilgrimage, but shall defer it too long and shall be prevented from doing so by his death.

54

Soubs la couleur de traicte mariage,
Fait magnanime par grand Chyren
* Selin,*
Quintin, Arras recouvrez au voyage,
D'Espagnols fait second banc
* Macelin.*

Under the pretence of a treaty of
  marriage,
A magnanimous act shall be done
  by Henry the Great,
St Quentin and Arras, recovered in
  the journey,
Of Spaniards shall be made a
  second Macelin bench.

A King of France, Henry the Great, through a pretended treaty of
marriage, shall acquire new territories. The word Macelin is from the Latin
word *Macellum* which means shambles. And the meaning here is that there
will be a war and subsequent havoc in Spain.

55

Entre deux fleuves se verra enserre,
Tonneaux a caques unis a passer
* outre,*
Huict ponts rompus chef a tant en-
* ferre,*
Enfans parfaicts sont jugulez en coul-
* tre.*

Between two rivers he shall find
  himself shut up,
Tuns and casks put together to pass
  over,
Eight bridges broken, the chief at
  last in prison,
Perfect children shall have their
  throats cut.

A commander of an army, about to launch an attack, shall be tempor-
arily stopped by the destruction of all bridges across the river near which
the enemy is encamped. Causing a pontoon bridge to be built, he and his
men will cross over and by surprise attack will overcome and capture the
enemy.

56

La bande foible le terre occupera,
Ceux du haut lieu feront horribles cris,
Le gros troupeau d'estre coin troub-
* lera,*
Tombe pres D. nebro descouvert les
* escrits.*

The weak party shall occupy the
  ground,
Those of the high places shall make
  horrible cries,
It shall trouble the great flock in the
  right corner,
He falleth near D. nebro dis-
  covereth the writings.

The continuing struggles between 'left' and 'right' political parties are
here predicted. The obscurely worded last line leads us to believe that
Nostradamus purposely wished to withhold his views as to the ultimate
outcome.

57

De soldat simple parviendre en empire,	From a simple soldier, he shall come to have supreme command,
De robe courte parviendra a la longue,	From a short gown he shall come to a long one,
Vaillant aux armes, en eglise ou plus pire,	Valiant in arms, no worse man in the church,
Vexer les prestres comme l'eau faict l'esponge.	He shall vex the priests, as water does a sponge.

A perfect picture of Oliver Cromwell: From a simple soldier he rose to be Lord Protector; from a student in the university he became a graduate of Oxford; and as for vexing the clergy, there was no one of his day who caused them more trouble.

58

Regne en querelle aux freres divise,	A kingdom in dispute and divided between the brothers,
Prendre les armes & le nom Britannique,	To take the arms and the Britannic name,
Tiltre d'Anglican sera tard advise,	And the English title, he shall advise himself late.
Surprins de nuict, mener a l'air Gallique.	Surprised in the night and carried into the French air.

This predicts the abdication of King Edward VIII, and the accession to the throne of his brother, Duke of York, who became George VI.

59

Par deux fois haut, par deux fois mis a bas,	Twice set up high, and twice brought down,
L'Orient aussi l'Occident foiblira,	The East also the West shall weaken,
Son adversaire apres plusieurs combats,	His adversary after many fights,
Par mer chasse au besoing faillira.	Expelled by sea, shall fail in need.

The role of Germany in World Wars I and II is predicted. Both times the goal of that country was world domination, and both times she was defeated by the combined efforts of East and West.

60

*Premier en Gaule, premier en Roma-
nie,*
Par mer & terre aux Anglois & Paris,
*Merveilleux faits par celle grand
mesnie,*
Violant, Terax perdra le Norlaris.

The first in France, the first in
Romania,
By sea and land to the English and
Paris,
Wonderful deeds by that great
company,
By ravishing, Terax shall ruin Nor-
laris.

The rapidity of the Nazi expansion (the 'blitz' technique) both East and
West during the dark days of World War II, the wonderful yet vain
resistance of the conquered peoples, the ravishing of the countries – all is
here prognosticated.

61

Jamais par le decouvrement du jour
Ne parviendra au signe sceptrifere
Que tous ses siege ne soient en sejour,
Portant au coq don tu Tag amisere.

Never by the discovering of the day
He shall attain to the sceptre bear-
ing sign,
Till all his martial trials be settled,
Carrying to the cock, a gift from
Der Tag of misery.

Three factors in this verse – the use of the alien word 'Tag', the warning
of war, and the reference to the 'Cock' (France) – lead us to believe that
here is a prognostication of the now infamous words 'Der Tag', which was
Germany's rallying cry for the day of vengeance and hoped-for triumph
over the democracies.

62

*Lors qu'on verra expiler le sainct
temple,*
*Plus grand du Rhosne & sacres
prophaner,*
Par eux naistra pestilence si ample,
Roy faict injuste ne fera condamner.

When one shall see spoiled the holy
temple,
The greatest of the Rhone, and
sacred things profaned,
From them shall come so great a
pestilence,
That the King being unjust shall
not condemn them.

When the city of Lyons, the greatest on the Rhone River, is invaded and
pillaged, a pestilence will descend upon the city, destroying both inhabitants and invaders.

63

Quand l'adultere blesse sans coup aura	When the adulterer wounded without a blow,
Meurdry la femme & le fils par despit,	Shall have murdered the wife and son by spite,
Famme assoumes l'enfant estranglera;	The woman knocked down, shall strangle the child,
Huict captifs prins s'estouffer sans respit.	Eight taken prisoners, and stifled without tarrying.

A tragic story is told here, of an adulterer who, through his philandering, contracts a contagious disease and in turn infects his wife and child. Being upbraided by his wife, he attempts to murder her and his son and then flees from the scene. She, dying, strangles her child. Without attempting to investigate the facts of the case, eight innocent persons are hanged for these two murders.

64

Dedans les Isles les enfans transportez,	In the Islands the children shall be transported,
Les deux de sept seront en desespoir;	The two of seven shall be in despair,
Ceux du terrouer en seront supportez,	Those of the company shall be supported by
Nom pelle prins, des ligues fuy l'espoir.	Nompelle taken, avoid the hope of the league.

As usual, during wartime the children of the British Isles are to be evacuated from London and other major cities to the countryside.

65

Le vieux frustre du principal espoir,	The old man frustrated of his chief hope,
Il parviendra au chef de son empire;	He shall attain to the head of the empire,
Vingt mois tiendra le regne a grand pouvoir,	Twenty months he shall keep the kingdom with great power,
Tiran, cruel en delaissant un pire.	Tyrant, cruel, and leaving a worse one.

Ayatollah Khomeini returns from exile in France to lead the Islamic revolution in Iran. However, he is destined to die in the 1980s and leave Iran in chaos.

66

Quand l'escriture D. M. trouvee,	When the writing D. M. shall be found,
Et cave antique a lamp descouverte,	And an ancient cave discovered with a lamp.
Loy, Roy & Prinse Ulpian esprouvee,	Law, King, and Prince Ulpian tried,
Pavillon Royne & Duc sous la couverte.	Tent, Queen and Duke under the cover.

Nostradamus here predicts the event of the re-discovery of his writings and the great new meanings that will be found contained in them.

67

Par. Car. Nersas, a ruine grand discorde,	Par. Car. Nersas, to ruin great discord
Ne l'un ne l'autre n'aura election,	Neither one nor the other shall be elected,
Nersas du peuple aura armour & concorde,	Nersas shall have of the people love and concord,
Ferrare, Collone grand protection.	Ferrara, Colonna shall have great protection.

A great variance of opinion shall lead to strife over the election of a Pope, and as a result the two leading candidates will be defeated and a hitherto unknown will gain that high honour. This, in fact, did occur in 1978 when John Paul II from Wadowice, Poland, was elected.

68

Vieux Cardinal par le jeune deceu,	An old Cardinal, by a young one shall be deceived,
Hors de sa charge se verra desarme,	And shall see himself out of his position,
Arles ne monstres double soit aperceu,	Arles do not show, a double strength perceived,
Et l'Aqueduct & le Prince embaume.	And the Aqueduct, and the embalmed Prince.

This prophesies the rivalry between (old) Cardinal Richelieu and his young successor, twenty-two-year-old Cinq-Mars. Richelieu died on December 4, 1642, and was embalmed.

69

Aupres du jeune se vieux Ange baisser,	Near the young one the old angel shall bow,
Et le viendra sur monter a la fin;	And shall at last overcome him,
Dix ans esgaux aux plus vieux rabaisser,	Ten years equal, to make the old one stoop,
De trois deux l'un huictiesme Seraphin.	Of three, two, one, the eighth a Seraphin.

An old man (referred to as an angel) shall humbly defer to a young man, even though he is aware that he is being cheated. After ten years the old one shall turn upon and overcome the young villain. (The mythical allusions in the last line seem to have no particular meaning.)

70

Il entrera vilain, meschant, infame	He shall come in villain, wicked, infamous,
Tyrannisant la Mesopotamie	To tyrannize Mesopotamia,
Tous amis faict d'adulterine dame,	He maketh all friends by an adulterous lady,
Terre horrible noir de physiognomie.	Foul, horrid, black, in his physiognomy.

The country near Babylon shall be terrorized by a person of the Negro race.

71

Croistra le nombre si grand des Astronomes,	The number of Astronomers shall grow so great,
Chassez, bannis & livres censurez,	Driven away, banished, books censured,
L'an mil six cens & sept par sacre Glomes,	The year one thousand six hundred and seven years by Glomes,
Que nul aux sacres ne seront asseurez.	That none shall be secure in sacred places.

Nostradamus dates all events from A.D. 325 (Council of Nicaea); thus 1607 plus 325 equals 1932. On January 30 1933, Hitler became Chancellor of Germany, ushering in the era of the burning of books, the banishment of men of science, religion and art, the crushing of all culture that did not concur with Nazi doctrines.

72

Champ Perugin O l'enorme deffaite
Et le conflit tout aupres de Ravenne,
Passage sacre lors qu'on fera la feste,
Vainqueur vaincu, cheval manger
l'avenne.

Perugian field, O the enormous defeat,
And the fight about Ravenna,
Sacred passage when the feast shall be celebrated,
The victorious vanquished, the horse to eat up his oats.

Perugia and Ravenna are cities in Italy, where a decisive battle will be fought on a holiday.

73

Soldat barbare le grand roy frappera,
In justement non eslongne de mort,
L'avare mere du faict cause sera,
Conjurateur & regne en grand remort.

A barbarous soldier shall strike the king,
Unjustly, not far from death,
The covetous mother shall be the cause of it,
The conspirator and kingdom in great remorse.

Mussolini ruled Italy from 1922 until 1945. He was hanged on April 28, 1945. Later, King Victor Emmanuel III abdicated and installed his son, King Humbert II, only to have him sent into exile with the establishment of the Republic.

74

En terre neuve bien avant Roy entre,
Pendant subges luy viendront faire
acueil,
Sa perfidie aura tel recontre,
Qu'aux citadins lieu de feste & re-
ceuil.

In a new land, well after a King enters,
Whilst his subjects shall come to welcome him,
His perfidy shall find such an accident,
To the citizens it shall be received instead of feasts.

An unpopular ruler shall die while on tour in a conquered land. The citizens shall be joyful thereat.

75

Le pere & fils seront meurdris ensemble,	The father and son shall be murdered together,
Le prefecteur dedans son pavillon	The governor shall be so in his tent,
La mere a Tours du fils ventre aura enfle,	At Tours the mother shall be got with child by her son,
Cache verdure de fueilles papillon.	Conceal the greenness with butterfly leaves.

This depicts murder, violence and incest in the city of Tours – and the fruit of the incest shall be strangled at birth and secretly buried, the small grave covered with grass and leaves and left forever unmarked.

76

Plus Macelin que Roy en Angleterre,	More Macelin than King in England,
Lieu obscur nay par force aura l'empire,	Born in obscure place, by force shall rule the empire,
Lasche, sans foy, sans loy, seignera terre,	Of loose morals, without faith, without law, the ground shall bleed.
Son temps s'approche si pres que je souspire.	His time is drawing so near that I sigh.

Macelin is from the Latin word *Macellum*, meaning shambles. A ruler of England is to come, who will be one of the world's worst tyrants and will bring about the near ruin of his country.

77

L'Antechrist trois bien trois annichilez,	By Antichrist, three shall be brought to nothing,
Vingt & sept ans sang durera sa guerre,	His war shall last seven and twenty years,
Les heretiques morts; captifs exilez,	The heretics dead, prisoners exiled,
Son corps humain eau rouge, gresler terre.	Blood, human body, water made red, earth shrunk.

In 1918, defeated Germany (Antichrist) laid the foundations for her dream of world conquest, which came to an end exactly as Nostradamus predicted, twenty-seven years later in 1945.

78

Un Bragamas avec la langue torte	A Bragamas with his harmful tongue,
Viendra des dieux rompre le sanc- *tuaire,*	Shall come and break the God's sanctuary,
Aux heretiques il ouvrira la porte,	He shall open the gates to heretics,
En suscitant l'eglise militaire.	By raising the militant church.

The word 'Bragamas' denotes a braggard, and the meaning of the verse is that he shall cause great harm to God's sanctuary (the Roman Catholic Church) by his boastful and false claims of great power.

79

Qui par fer pere perdra, nay de Non- *naire,*	He who by iron shall destroy his father, born in Nonnaire,
De gorgon sur la fera sang perfetant,	Shall in the end carry the blood of the gorgon,
En terre estrange fera si tout de taire,	Shall in a strange country make all so silent,
Qui bruslera luy mesme & son en- *tante.*	That he shall burn himself, and his double talk.

Adolf Hitler, born in Austria, ruled Germany, and in the end perished in a bomb cellar in Berlin, probably burned to death.

80

Des innocens le sang de vefue & *vierge,*	The blood of the innocent widow and virgin,
Tant de maux faicts par moyen de *grand Roge,*	Much evil committed by the means of that great rogue,
Saints simulachres trempez en ardant *cierge,*	Holy images, dipped in burning wax candles,
De frayeur crainte ne verra nul que *boge.*	For fear, nobody shall be seen to stir.

A band of marauders shall roam the countryside, despoiling the inno-cent. Church property shall be unsafe and the populace shall be in great fear.

81

Le neur empire en desolation	The new empire in desolation,
Sera change du pole aquilonaire,	Shall be changed from the Northern Pole,
De la Sicile viendra l'emotion,	The commotion shall come from Italy,
Troubler l'emprise a Philip, tributaire.	To trouble the undertaking, tributary to Philip.

The empire of Germany shall be laid waste by invaders from both the north and south. Spain, her spiritual ally, shall be troubled at the same time.

82

Ronge long, sec, faisant du bon vallet,	Long devourer, dry, cringing and fawning,
A la parfin n'aura que son congie,	In conclusion shall have nothing, but leave to be gone,
Poignant poyson, lettres au collet,	Piercing poison and letters in his collar,
Sera saisi, eschappe, en dangie.	Shall be seized, escape and in danger.

This depicts the downfall, capture and escape of a tyrant, before whom people had cringed in fear for many years. Although he is never apprehended, he lives out his years in constant fear and danger and dies a miserable death.

83

Le plus grand voile hors du port de Zara,	The greatest sail out of the port of Zara,
Pres de Bisance fera son entreprinse,	Near Turkey shall make his undertaking,
D'ennemy perte & l'amy ne fera,	There shall be no loss of foes or friends,
Le tiers a deux fera grand pille & prise.	The third shall make a great pillage upon the two.

The Venetians (Zara) shall take the Island of Tenedos, near Constantinople, without loss of life on either side.

84

Paterne aura de la Sicile crie,	Paterno shall have out of Sicily screaming,
Tous les aprests du Goulphre de Trieste,	All the preparations of the Gulf of Trieste,
Qui s'entenda jusques a la Trinacria,	That shall be heard as far as Trinacria,
De tant de voiles, fuy, fuy, l'horrible peste.	Of so many sails, fly, fly, the horrible plague.

There seems to be a misspelling here in the word Paterno. We believe it refers to Palermo, and warns of a plague that shall strike around that vicinity.

85

Entre Bayonne & a Saincte Jean de Lux,	Between Bayonne and St Jean of Lux,
Sera pose de Mars le promottoire;	Shall be put down the promoting of Mars,
Aux Hanix d'Aquilon, Nanar hostera Lux,	From the Hunix of the North, Nanar shall take away Lux,
Puis suffoque au lict sans adjutoire.	Then shall be suffocated in bed without help.

After many years of war between France and Spain, peace was declared and a marriage arranged between the King of France and the Infanta of Spain. The last two lines have no significance and we believe they were put in merely to make up the rhyme.

86

Par Arnani, Tholose, Ville Franque,	By Arnani, Toulouse and Villefranche,
Bande infinie par le Mont Adrian,	An infinite number of people by Mont Adrian,
Passe riviere, hutin par pont la planque,	Cross rivers, noise upon the bridges and planks,
Bayonne entrer tous Bichoro criant.	Come all into Bayonne crying Bichoro.

'Bichoro' is an old French word for Victory. Bayonne, on the border of Spain, shall be successfully invaded by the French.

87

Mort conspiree viendra en plein effect,	A conspired death shall come to an effect,
Charge donnee & voyage de mort,	Charge given, and a journey of death,
Esleu, cree, receu, par siens deffaict,	Elected, created, received, by his own defeated,
Sang d'innocence devant soy par remort.	Blood of innocence before him by remorse.

A conspiracy against an elected one is here foreshadowed.

88

Dans le Sardaigne un noble Roy vien-dra,	Into Sardinia shall come a noble King,
Qui ne tiendra que trois ans le Royaume,	Who shall hold the Kingdom only three years,
Plusieurs couleurs avec soy conjoin-dra,	He shall join many colours to his own,
Luy mesme apres soin matriscome.	Himself afterwards, care, sleep, repentance come.

The Kingdom of Sardinia was created in 1720, more than 150 years after Nostradamus predicted this occurrence.

89

Pour ne tomber entre mains de son oncle,	That he might not fall into the hands of his uncle,
Qui les enfans par regner trucidez,	That had murdered his children for to rule,
Orant au peuple mettant pied sur Peloncle,	Taking away from the people, and putting his foot on the bald-headed one.
Morts & traisne entre chevaux barbez.	Killed and drawn among horses.

A bald-headed tyrant shall be killed in a dishonourable manner after having misruled the country.

90

Quand des croisez un trouve de sens trouble,	When of the crossed, one of a troubled mind,
En lieu du sacre verra boeuf cornu,	In a sacred place, shall see a horny ox,
Par vierge porc son lieu lors sera double	By virgin swine then shall his place be double,
Par Roy plus ordre ne sera soustenu.	By King henceforth, order shall not be sustained.

A madman, whose symbol is a strange cross, shall be aided in his schemes of conquest by unmitigated scoundrels (pure swine), but his power will be short-lived.

91

Parmy les champs de Rodanes entrees,	Through the fields where the Rhone meanders,
Ou les croisez seront presque unis,	Where the crossed shall be almost united,
Les deuz Brassiers en Pisces rencontrees,	The two Brassiers met in Pisces,
Et un grand nombre par deluge punis.	And a great number punished by a flood.

This quatrain continues from the preceding one, indicating the near-success of the plots of the 'madman' and his cohorts and predicting their final overthrow.

92

Loin hors du regne mis en hazard voyage,	Far from the kingdom a hazardous journey undertaken,
Grand ost duyra, pour soy l'occupera,	He shall lead a great army, which he shall make his own,
Le Roy tiendra les siens captif, ostage,	The King shall keep his prisoners and pledges,
A son retour tour pays pillera.	At his return he shall plunder all the country.

A General shall mutiny against a King. In retaliation, the King shall hold his relatives hostage; but on the General's return he shall pillage the country.

93

Sept mois sans plus obtiendra prelature	Seven months and no more he shall obtain the prelacy,
Par son decez grand scisme fera naistre,	By his decease he shall cause a great schism,
Sept mois tiendra un aurte la preture,	Another shall be seven months governor,
Pres de Venise paix union renaistre.	Near Venice peace and union shall grow again.

A sharp division of opinion will occur on the death of a Pope after only seven months in office. It will be further aggravated by the death of a governor who also held office for only seven months. When both offices are again filled, to the satisfaction of the dissenting parties, peace will reign once more.

94

Devant le lac ou plus cher fut gette,	Before the lake, wherein most dear was thrown,
De sept mois, & son ost desconfit,	Of seven months and his army discomfited,
Seront Hispans par Albannois gastez,	Spaniards shall be spoiled by Albanians,
Par delay perte en donnant le conflit.	By delaying, loss in giving the battle.

The League of Nations at Lake Geneva is meant here. Spain shall delay giving battle to the English and be the loser thereby.

95

Le seducteur sera mis dans la fosse,	The deceiver shall be put into the dungeon,
Et estache jusques a quelque temps,	And bound fast for a while,
Le clerc uny, le chef avec sa crosse,	The clergy united, the chief with his cross emblem,
Pycante droite attraira les contens.	Pointing upright, shall draw in the contented.

Those of the party of the Cross shall be supported by the rich. Dissenters shall be thrown into jail in order to keep them from spreading their doctrines of heresy.

96

La Synagogue sterile sans nul fruit,	The Synagogue barren, without fruit,
Sera recue entre les infideles,	Shall be received among the infidels,
De Babylon la fille du persuit,	In Babylon, the daughter of the persecuted,
Misere & triste luy trenchera les aisles.	Miserable and sad shall cut her wings.

There will be a period of great persecution of the Jews, and their Synagogue will become empty and desolate because of it.

97

Aux fins du var changer le pempotans,	At the finish of the war, to change the glory,
Pres du rivage, le trois beaux enfans naistre,	Near the shore shall three fair children be born,
Ruyne au peuple par aage competans,	Ruin to the people, by competent age,
Regne au pays charger plus croistre.	To change that country's Kingdom and see it grow no more.

Truly a fantastic prediction of the three Kennedy brothers involved in the affairs of government. The recessions of 1970 and 1982 are also forecast.

98

Des gens d'Eglise sang sera espanche,	The blood of churchmen shall be spilt,
Comme de l'eau en si grand abondance,	As water in such great abundance,
Et d'un long temps ne sera restranche,	And for a long time shall not be stayed,
Veue au clerc ruine & doleance.	Ruin and grievance shall be seen to the clergy.

The persecution of the clergy in Soviet-dominated countries is here anticipated.

99

Par la puissance de trois Roys temporels,	By the power of three temporal Kings,
En autre lieu mis le Sainct Siege;	The Holy See shall be put in another place,
Ou la substance de l'esprit corporel,	Where the substance of the corporeal spirit,
Sera remis & receu pour vray siege.	Shall be restored, and admitted for a true seat.

A coalition of three temporal rulers shall attempt to change the location of the Holy City.

100

Pour l'abundance de l'arme respandue,	Through the abundance of the army scattered,
Du haut en bas, par le bas au plus haut,	High will be low, low will be high,
Trop grande foy par jeu vie perdue,	Too great a faith, a life lost in jesting,
De soif mourir par abondant deffaut.	To die by thirst, through abundance of want.

Nations will increase their military might and great armies will be scattered throughout the world. The people, burdened with the increased taxes for the maintenance of these armies, will finally rebel, and world-wide revolution will follow.

Automation and the discovery of new sources of energy will make it possible to reduce all of our power requirements to a point where labour will not have to be employed more than twelve hours per week. This will eliminate the chief cause of the wars of aggression that have plagued the world since the industrial revolution for the diminishing natural resources but will also create a new and powerful Politico-Labour group that will hold the balance of power.

In the United States this shall manifest itself in a new third party built on the foundations of the Union Labor movement.

1

Seront confus plusieurs de leurs attente,
Aux habitants ne sera pardonne,
Qui bien pensoient perseverer l'attente,
Mais grand loisir ne leur sera donne.

Many shall be confounded in their expectation,
The people shall not be pardoned,
Who thought to persevere in their resolution,
But there shall not be given them a great leisure for it.

The collaborationists shall not escape; they shall be sought out and prosecuted.

2

Plusieurs viendront, & parleront de paix,
Entre Monarques & Seigneurs bien puissans,
Mais ne sera accorde de si pres,
Que ne se rendent, plus qu'autres obeissans.

Many shall come and talk of peace,
Between Monarchs and Lords very powerful,
But it shall not be agreed to it so soon,
If they do not show themselves more obedient than others.

We are just on the verge of the fulfilment of this prophecy; relations between powerful industrialists and leaders of the labour organizations shall not be settled soon, unless a greater spirit of cooperation develops.

3

Las quelle fureur, helas quelle pitie,
Il y aura entre beaucoup de gens!
On ne vit onc une telle amitie,
Qu'auront les loups a courir diligens.

See! what fury, alas what pity,
There shall be betwixt many people,
There never was seen such a friendship,
As the wolves shall have in being diligent to run.

Under the guise of political organizational activity, various elements of society shall be set at each other's throats.

4

Beaucoup de gens viendront parle-menter, *Aux grands seigneurs qui leur feront la guerre,* *On ne voudra en rien les escouter,* *Helas! si Dieu n'enuoye paix en terre.*	Many peoples shall come to speak, To great lords that shall make war against them, They shall not be admitted to a hearing, Alas! If God does not send peace upon earth.

The United Nations debates peace among warlike nations but fails to prevent or stop war.

5

Plusieurs secours viendront de tous costez, *De gens loingtains qui voudront resister;* *Ils seront tout a coup bien hastez,* *Mais ne pourront pour celte heure assister.*	Many helps shall come on all sides, Of peoples far off, that would want to resist, They shall be upon a sudden all very hasty, But for the present they shall not be able to assist.

At a time of need, when a great emergency threatens, the nations of the world will promise to aid the needy, but will not be in a position to give immediate help.

6

Las quel plaisir ont Princes estran-gers! *Garde toy bien qu'en ton pays ne vienne,* *Il y auroit de terribles dangers,* *En maints contrees, mesme en la Vienne.*	Ha! Pleasure take foreign Princes, Guard thyself lest any should come into thy country, There should be terrible dangers, In several countries, and chiefly in Vienna.

A clear warning to the nations of the world to profit by the example of Austria, and to arm themselves against subversive foreign propaganda.

CENTURY IX

1

Dans la maison du traducteur de
Boure,
Seront les lettres trouvees sur la table,
Borgne, roux blanc, chenu tiendra de
cours,
Qui changera au nouveau Connes-
table.

In the house of the translator of
Boure,
The letters shall be found upon the
table,
Blind of one eye, red, white, hoary,
shall keep its course,
Which shall change at the coming
of the new constable.

A disseminator of subversive propaganda will be exposed upon the election of a new local governor.

2

Du haut du Mont Aventin voix ouye
Vuides, vuidez de tous les deux costes,
Du sang des rouges sera l'ire assomie,
D'Arimin, Prato, Columna debotez.

From the top of Mount Aventine, a
voice was heard,
Get you gone, get you gone on all
sides,
With the blood of the red one, the
passions shall be glutted.
From Arimini and Prato, the Col-
onnas shall be driven away.

Mt Aventine is one of the seven hills of Rome. A fratricidal struggle shall take place in Italy resulting in the ruin of the Colonna family.

3

La magna vaqua a Ravenne grand trouble,	The *magna vaqua* great trouble at Ravenna,
Conduicts par quinze enserrez a Fornase;	Conducted by fifteen, shut up at Fornase,
A Rome naistra deux monstres a teste double,	At Rome, shall be born two monsters with a double head,
Sang, feu, deluge, les plus grands l'espase.	Blood, fire, flood, the greater ones astonished.

The expression 'magna vaqua' is a derisive term, meaning a great nothing. The significance of the quatrain lies in the prediction of the monstrous Rome-Berlin Axis, and the indication of its short but bloody period of existence.

4

L'an ensuyvant descouverts par deluge,	The year following being discovered by a flood,
Deux chefs esleuz, le premier ne tiendra,	Two chiefs elected, the first shall not hold,
De fuyr ombre a l'un d'eux le refuge,	To fly from shade, to one shall be a refuge
Saccagee case qui premier maintiendra.	That house shall be plundered which shall maintain the first.

A follow-up of the preceding stanza, this predicts the flight of Mussolini to Germany, after the crumbling of his power, and the eventual ruin of both him and Hitler.

5

Tiere doibt du pied au premier semblera	The third toe shall be like the first,
A un nouveau Monarque de bas haut	To a new high monarch come from a low estate,
Qui Pise & Luiques tyran occupera,	Who being a tyrant shall occupy Pisa and Lucca,
Du precedent corriger le deffault.	To correct the faults of him that preceded him.

One of low estate, pretending to improve conditions in Italy, shall seize power and become a dictator.

6

Par la Guyenne infinite d'Anglois	There shall be in Guyenne an infinite number of English,
Occuperont par nom d'Angle Aquitaine,	Who shall occupy it by the name of Aquitanian England,
Du Languedoc, I, palme Bourdelois,	On Languedoc, near the land of Bordeaux,
Qu'ils nommeront apres Barboxit-aine.	Which afterwards they shall call Barboxitain.

The prediction here is that the English will invade and occupy the west coast of France near Bordeaux. This was fulfilled in the twelfth, thirteenth, fourteenth, fifteenth, and twentieth centuries.

7

Qui ouvrira le monument trouve,	He that shall open the found sepulchre,
Et ne viendra le serrer promptement,	And shall not close it again promptly,
Mal luy viendra, & ne pourra prouve,	Evil will befall him, and he shall not be able to prove
Si mieux doit estre Roy Breton ou Normand.	Whether is best, a British or Norman King.

The discovery and opening of the tomb of Tutankhamen brought sudden and mysterious death to the discoverer and to members of his family.

8

Puisnay Roy fait son pere mettre a mort,	A Younger King causeth his father to be put
Apres conflit de mort tres in honeste:	To a dishonest death, after a battle,
Escrit trouve soupcon, donra remort,	Writing being found shall give suspicion and remorse,
Quand loup chasse pose sur la couchette.	When a hunted wolf shall pose on the cot.

A young prince, during the action of a battle, shall turn and, unseen by others, shall kill his father. However, after a short time, documents will turn up in which his murderous intentions are clearly outlined, and he shall be overthrown.

9

Quand lampe ardente de feu inexting-uible	When a lamp burning with an un-quenchable fire,
Sera trouvee au Temple des Vestales,	Shall be found in the Temple of the Vestals,
Enfant trouve, feu, eau passant par crible;	A child shall be found, water running through a sieve,
Nismes eau perir, Tholose cheoir les hales.	Nismes to perish by water, the city hall shall fall at Toulouse.

There was a custom among the Vestal Virgins of ancient Rome, pertaining to the punishment of those among them who had forfeited their honour. They were buried alive in a cave, with some bread and water and a lamp with an infinitesimal amount of oil. Beyond this reference, this quatrain holds no greater meaning.

10

Moine, Moinesse d'enfant mort expose,	Monk and Nun having exposed a dead child,
Mourir par ourse ravy par verrier,	To be killed by a bear and be carried away by a glazier,
Par Foix & Panniers le camp sera pose,	The camp shall be pitched at Foix and Panniers,
Contre Tholose, Carcas, dresser sor-rier.	Against Toulouse, Carcassone shall be against them.

Neglect of the teaching of spiritual values shall cause innocent children to fall prey to false doctrines.

11

Le just a tort a mort l'on viendra mettre	The just shall be put to death wrongfully,
Publiquement, & du milieu estaint;	Publicly, and being taken out of the midst,
Si grand peste en ce lieu viendra naistre,	So great a plague, shall break into that place,
Que les jugeans fouyr seront con-traints.	That the judges shall be compelled to run away.

Charles I was executed in 1649 in England, and the great plague occurred in 1665–1666.

12

Le tant d'argent de Diane & Mercure,	The so much silver of Diana and Mercury,
Les simulachres au lac seront trouvez;	The statues shall be found in the lake,
Le figulier cherchant argille neuve,	The potter seeking for a new clay,
Luy & les siens, d'or seront abbreuvez.	He and his, shall be filled with gold.

A smooth-tongued demagogue, ever seeking new victims under the pretence of reform, shall be shown to have betrayed and looted all.

13

Les exilez autour de la Solongne	The exiles in the tower of Sologne,
Conduicts de nuict pour marcher en l'Auxois,	Being conducted by night to go into Auxois,
Deux de Modene truculent de Bologne,	Two of Modena, the cruel of Bologna,
Mis, descouverts par feu de Burancois.	Shall be discovered by the fire of Burancois.

Pertaining to a local incident of Nostradamus's time, this merely describes the escape and eventual capture of some criminals.

14

Mis en planure chauderon d'infecteurs,	On the plain shall be put a great dyer's vat,
Vin, miel, & huyle, & bastis sur fourneaux,	Filled with wine, honey and oil and built on a furnace,
Seront plongez, sans mal dit malfacteurs,	In it shall be plunged without evil, those called malefactors,
Sept, fum, extaint au canon des Bordeaux.	Seven, summoned, at the law of Bordeaux.

Boiling in oil, a favourite punishment reserved for counterfeiters in ancient France, shall be meted out to seven persons at Bordeaux.

15

Pres de Parpan les rouges detenus,	Near unto Parpan, the red ones detained,
Ceux du milieu parfondrez menez loing;	Those of the middle sunk and carried far away,
Trois mis en pieces, & cinq mal soustenus,	Three cut in pieces and five ill sustained,
Pour le Seigneur & Prelat de Bourgoing.	For the Lord and Prelate of Bourgoing.

One of the many feuds among the cardinals and lesser clergymen is herein described.

16

De Castel Franco sortira l'assemblee,	From Spanish Franco shall come the assembly,
L'ambassadeur non plaisant fera scisme;	The Ambassador not pleased, shall make a separation,
Ceux de Riviere seront en la meslee,	Those of the Riviera, shall be in the melee,
Et au grand goulphre desnier ont l'entree.	And shall deny entry into the great gulf.

This quatrain is remarkable in that it exactly names the protagonist involved. The reference is, of course, to Franco, the Spanish Civil War and its repercussions. It also refers to the Axis powers who, after consultation with Franco, were denied domination of Gibraltar and entrance into the ('great gulf') Mediterranean.

17

Le tiers premier, pis que ne fit Neron,	The third first, worse than ever did Nero,
Vuidez vaillant que sang humain respandre,	Go out of the valiant, he shall spill much human blood,
R'edificer fera le Forneron,	He shall cause the Forneron to be rebuilt,
Siecle d'or, mort, nouveau Roy grand esclandre.	Golden age dead, new King great troubles.

'The third first' – the Third Reich (Nazi Germany), worse than Nero with massacres of Central European Jews and political dissidents.

18

Le lys Dauffois portera dans Nancy,	The Dauphin shall carry the lily into Nancy,
Jusques en Flandres Electeur de l'Empire,	As far as Flanders the Elector of the Empire,
Neufue obturee au grand Montmorency,	New hindrance to great Montmorency,
Hors lieux prouvez delivre a clere peyne.	Out of proved places, delivered to a clear pain.

An incident in the reign of Louis XIII when Nancy was conquered by the Dauphin. The events forecast occurred some ninety years after Nostradamus wrote this quatrain. Montmorency was charged with rebellion against Louis XIII and was subsequently beheaded.

19

Dans le milieu de la Forest Mayenne,	In the middle of the Forest of Mayenne,
Sol au Lyon la fourdre tombera,	Sol being in Leo, the lightning shall tumble,
Le grand bastard issu du grand du Maine,	The great bastard, begat by the great du Main,
Ce jour Fougere pointe en sang entrera.	That day Fougeres shall enter its point into blood.

An incident pertaining to one of the noble families of ancient France, this needs no further interpretation.

20

De nuict viendra par la forest de Reines,	By night shall come through the forest of Reines,
Deux pars Voltorte Herne, la pierre blanche,	Two parts Voltorte Herne, the white stone,
Le moine noir en gris dedans Varennes,	The black monk in gray within Varennes,
Esleu cap. cause tempeste, feu, sang tranche.	Elected captain, causeth tempest, fire, blood running.

At Varennes, Louis XVI, disguised in a monk's cloak, was intercepted as he attempted to escape from the Revolutionists.

21

Au temple haut de Bloys sacre Salonne,	At the high temple of Blois sacred Salon,
Nuict pont de Loyre, Prelat, Roy pernicant;	In the night the bridge of Loire, Prelate, King pernicious,
Cuiseur victoire aux marests de la Lone	A poignant victory in the marshes of Lone,
D'ou Prelature de blancs abormeant.	Whence Prelature of white shall be abortive.

During the course of one night, both a Prelate and a King will meet their deaths on a bridge, much to the rejoicing of the lesser clergy of the region.

22

Roy & sa court au lieu de langue halbe,	King and his court in the place of half language,
Dedans le temple vis a vis du palais,	Within the church, near the palace,
Dans le jardin Duc de Mantor & d'Albe,	In the garden, Duke of Mantor and of Alba,
Albe & Mantor, poignard, langue & palais.	Alba and Mantor, dagger, tongue in the palace.

This continues the story of the previous quatrain, describing the intrigue and scandal that prevailed in both the church and the palace.

23

Puisnay jouant au fresch dessous la tonne,	The youngest son playing under the tun,
Le haut du toit du millieu sur la teste,	The top of the house shall fall on his head,
Le pere Roy au temple sainct Salonne,	The king, his father, in the temple of Saint Soulaine,
Sacrifiant sacrera fum de feste.	Sacrificing shall make festival smoke.

A young prince shall be injured by the cave-in of a house. No greater significance can be gathered from this obscure verse.

24

Sur le palais au rocher des fenestres	Upon the palace at the rock of the windows,
Seront ravis les deux petits royaux,	
Passer Aurelle, Lutece, Denis clois-tres,	Shall be carried the two little royal ones,
Nonnain, Mallods avalle verts noy-aux.	To pass Aurele, Lutece, Denis cloisters,
	Nonnain, Mallods to swallow green kernels of fruit.

The journey of two children of a royal household is herein described.

25

Passant les Ponts, venir pres des ro-siers,	Going over the bridge, to come near the rose-trees,
Tard arrive plustost qu'il cuydera,	Arriving late, much sooner than he thought,
Viendront les noves Espagnols a Be-siers,	Shall come the news of Spaniards to Beziers,
Qui icelle chasse emprinse cassera.	Who shall chase this hunting undertaking.

In this particular section Nostradamus seems concerned merely with trivial events of his day; this quatrain continues in that vein, describing an incident in a hunting expedition.

26

Nice sortie sur nim des lettres aspres,	A foolish going out, caused by sharp letters,
La grand cappe fera present non sien;	The great cap shall give what is not his,
Proche de vultry aux murs de vertes capres,	Near Vultry by the walls of green capers,
Apres Plombin le vent a bon escient.	About Piombino the wind shall be in good earnest.

The Pope is here referred to as 'the great cap', and the meaning is that he shall be the arbitrator in a dispute between the Italian cities of Velitrum and Piombino.

27

De bois la garde, vent clos rond pont sera,
Haut le receu frappera de Dauphin,
Le vieux Teccon bois unis passera,
Passant plus outre du Duc le droict confin.

The fence being of wood, close wind, bridge shall be broken,
He that is received high, shall strike at the Dauphin,
The old Teccon shall pass over smooth wood,
Going to the right on the side of the Duke.

Malcontents shall attempt to form a conspiracy against the government, but it shall be put down almost immediately due to the leaders betraying their cause and going over to the side of the Duke.

28

Voille Symacle, Port Massiliolique,
Dans Venise port marcher aux Pannons,
Partir du goulfre & Synus Illyrique,
Vast a Sicille, Ligurs coups de cannons.

Symaclian sail, Massillion port,
In Venice to march towards the Hungarians,
To go away from the Gulf and Illyrian Straits,
Towards Sicily, the Genoese, with cannon shots.

A great expedition from Marseilles, arriving at Venice, shall march towards the Hungarians. The Genoese will be driven from Sicily by cannon shots.

29

Lors que celuy qu'a nul ne donne lieu,
Abandonner voudra lieu prins non pris;
Feu, nef, par saignes, bitument a Charlieu,
Seront Quintin, Balez reprins.

When he that giveth place to nobody,
Shall forsake the place taken and not taken,
Fire, ship, by bloody bitumen at Charlieu,
Then St Quentin and Calais shall be taken.

The powerful dictator shall retreat from northern France, and Calais shall be retaken from him.

30

Au port de Puola & de Sainct Nicolas,	At the harbour of Puola and St Nicolas,
Perir Normandie au Goulfre Phanatique,	A Norman ship shall perish in the Fanatic Gulf,
Cap de Bizance rues crier helas!	At the Cape of Byzantia, the streets shall cry 'Alas!'
Secors de Gaddes & du grand Philippique.	Help from Cadiz and from the Spanish King.

The reference here is to the port of Malta, which was besieged by the Turks. Philip II, King of Spain, sent an army to relieve it, which caused a great commotion among the people of Constantinople.

31

Le tremblement de terre a Mortars,	There shall be an earthquake by mortars,
Cassich, Sainct Georges a demy perfondrez,	Cassich, St George shall be half swallowed up,
Paix assoupie, la guerre esueillera,	The war shall awake the sleeping peace,
Dans temple a Pasques abysmes enfondrez.	On Easter Day, shall be a great hole sunk in the temple.

Terrific artillery fire shall shake the earth; England (St George) shall be almost defeated; the war shall spread to the ends of the earth. This refers to the bombing of the Cathedral at Coventry at Eastertime in 1941. An extremely accurate prediction.

32

De fin porphire profond collon trouvee	A deep column of fine Porphyry shall be found,
Dessous la laze escripts capitolin;	Under whose base shall be important writings,
Os, poil retors, Romain force prouvee,	Bones, hairs twisted, Roman force tried,
Classe agiter au port de Methelin.	A fleet about the port of Methelin.

The Rosetta Stone, with its important writing, was discovered in 1799 and describes events that took place in 197–196 B.C. The stone was probably ruined and buried by Roman legions in the early Christian era.

33

Hercules Roy de Rome & Danne-marc,	Hercules, King of Rome, and Denmark,
De Gaule trois Guion surnomme,	Of France three Guyon surnamed,
Trembler l'Italie & l'un de sainct Marc,	Shall cause Italy to quake and one of Venice,
Premier sur tous Monarque renomme.	He shall be above all a famous monarch.

We believe that the 'Hercules' referred to indicates the powerful and famous Napoleon, before whom all Europe quaked.

34

La parte solus mary sera mittre,	The separated husband shall wear a mitre,
Retour conflit passera sur la tuille;	Returning, battle, he shall go over the tiles,
Par cinq cens un trahye sera tiltre,	By five hundred, one dignified shall be betrayed,
Narbon & Saulce par coutaux avons d'huille.	Narbon and Saulce shall have oil by Quintal.

Here is one of the most famous and most discussed prophecies of Nostradamus, and the most remarkable for its mention of so many actual names – Narbon (Narbonne), Louis XVI's minister of war; Saulce, oilman and mayor of Varennes; and the reference to 'over the tiles' (Tuileries), which was not a palace when Nostradamus was alive, but was the location of kilns for tiles. The interpretation, then, is that the king and queen were arrested at Varennes because Saulce betrayed them to the soldiers when they came to his shop. The five hundred men were the Marseillais who attacked the palace of Tuileries and formally put the king under arrest. At that time the king was wearing the red 'mitre' of the Revolution.

35

Et Ferdinand blond sera descorte,	And Ferdinand having a troop of blond men,
Quitter la fleur, suyure le Macedon,	Shall leave the flower to follow the Macedonian,
Au grand Besoing defaillira sa routte,	At his great need his road shall fail him,
Et machera contre le Myrmidon.	And he shall go against the Myrmidon.

King Ferdinand of Bulgaria, with a German Army at his command, shall campaign against the Greeks and Macedonians, but he shall fail to conquer them.

36

Un grand Roy prins entre les mains d'un jeune,	A great King taken in the hands of a young one,
Non loin de Pasques, confusion, coup cultre,	Not far from Easter, confusion, of a knife,
Perpet. cattif temps, que foudre en la hune,	Shall commit, pitiful time, the fire at the top of the mast,
Trois freres lors se blesseront, & meurtre.	Three brothers then shall wound one another, and murder done.

The reference here is to the execution of Louis XVI, on January 21, 1793; and also indicating the confusing state of affairs in France at that time.

37

Pont & molins en Decembre versez	Bridges and mills in December overturned,
En si hault lieu montera la Garonne;	In so high a place the Garonne shall come,
Murs, edifice, Tholose renversez,	Walls, buildings, Toulouse overturned,
Qu'on ne scaura son lieu autant matronne.	So that no one shall know its place, so much Matrone.

A tremendous overflowing of the Garonne River shall occur in December with disastrous destruction of life and property.

38

L'entree de Blaye, par Rochelle & l'Anglois,	The entrance of Blaye, by Rochelle and the English,
Passera outre le grand Aemathien,	Shall go beyond the great Aemathien,
Non loing d'Agen attendra le Gaulois,	Not far from Agen shall expect the French,
Secours Narbonne deceu par entretien.	Help from Narbonne deceived by entertainment.

The English will attempt an invasion of France by way of Bordeaux (Blaye). The French will issue a call for help to the people of southern France, but, spurred on by traitors in their midst, they shall refuse to aid their countrymen.

39

En Arbissela, Vezema & Crevari	By Arbisella, Vezema and Crevari,
De nuict conduicts par Savone at-traper,	Being conducted by night to take Savonna,
Le vif Gascon, Giury & la Charry,	The quick Gascon, Giury and the Charry,
Derrier mur vieux & neuf palais grip-per.	Behind old walls and new palaces to grapple.

An incident concerning the minor disturbances between the Italians and Gascons in Nostradamus's day is described.

40

Pres de Quentin dans la forest Bour-lis,	Near St Quentin in the forest of Bourlis,
Dans l'Abbaye seront Flamens tran-chez,	In the Abbey the Flemish shall be slashed,
Les deux puisnais de coups my estour-dis,	The two younger sons half aston-ished with blows,
Suitte oppressee & garde tous haches.	The followers oppressed, and the guards cut to pieces.

An incident during the war in the Flemish lowlands between Flemings and the Spaniards, this concerns a peculiar accident which caused much talk at that time.

41

Le grand Chyren soy saisir d'Avig-non,	The great Henry shall seize upon Avignon,
De Rome lettres en miel plein d'amertume,	Letters from Rome shall come full of bitterness,
Lettre ambassade partir de Chanig-non,	Letters and embassies shall go to Chanignon,
Carpentras pris par Duc noir rouge plume.	Carpentras taken by a black Duke with a red feather.

This prophecy was fulfilled when Avignon, the one-time seat of Papal power, was seized by the French King.

42

De Barcelonne, de Gennes & Venise,	From Barcelona, from Genoa and Venice,
De la Sicille pres Monaco unis,	From Sicily near Monaco united,
Contre Barbare classe prendront la vise,	Against the Barbarians the fleet shall take her aim,
Barbar poulse bien loing jusqu'a Thunis.	The Barbarians shall be driven back as far as Tunis.

Spain and Italy, united in war, shall be driven back in Africa as far as Tunis.

43

Proche a descendre l'armee crucigere,	The crusading army being about the land,
Sera guettee par les Ismaelites,	Shall be watched by the Ismaelites,
De tous costez batus par nef Raviere,	Being beaten on all sides, the ship carried away,
Prompt assaillis de dix galeres d'eslites.	Presently assaulted by ten chosen warships.

A crusading (Christian) army shall attempt an incursion against non-believers. They shall meet with great resistance and will be forced to withdraw.

44

Migrez, migres de Geneve trestous,	Leave, leave, go forth out of Geneva, all,
Saturne d'or en fer se changera,	Saturn of gold, shall be changed into iron,
Le contre Raypoz exterminera tous,	The contrary of the positive ray shall exterminate all,
Avant l'advent le Ciel signes fera.	Before it happens, the Heavens shall show signs.

Startling! Nostradamus here foretells the advent of atomic power. He indicates clearly that this force *can* be used for useful or destructive purposes. But, with terrifying finality, he warns of the eventual destruction of our civilization by means of the release of atomic energy – holding out but one ray of hope, 'the Heavens shall show signs', meaning that we will be given one final chance to determine our destiny.

45

Ne sera soul jamais de demander,	He shall never be weary of asking,
Grand Mendosus obtiendra son empire,	Great Liar shall obtain his dominion,
Loing de la court fera contremander,	Far from the court he shall be countermanded,
Piedmont, Picart, Paris, Tyrhen le pire.	Piedmont, Picardy, Paris, Tyrrhenia the worse.

This points to the doctrine of lies and deceit which was the cornerstone of the Nazi philosophy; and indicates the final downfall of the regime.

46

Vuydez, fuyez, de Tholose les rouges,	Get you gone, fly from Toulouse, ye red ones,
Du sacrifice faire expiation,	There shall expiation be made of the sacrifice,
Le chef du mal dessous l'ombre des courges,	The chief cause of the evil under the shadow of the gourds,
Mort estrangler carne omination.	Shall be strangled, a presage to the destruction of much flesh.

In Toulouse, the red ones (cardinals) are warned of an imminent onslaught against members of the clergy.

47

Les soub signez d'indigne delivrance,	The undersigned to a worthless deliverance,
Et de la multe auront contre advis,	Shall have from the multitude a contrary advice,
Change monarque mis en perille pence,	Changing their monarch and put him in peril,
Serrez en cage se verront vis a vis.	They shall see themselves shut up in a cage.

The Islamic revolution in Iran is predicted here but the faithful end up isolated from the Arab world.

48

La grand cite d'ocean maritime,	The great maritime city of the ocean,
Environnee de marets en crystal;	Encompassed with marshes of crystal,
Dans le solstice hyemal & la prime,	In the winter solstice and the spring,
Sera tentee de vent espouvental.	Shall be tempted with a fearful wind.

The people of London are warned of the approach of a great hurricane which will cause much damage to the city.

49

Gand & Bruxles marcheront contre Anvers,	Ghent and Brussels shall march against Antwerp,
Senat de Londres mettront a mort leur Roy,	The Senate of London shall put their King to death,
Le sel & vin luy seront a l'envers,	The salt and wine shall not be able to do him good,
Pour aux avoir le regne en desarroy.	That they may have the kingdom into ruin.

This is a most remarkable prophecy, for here we have a concatenation of circumstances starting with the number of the quatrain itself, 49; and the unmistakable event referred to was the execution of King Charles I in the year 1649.

50

Mendosus tost viendra a son haut regne,	Mendosus shall soon come to his high government,
Mettant arriere un peuple Norlaris,	Putting aside a little the Norlaris,
Le rouge blesme, le mesle a l'inter-regne,	The red pale, the male at the inter-reigne,
Le jeune crainte & frayeur Barbaris.	The young fear, and dreadful barbarism.

The great liar (see Quatrain 45) shall gain supremacy, being especially successful in operations among young people.

51

Contre les rouges sectes se banderont,	Against the reds, sects shall gather themselves,
Feu, eau, fer, corde, par paix se minera,	Fire, water, iron, rope, by peace it shall be destroyed,
Au point mourir ceux qui machineront,	Those that shall conspire shall be put to death,
Fors un que monde sur tout ruynera.	Except one, who above all shall ruin the world.

The latter half of the twentieth century best fits this prophecy with the anti-Communist movement in eastern Europe and Latin America. Stalin or Hitler certainly fulfil line 4.

52

La paix s'approche d'un coste & la guerre,	Peace is coming on one side, the war on the other,
Oncques ne fut la poursuite si grande,	There never was so great a pursuit,
Plaindre homme, femme, sang innocent par terre,	Man, woman, shall bemoan, innocent blood shall be spilt,
Et ce sera de France a toute bande.	It shall be in France at all sides.

Nostradamus here foresees the conflict between peace groups and militants. Also bombing of civilians, particularly during the anti-French rebellion in Algeria in the 1960s.

53

Le Neron jeune dans les trois cheminees,	The young Nero in the three chimneys,
Fera de paiges vifs pour ardoir jetter,	Shall cause pages to be thrown to be burnt alive,
Heureux qui loing sera de tels menees,	Happy shall be he, who shall be far from this doing.
Trois de son sang le feront mort guetter.	Three of his own blood shall cause him to be put to death.

A tyrannical leader (here referred to as a Nero) shall cause much destruction of life and property. Three men of his own class shall destroy him.

54

Arrivera au port de Corsibonne,	There shall come into the port of Corsibonne
Pres de Ravenna qui pillera la dame,	Near Ravenna, those that shall plunder the lady,
En mer profonde legat de la Ulisbonne,	In the deep sea shall be the Ambassador of Lisbon,
Sous roc cachez raviront septante ames.	The hidden under the rock, shall carry away seventy souls.

Corsica shall be the birthplace of one (Napoleon) who shall plunder Italy and cause great damage to the whole of Europe.

55

L'horrible guerre qu'en occident s'appreste;	The horrible war is in preparation in the west,
L'an ensuivant viendra la pestilence,	The year following shall come the plague,
Si fort terrible, que jeune, vieil, ne beste,	So strangely terrible, that young, old, nor beast shall escape.
Sang, feu, Mercu, Mars, Jupiter en France.	Blood, fire, Mercury, Mars, Jupiter in France.

In the western area, a horrible war is in preparation; following this will come a terrible plague, such as the world has never seen before.

56

Camp pres de Noudam passera Goussanville,	A camp shall by Noudam pass Goussanville,
Et a Maiotes laissera son enseigne,	And shall leave its flag at Maiotes,
Convertira en instant plus de mille,	And shall in an instant convert more than a thousand,
Cherchant les deux remettre en chaine & legne.	Seeking to put the two parties in good understanding.

Events and towns related here are of no importance now, but had local significance in Nostradamus's day.

57

Au lieu de Drux un roy reposera,	In the place of Drux a king shall repose,
Et cherchera loy changeant d'ana-theme,	And shall seek a law changing anathema,
Pendant le ciel si tresfort tonnera,	In the meanwhile the heaven shall thunder so strongly,
Portee neufue Roy tuera soymesme.	That a new gate shall kill the King himself.

Drux is a city in Normandy; and in this region the King shall attempt to alter the local religious customs, without success.

58

Au coste gauche a l'endroit de Vitri,	On the left coast over against Vitry,
Seront guettez les trois rouges de France,	The three red ones of France shall be watched for,
Tous assoumez rouge, noir non meurdry,	All the red shall be beaten to death, the black not murdered,
Par les Bretons remis en asseurance.	By the Britons set up again in security.

The British shall re-establish a government in France; radicals shall be eliminated from any participation in it.

59

A le Ferte prendra la Vidame,	In the Ferte the Vidame shall take,
Nicol tenu rouge qu'avoit produit la vie,	Nicol, reputed red, who is the product of life,
La grand Loyse naistra que fera clame,	The great Louis shall be born, who shall lay claim,
Donnant Bourgongne a Bretons par envie.	Giving Burgundy to the Britons through envy.

The reds shall be beaten by the opposite party, with the aid of a British leader named Louis, who will ask for payment in the form of an alliance between France and England.

60

Conflit barbare, en la cornere noire,	A barbarous fight in the black corner,
Sang espandu trembler la Dalamatie,	
Grand Ismael mettra son promontoire,	Blood shall be spilt, Dalmatia shall tremble for fear,
Ranes trembler, secours Lusitanie.	Great Ishmael shall set up his promontory,
	Frogs shall tremble, Portugal shall bring succour.

Inter-sectional warfare among the Mohammedans is here predicted.

61

La pille faite a la coste marine,	The plunder shall be made on the sea coast,
Incite nova & parens amenez,	
Plusieurs de Malte par le fait de Messine,	Incited by new people and friends brought up,
Estroit serrez seront mal guerdonnez.	Many of Malta, for the fact of Messina,
	Being kept close, shall be ill rewarded.

A coalition of small nations, hitherto considered peaceful and harmless, shall attempt to gain control of Europe.

62

Au grand de Cheramonagora,	To the great one of Cheramonagora,
Seront croisez par rangs tous attachez,	
Le Pertinax Oppi, & Mandragora,	Shall be crossed by ranges, all tied up.
Raugon d'Octobre le tiers seront laschez.	The Pertinax Oppi, and Mandragora,
	Raugon the third of October shall be set loose.

There is a warning implicit in the words of this quatrain, of a world-shaking event that will take place on October third.

63

Plainctes & pleurs, cris & grands hurlements,	Complaints and tears, cries and great howlings,
Pres de Narbon a Bayonne & en Foix,	Near Narbonne, Bayonne and in Foix,
O quel horribles, calamitez, change-mens,	O what horrid calamities and changes,
Avant que Mars revolu quelquefois	Before Mars has made somewhat his revolution.

Much disturbance in France is foreseen, with many changes taking place, leading to a completely reorganized government.

64

L'Aemathion passer monts Pyrenees,	The invader shall pass the Pyrenean Mountains,
En Mars Narbon ne fera resistance,	In March Narbonne shall make no resistance,
Par mer & terre fera si grand menee,	By sea and land he shall make so much ado,
Cap. n'ayant terre seure pour demeurance.	Cap. shall not have safe ground to live in.

An invasion shall come to France, by way of the Spanish frontier.

65

Dedans le coing de Luna viendra rendre,	He shall come into the corner of Luna,
Ou sera prins & mis en terre estrange,	Where he shall be taken and put in a strange land,
Les fruicts immeurs seront a grand esclandre,	The green fruits shall be in great disorder,
Grand vitupere, a l'un grande louange.	A great shame, to one shall be great praise.

The moon landing is predicted in lines 1 and 2. A remarkable forecast.

66

Paix, union sera & changement,	Peace, union, shall be and profound changes,
Estats, offices, bas hault, & hault bien bas,	Estates, offices, the low high and the high very low,
Dresser voyage, le fruict premier, torment,	A journey shall be prepared for, the first fruit, pains,
Guerre cesser, civils proces, debats.	War shall cease, also civil processes and strife.

A Utopian age shall come into being in the course of time, but not without pain.

67

Du hault des monts a l'entour de Dizere,	From the top of the mountains about Dizere,
Port a la roche Valent, cent assemblez,	Gate at the rock Valence, a hundred gathered together,
De Chasteau-Neuf, Pierrelate, en Douzere,	From Chateau Neuf, Pierrelate, in Douzere,
Contre le Crest, Romains for assemblez.	Against the Crest, Romans shall be assembled.

This prophecy, obscure and meaningless to us, was directed to the people in the provinces of Dauphiné and Languedoc, in which all the towns and rivers mentioned were situated.

68

Du mont Aymar sera noble obscurcie,	From Mount Aymar shall proceed a noble obscurity,
Le mal viendra au joinct de Saone & Rhosne,	The evil shall come to the joining of the Saone and Rhone,
Dans bois cachez soldats jour de Lucia,	Soldiers shall be hid in the wood on St Lucia's Day,
Que ne fut onc un si horrible throsne.	So that there was never such a horrible throne.

A group of men, banded together in a conspiracy to overthrow the local government, shall attempt a march on the city of Lyons, but shall be overcome by soldiers during a battle in the forest just outside the city.

69

Sur le mont de Bailly & la Bresse,
Seront cachez de Grenoble les fiers,
Outre Lyon, Vien, eulx si grand gresle,
Langoult en terre n'en restera un tiers.

Upon the Mount of Bailly and the country at Bresse,
Shall be hidden the fierce ones of Grenoble,
Beyond Lyons, Vienna, upon them shall fall such a hail,
That languishing on the ground, not even a third shall be left.

A fearful hail (bombardment) shall fall on parts of Italy and Austria, destroying two-thirds of the population.

70

Harnois trenchans dans les flambeaux cachez
Dedans Lyon le jour de Sacrement,
Ceux de Vienne seront trestour hachez,
Par les Cantons Latins, Mascon eront.

Sharp weapons shall be hidden in burning weapons,
In Lyons the day of the Sacrament,
Those of Vienna shall be cut to pieces,
By the Latin Cantons, after the example of Mascon.

This foretells the advent of terrible incendiary weapons; and deplores the rise of a science that may lead mankind to ultimate destruction.

71

Aux lieux sacrez, animaux veu a Trixe,
Avec celuy qui n'osera le jour,
A Carcassonne pour disgrace propice,
Sera pose pour plus ample sejour.

The place of sacred objects shall be seen at Trixe,
With him that shall not dare in the day,
In Carcassone for a favourable disgrace,
He shall be set to make a longer stay.

Holy objects in France shall be defiled, by temporary invaders.

72

Encor seront les saincts temples pollus,
Et expillez par Senat Tholosain,
Saturne deux trois siecles revollus,
Dans Avril, May, gens de nouveau
    levain.

Once more shall the Holy Temple
    be polluted,
And depredated by the Senate of
    Toulouse,
Saturn two, three cycles revolving,
In April, May, people of a new
    leaven.

According to this prophecy, there will be a complete revision of the basic concepts of religion about the year 2150 (600 years after it was written), and a new world order will arise (possibly one religion for all).

73

Dans Fois entrez Roy cerule Turban,
Et regnera moins evolu Saturne,
Roy turban blanc, Bizance coeur ban,
Sol, Mars, Mercure, pres la hurne.

In Foix shall come a King with a
    blue Turban,
And shall reign before Saturn is
    revolved,
Then a King with a white turban
    shall make Turkey quake,
Sol, Mars, Mercury being near the
    top of the mast.

Foix, a city in southern France, shall be the centre of military disturbances, culminating in the selection of a ruler who will bring great prosperity.

74

Dans la cite de Fertsod homicide,
Fait & fait multe beuf arant ne
    macter,
Retours encores aux honneurs d'Arte-
    mide,
Et a Vulcan corps morts sepulturer.

In the city of Fertsod, murder shall
    be done,
Causing a fine to be laid for killing a
    plow ox,
There shall be a return of the hon-
    ours due to Artemide,
And Vulcan shall bury dead bodies.

In this quatrain, Nostradamus pays honour to a spiritual 'contemporary', the writer Artemidorus (100 B.C.), who was widely known in his day for his writings on augurs, and whose books on dream interpretation are still extant.

75

De l'Ambraxie & du pays de Thrace,	From Ambraxia, and from the country of Thracia,
Peuple par mer, mal & secours Gaulois,	People by sea, evil and French assistance,
Perpetuelle en Provence la trace,	The trace of it shall be perpetual in Provence,
Avec vestiges de leur coustumes & loix.	The footsteps of their customs and laws remaining.

Provence is shown here by Nostradamus to have been settled originally by Thracians, with vestiges of the original laws and customs still remaining.

76

Avec le noir rapax & sanguinaire,	With the black and rapacious near a bloody peace,
Yssu de peaultre de l'inhumain Neron,	Descended from the hide of the inhuman Nero,
Emmy deux fleuves main gauche militaire,	Between two rivers, by the left military hand,
Sera meurtry par Joyne Chaulveron.	He shall be murdered by Joyn Caulveron.

One of a like character to Nero, black and rapacious, shall meet a violent death at the hands of revolutionaries.

77

Le regne prins le Roy conviera,	The Kingdom being taken the King shall invite,
La dame prinse a mort jurez a sort,	The lady taken to death,
La vie a Royne fils on desniera,	The life shall be denied unto the Queen's son,
Et la pillex au forte de la consort.	And the Pellex shall be at the height of her ease.

This is a prophecy of the French Revolution. The government was overthrown by revolutionaries, the King deposed, and the Queen guillotined.

78

La Dame Greque de beaute laydique,	The Grecian Lady of exquisite beauty,
Heureuse faicte de proces innumerable,	Made happy from innumerable quarrels,
Hors translatee au Regne Hispanique,	Being translated into the Spanish Kingdom,
Captive prinse mourir mort miserable.	Shall be made a prisoner, and die a miserable death.

The reference here is to Elizabeth of Valois who was married to King Philip II of Spain. According to historical gossip she was in love with another and never found any happiness in her royal liaison.

79

Le chef de classe, par fraude stratageme,	The commander of the fleet by fraud and stratagem
Fera timides sortir de leurs galleres,	Shall cause the timid ones to come out of their galleys,
Sortis meurtris chef renieux de cresme,	Come out murdered, chief renouncer of baptism,
Puis par l'embusche luy rendront les saleres.	After that, by an ambush, they shall give him his salary.

In 1932 Nordhoff and Hall related the famous story of the mutiny on the *Bounty*, which occurred in 1789, and recalled the setting adrift of the infamous Captain Bligh by his galley crewmen.

80

Le Duc voudra les siens exterminer,	The Duke shall endeavour to exterminate his own,
Envoyera les plus forts, lieux estranges,	And shall send away the strongest of them into strange places,
Par tyrannie Bize & Luc ruyner,	By tyranny Pisa and Lucca will be ruined,
Puis le Barbares sans vin feront vendanges.	The Barbarians shall make vintage without wine.

The ruthless plans for conquest of an Italian Duke are here described.

81

Le Roy ruse entendra ses embusches,
De trois quartiers ennemis assaillir,
Un nombre estrange larmes de co-
queluches,
Viendra Lamprin de tracteur faillir.

The King by a ruse, shall hear of
the ambushes,
And shall assail his enemies on
three sides,
A strange number of friars' tears,
Shall cause Lamprin to desert the
traitor.

The King shall use strategy to defend himself, and the influence of the
clergy shall cause the 'Light Prince' to come to the King's aid.

82

Par le deluge & pestilence forte,
La cite grande de long temps assiegee,
La sentinelle & garde de main morte,
Subite prinse, mais de nul outragee.

By the deluge and violent plague,
The great city having been long
besieged,
The sentinel and watch being surprised,
Shall be taken suddenly, but hurt
by nobody.

A violent earthquake shall crack dams and thereby inundate a great city
(Los Angeles? Teheran?). Mountains of water shall drown the city.

83

Sol vingt de Taurus si fort terre trembl-
er,
Le grand theatre remply ruinera,
L'air, ciel & terre, obscurcir & troub-
ler,
Lors l'infidele Dieu, & saincts vo-
guera.

The sun being in the 20th of
Taurus, the earth shall so quake,
That it shall fill and ruin the great
theatre,
The air, the heaven and the earth
shall be so obscured and
troubled,
That unbelievers shall call upon
God, and his saints.

The tenth of May is foretold as the exact day of the great Cataclysm.

84

Roy espose parfaira l'Hecatombe,	The King exposed shall fulfil the Hecatomb,
Apres avoir trouve son origine,	After he has found out his off-spring,
Torrent ouvrir de marbre & plomb la tombe,	A torrent shall open the sepulchre, made of marble and lead,
D'un grand Romain d'enseigne Medusine.	Of a great Roman, with a Medusian design.

A so-called revolutionary movement, based on the ideas advocated in Ancient Rome, is here compared to the Medusa's head, in that it turns the beholders thereof into stone, meaning that its concepts will lead to a static and unprogressive society.

85

Passer Guienne, Languedoc & le Rhosne,	They shall pass over Gascony, Languedoc, and the Rhone,
D'Agen tenans de Marmande & la Reole,	From Agen keeping Marmande, and the Reale,
D'ouvrir par for parroy, Phocen tiendra son throsne,	To open the wall by faith Phocen shall keep his throne.
Conflict aupres sainct Pol de Manseole.	A battle shall be by St Paul of Manseole.

Armies shall pass through all the above-mentioned French towns, during the course of a great war.

86

Du Bourg La Reyne parviedrot droit a Chartres,	From Bourge, La Reyne they shall come straight to Chartres,
Et feront pres du Pont Anthony pause,	And shall make a stand near Anthony's Bridge,
Sept pour la paix cauteleux comme Martres,	Seven for peace as crafty as Martres,
Feront entree d'armes a Paris clause.	They shall enter in Paris besieged with an army.

This continues the story in the preceding stanza, and foretells a march on Paris, culminating in its taking.

87

Par la forest de Touphon essartee
Par hermitage sera pose le temple,
De Duc d'Estampes per sa ruse inven-
tee,
De Montleheri prelat donra exemple.

By the forest of Touphon cut off,
At the hermitage shall the temple
be set,
The Duke of Prints by his invented
ruse,
Shall give an example to the prelate
of Montleheri.

By the ruse of inflated money, the temporal governments shall overcome the authority of the Church.

88

Calais, Arras secours a Theroanne,
Paix & semblant simulera l'escoute,
Soul de d'Alobrox descendre par
Roane,
Destornay peuple qui defera la routte.

Calais, Arras shall give help to the
Theroanne,
Peace or the like, shall dissemble
the hearing,
Soldiers of Allobrox shall descend
by Roanne,
People persuaded, shall spoil the
march.

An incident in a war between France and Spain, concerning the Netherlands.

89

Sept ans sera Philip, fortune prospere,
Rabaissera des Barbares l'effort,
Puis son midi perplex, revours af-
faire,
Jeune Ogmion abysmera son fort.

Seven years of prosperous fortune
shall Philip have,
And shall beat down the attempt of
the Barbarians,
Then in his heyday, perplexed with
misdirections,
Young Ogmion shall pull down his
strength.

The story here is clearly that of the career of Philip II of Spain.

90

Un grand Capitaine de la grand Germanie,	A Captain of great Germany,
Se viendra rendre par simule secours,	Shall come to yield himself by simulating help.
A Roy des Roys, ayde de Pannonie,	To the King of Kings, with the help of Hungary,
Que sa revolte fera de sang grand cours.	So that his revolt shall cause great bloodshed.

Hitler, offering help to Hungary, shall involve her in the general ruin that follows.

91

L'horrible peste Perynthe & Nicopolle,	The horrid pestilence shall be in Corinth and Nicopol,
Le Chersonnez tiendra & Marceloune,	The Crimeans and the Macedonians also,
La Thessalie vestera l'Amphipolle,	It shall waste Thessaly and Amphipolis,
Mai incogneu, & le refus d'Anthoine.	An unknown evil and the refusal of Anthony.

A great plague shall befall the places mentioned.

92

Le Roy voudra dans cite neufve entrer,	The King shall desire to enter into the New City,
Par ennemis expugner l'on viendra,	With foes they shall come to overcome it,
Captif libere faulx dire & perpetrer,	The prisoner being freed, shall speak and act falsely,
Roy dehors estre, loin d'ennemis tiendra.	The King being gotten out, shall keep far from enemies.

The New City shall be besieged by a powerful person helped by spies within.

93

Les ennemis du fort bien esloignez,	The enemies being a good way from the fort,
Par chariots conduict le Bastion,	By chariots shall be conducted to the Bastion,
Par sur les murs de Bourges esgrong-nez	From the top of Bourges' walls they shall be cut less,
Quand Hercules battra l'Haema-thion.	When Hercules shall beat the Bloody One.

Bourges, a city in France, south of Paris, shall be in the direct path of a march on Paris, and shall be devastated by the invading army.

94

Foibles galeres seront unis ensemble,	Weak ships shall be united together,
Ennemis faux, le plus fort en rempart,	False enemies, the strongest shall be fortified,
Foible assaillies Vratislave tremble,	Weak assaults, and yet Bratislava quakes for fear,
Lubecq & Mysne tiendront Barbare part.	Lubeck and Misne shall take the part of the Barbarians.

Weak nations, although not trusting each other, shall be forced to unite. Bratislava, a Czecho-Slovakian city, Lubeck and Misne shall be in the hands of the Germans.

95

Le nouveau faict conduira l'exercite,	The New Man shall lead up the Army,
Proche Apame jusqu'aupres du rivage,	Near Apame, till near the bank,
Tendant secours de Milanoise eslite,	Carrying aid of elite forces from Milan,
Duc yeux prive, a Milan fer de cage.	The Duke deprived of his eyes, and an iron cage at Milan.

A mob of rebellious soldiers aided by civilians captured and lynched Mussolini and his paramour at Milan in April, 1945.

96

Dans cite entrer exercit desniee,	Being denied entrance into the city,
Duc entrera par persuasion,	The Duke shall enter by persuasion,
Aux foibles portes clam armee amenee,	To the weak gates, secretly the army being brought,
Mettront feu, mort, de sang effusion.	Shall put all to fire and sword.

Because of the clarity of the English verse, we feel that this needs no further interpretation.

97

De mer copies en trois parts divisees,	A fleet being divided into three parts,
A la seconde les vivres failleront,	The living shall fail the second part,
Desesperez cherchant Champs Elisees,	Being in despair, they shall seek the Champs Elysées,
Premiers en breches entrez victoire auront.	And entering the breach first, shall obtain victory.

Three armies shall converge at Paris; the second one will enter it first, and parade on the Champs Elysées.

98

Les affligez par faut d'un seul taint,	The afflicted by fault of one, only died,
Contremanant a partie opposite,	Carrying against the opposite part,
Aux Lygonnois mandera que contraint,	Shall send word to those of Lyons, they shall be compelled,
Seront de rendre le grand chef de Molite.	To surrender the great chief of Molite.

The reference here, we believe, is to Laval and the role he played in the betrayal of France.

99

Vent Aquilon fera partir le siege,
Par murs jetter cendres, chaulx, &
poussiere,
Par pluye apres qui leur fera bien
piege,
Dernier secours encontre leur frontiere.

The North Wind shall cause the
siege to be raised
They shall throw ashes, lime and
dust,
By a rain after they shall be a trap to
them,
It shall be the last help against the
frontier.

The siege of a city will be lifted and an enemy driven back by a wind storm of such ferocity as to make it impossible for the armies to make use of their weapons.

100

Navalle pugne nuict sera superee,
Le feu, aux naves a l'Occident ruine;
Rubriche neuve, la grand nef coloree,
Ire a vaincu, & victoire en bruine.

In a sea fight night shall be overcome,
By fire, to the ship of the west, ruin
shall happen,
A new stratagem, the great ship
coloured,
Anger to the vanquished, and victory in a fog.

This tells of a naval battle which took place at night, in which the firing from both sides was so constant and fierce, that it literally turned night into day.

CENTURY
X

1

A l'ennemy, l'ennemy foy promise,
Ne se tiendra, les captifs retenus;
Prins preme mort, & le reste en che-
mise,
Donnant le reste pour estre secourus.

To the enemy, the enemy faith
promised,
Shall not be kept, the captives will
be detained,
The first taken, put to death, and
the rest stripped,
Giving the rest that they may be
rescued.

American embassy personnel were held hostage in Iran for over a year
and then, fortunately, were released.

2

Voile gallere voil de net cachera,
La grande classe viendra sortir la
moindre,
Dix naves proches le tourneront
poulser,
Grand vaincue, unies a soy joindre.

The galley and the ship shall hide
their sails,
The great fleet shall make the little
ones come out,
Ten ships approaching shall turn
and push it,
The great being vanquished, they
shall unite together.

This is a prophetic description by Nostradamus of the defeat of the
Spanish Armada, August, 1588.

3

En apres cinq troupeau ne mettra hors,	After five he shall not put out his flock,
Un fuytif pour Penelon laschera,	He will let loose a runaway for Penelon,
Faux murmurer secours venir par lors,	There shall be a false rumour, help shall then come,
Le chef, le siege lors abandonnera.	The commander shall forsake the siege.

A small group of men, defending their city against a large enemy army, sends out a scout who succeeds in getting through the enemy lines and in bringing back enough reinforcements to drive back the enemy and lift the siege.

4

Sur la minuict conducteur de l'armee,	About midnight the leader of the army,
Se sauvera subit esvanovy,	Shall save himself, vanishing suddenly,
Sept ans apres la fame non blasmee,	Seven years after his fame shall not be blamed,
A son retour ne dira oncq ouy.	And at his return he shall never say yes.

The career of General Douglas MacArthur fulfils this prophecy. In March 1942 he withdrew from Corregidor in the Philippines only to return, invade, and recapture the islands in 1944; however, seven years later he was relieved of his command. And to his quest for the presidency, he never did say yes.

5

Albi & Castres seront nouvelle ligue,	Albi and Castres shall make a new league,
Neuf Arriens, Lisbon & Portuges,	Nine Aryans, Lisbon and Portuguese,
Carcas, Tholose consurmeront leur brigue,	Carcassone, Toulouse, shall make an end of their confederacy,
Quand chef neuf monstre de Lauragues.	When the new chief shall come from Lauragais.

Although this verse is most obscurely worded and weighed down with many seemingly unconnected names, we gather from it the prognostication of the rise of the theory of Aryan supremacy which was one of the basic concepts of the Hitler regime.

6

Gardon a Nemans, eaux si hault desborderont, *Qu'on coidera Deucalion renaistre,* *Dans le colosse la plus part fuyront,* *Vesta sepulchre feu estaint apparoistre.*	Gardon at Nismes, waters shall overflow so high, That they think Deucalion be born again, Most of them will run into the colossus, And a sepulchre, and fire extinguished, shall appear.

The description here is of the great flood of the River Gardon, in 1557, which Nostradamus likens to that which was sent upon the world by Zeus and of which Deucalion and his wife were the sole survivors.

7

Le grand conflit qu'on apreste a Nancy, *L'Aemathien dira tout le soubmets,* *L'Isle Britanne par vin, sel en soley,* *Hem. mi. deux Phi. long temps ne tiendra Mets.*	A great war is in preparation at Nancy, The Aemathien shall say, submit to all, to me, The British Isle shall be put in want for salt and wine, The two bloody friends shall keep Metz long.

A war between France and Germany, instigated by the arrogant demands on the part of the rulers of Germany, is forecast. The British Isles will be involved much to the distress and suffering of the English people. France will be occupied for some years by the 'two bloody friends', but will finally be liberated by the joint efforts of her allies.

8

Index & Poulse parfondera le front, *De Senegalia le Compte a son fils propre,* *La Myrnamee par plusieurs de plain front,* *Trois dans sept jour blessez more.*	Index and Poulse shall break the forehead, Of the son of the Earl of Senegal, The Myrnamee by many at a full bout, Three within seven days shall be wounded to death.

The reference here seems to be almost purposely obscured by apparently meaningless names; nevertheless, it seems clear to me that it points directly to the situation in North Africa during the early days of World War II, especially pertaining to the death of Admiral Darlan.

9

De Castillon figuires jour de brune,
De femme infame naistra souverain prince,
Surnom de chausses per hume luy posthume,
Onc Roy ne fut si pire en sa province.

Out of Castilon, signalized on a misty day,
From an infamous woman shall be born a sovereign Prince,
His surname shall be from breeches, born after his father's death,
Never a King was worse in his province.

The story told in this and the following two stanzas concerns the illegitimate son of a woman of ill repute, born after the death of his father, who grows up to be a powerful and tyrannical figure in the politics of his day.

10

Tasche de murdre, enormes adultres,
Grand ennemy de tout le genre humain,
Que sera pire qu'ayeuls, oncles, ne peres,
En fer, feu, sanguin & inhumain.

Endeavour of murder, enormous adulteries,
A great enemy of all humanity,
That never saw worse grandfathers, uncles, or fathers,
In iron, water, bloody and inhumane.

Continuing the story told above, the infamous deeds of this tyrant are further described.

11

Dessous jonchere du dangereux passage,
Fera passer le Posthume sa bande,
Les monts Pyrens passer hors son bagage,
De Parpignan couvrira Duc a Tende.

Below Jonchere a dangerous passage,
The Posthume shall cause his army to go over.
And his baggage to go over the Pyrenean Mountains,
A Duke shall run from Perpignan to Tende.

Here we are told that the tyrant becomes the leader of an army, powerful enough to conquer Spain and cause other nations to fear him.

12

Esleu en Pape, d'esleu sers mocque,	Elected for a Pope, from elected shall be baffled,
Subit soudain, esmeu prompt & timide,	Upon a sudden, moved promptly and fearful,
Par trop bon doux a mourir provoque,	By too much sweetness provoked to die,
Crainte estainte la nuit de sa mort guide.	His fear being out in the night, shall make a guide.

After the death of Pope Innocent IX, Cardinal Santa Severina was elected Pope. However, his election was declared illegal and Clement VIII was chosen in his place, for which shortly after the deposed one died of grief.

13

Soubs la pasture d'animaux ruminants,	Under the pasture of cud-chewing animals,
Par eux conduicts au ventre Herbipolique,	Conducted by them to the Herbipolique belly
Soldats cachez, les armes bruit menants,	Soldiers hidden, the weapons making a noise,
Non loing temptez de cite Anti-polique.	Shall be attempted not far from the Free City.

The shepherds of the Falkland Islands shall counterattack the insurgent Argentinians. All of this is predicted 'not far from the Free City' of Port Stanley. Much bloodshed, although a limited operation.

14

Urnel Vaucile sans conseil de soy mesmes,	Urnel-Vaucile, without advice of his own,
Hardit timide, par crainte prins vaincu,	Stout and fearful, by fear taken and overcome,
Accompagne de plusieurs putains blesmes,	Pale and in company of many whores,
A Barcellone aux Chartreux connaincu.	Shall be convicted at Barcelona by the Charterhouse.

This stanza is a reading of the horoscope of a contemporary of Nostradamus, Urnel Vaucile.

15

Pere Duc vieux d'ans & de soif charge,	A Father Duke aged and very thrifty,
Au jour extreme fils desniant les guiere,	In his extremity his son denying him the pail,
Dedans le puis vif mort viendra plonge,	Alive into a well, where he shall be drowned,
Senat au fil la mort longue & legere.	The Senate shall give to the son a death sentence.

An ungrateful son shall lead his father to a well and drown him; he is later put to death for the crime.

16

Heureux au Regne de France heureux de vie,	Happy in the Kingdom of France in his life,
Ignorant sang, mort fureur, & rapine,	Ignorant of blood, death, fury of taking by force,
Par non flateurs seras mis en envie,	By no flatterers shall be envied,
Roy desrobe, trop de foy en cuisine.	King robbed, too much faith in kitchens.

This quatrain deals with Louis XVIII, an excessive wine-consuming gourmet, who mounted the throne in 1814 while Napoleon was in exile on Elba. However, after Napoleon's escape from Elba and the ensuing famous 100 days, Louis fled. After Waterloo, Louis again assumed the throne and ruled from 1814–1824.

17

La Reyne Ergaste voyant sa fille blesme,	Queen Ergast seeing her daughter pale,
Par un regret dans l'estomach enclos,	By a regret contained in her breast,
Crys lamentables seront lors d'Angolesme,	Then shall lamentable cries come out of Angolesme,
Et au germain mariage forclos.	And the marriage shall be denied to the German.

Marie Antoinette's daughter, Madame Royale, was married to the Count of Angoulême in 1799.

18

Le rang Lorrain fera place a Vandosme,	The house of Lorraine shall give place to Vendôme,
Le haut mis bas, & le bas mis en haut,	The high pulled down, the low raised up,
Le fils d'Hamon sera esleu dans Rome,	The sons of Haman shall be elected in Rome,
Et les deux grands seront mis en defaut.	And the two great ones shall not appear.

The reference here is to the downfall and subsequent triumph of two rival ruling Houses of France.

19

Jour que sera par Royne saluee,	The day that she shall be saluted Queen,
Le jour apres le salut, la priere;	The next day after the evening prayer,
Le compte fait raison & valbuee,	The account being settled and paid,
Par avant humble oncques ne fut si fiere.	She that was humble before, never was so proud.

A woman of lowly birth shall become a Queen; and as soon as the crown is placed upon her head she shall assume a regal and arrogant manner. This refers to the Maharani of Sikkim (the former Hope Cooke of NY) and also Queen Noor al-Hussein of Jordan (the former Elizabeth Halaby).

20

Tous les amys qu'auront tenu party,	All the friends that shall have taken the part,
Pour rude en lettres mis mort & saccage	Of the unlearned, put to death and robbed,
Biens publiez par fixe, grand neanty,	Goods sold at public auction, great emptiness,
Onc Romain peuple ne fut tant outrage.	Never Roman people were so much outraged.

A period of oppression of liberals shall occur, accompanied by general confiscation of their property. Worldwide conservative and reactionary movements are underway.

21

Par le despit du Roy soustenant moindre,	To spite the King, who took the part of the weaker,
Sera meurdry luy presentant les bagues,	He shall be murdered, presenting the jewels,
Le pere & fils voulant noblesse poindre,	The father and the son going to vex the nobility,
Fait comme a Perce jadis feirent les Magues.	It shall be done to them as the Magi did at Persia.

A King and his son, taking the part of the people against the nobility, shall be murdered by a method once used by the ancient Persians when they desired to dispose of their rulers.

22

Pour ne vouloir consentir au divorce,	For not consenting to the divorce,
Qui puis apres sera cogneu indigne,	Which afterwards shall be acknowledged unworthy,
Le Roy des Isles sera chasse par force,	The King of the Island shall be expelled by force,
Mis a son lieu que de Roy n'aura signe.	And another subrogated who shall have no mark of the King.

Nostradamus here predicts the fate of Edward VIII, who abdicated the English throne in 1936 when he refused to give up Wallis Warfield Simpson, a divorcée and an American commoner.

23

Au peuple ingrat faictes les remonstrances,	The remonstrances being made to ingrates,
Par lors l'armee se saisira d'Antibe,	At the time the army shall seize Antibes,
Dans l'arc Monech feront les dolesances,	In the vault of Monaco, they shall make their complaints,
Et a Freius l'un l'autre prendra ribe.	And at Freius both of them shall take their share.

A period of unrest and inter-city warfare in Southern France is here described.

24

Le captif prince aux Itales vaincu,	The captive prince captured in Italy,
Passera Gennes par mer jusqu'a Marseille,	Shall pass by sea through Genoa to Marseilles,
Par grand effort des forens survaincu,	By great efforts of foreign forces overcome,
Sauf coup de feu, barril liqueur d'a-bielle.	A barrel of honey shall save him from fire.

Napoleon escaped from Elba on March 1, 1815, and landed near Marseilles at Cannes. His emblem was the bee ('barrel of honey').

25

Par Nebro ouvrir de Brisanne passage,	By Nebro to open the passage of Brisanne,
Bien esloignez el tago fara muestra,	A great way off, *el tago fara muestra,*
Dans Pelligouxe sera commis l'outrage,	In Pelligouxe the wrong shall be done,
De la grand dame assise sur l'orchestra.	On the great lady sitting in the orchestra.

The only clear reference here is to the 'great lady sitting in the orchestra', which means a woman of noble birth. The interpretation of the rest of the verse is hard to come by, but we believe there is no greater significance than that some harm shall befall this woman.

26

Le successeur vengera son beau frere,	The successor shall avenge his brother-in-law,
Occuper regne soubs ombre de vengeance,	And rule under the pretence of revenge,
Occis ostacle son sang mort vitupere,	That obstacle killed, his dead blood vituperated,
Long temps Bretagne tiendra avec la France.	A long time shall Brittany hold with France.

The prognosticated event and the fact that it refers to a quarrel between Brittany and other provinces in France are clearly described in the verse itself.

27

Charles Cinquiesme & un grand Hercules,	Charles the Fifth and a great Hercules,
Viendront le temple ouvrir de main bellique,	Shall open the temple with a warlike hand,
Un Colonne, Jule & Ascans reculez,	One Colonne, Julius and Ascan shall put back,
L'Espagne, clef, aigle, n'eurent onc si grand picque.	Spain, the key, and eagle never at such great pique.

It is here predicted that Charles V of Spain and Henry II of France will split the Church with their quarrels.

28

Second & tiers qui font prime musique	Second and third that make first music,
Sera par Roy en honneur sublimee,	Shall by the King be raised to high honours,
Par grasse & maigre presque a demy eticque,	By a fat one, and a lean one, and one emaciated.
Rapport de Venus faux rendra deprimee.	A false report of Venus shall pull her down.

Here we have a detailed prognostication of events and people involved in the French Revolution. Because of the hostility displayed by the nobility and clergy, two of the most powerful groups in France, toward the *Tiers Etat*, this 'third estate' constituted itself as a National Assembly and took one of the most active parts in the fomenting of the Revolution. The King (Louis XVI), during this time, was retained as 'ruler' of the country. Perhaps the most remarkable part of this prophecy is the clarity of the descriptions of Mirabeau (the fat one), Danton (the lean one), and Marat (the emaciated one), three of the leading figures in the Revolution.

29

De Pol Mansol dans caverne caprine,	From St Paul's house in a goats' cavern,
Cache & prins extraict hors par la barbe,	Hidden and taken, drawn out by the beard,
Captif meme comme beste mastine,	Captive, like unto an accursed beast,
Par Begourdans amenee pres de Tarbe.	By Begourdane shall be brought near to Tarbe.

One shall seek sanctuary in the Cathedral of St Paul, but he will be taken prisoner and subjected to great indignities.

30

Nepveu & sang du sainct nouveau venu,	Nephew and blood of the saint newly come,
Par le surnom soustient arc & couvert,	By the surname, upholds arches and covers,
Seront chassez mis a mort chassez nu,	They shall be driven, put to death, and chased out nude,
En rouge & noir convertiront leur vert.	They shall change their red and black to green.

The downfall of the totalitarian groups in Europe is here predicted; but there is also a warning that they will attempt to continue their operations even though they may change their 'colours'.

31

Le Sainct Empire viendra en Germaine,	The Holy Empire shall come into Germany,
Ismaelites trouveront lieux ouverts,	The Ismaelites shall find open places,
Asnes viendront aussie la Carmanie,	Asses shall also come out of Carmania,
Les soustenans de terre tous couverts.	Taking their part, and covering the earth.

The Germans, imbued with the spirit of barbarism, shall embark on a conquest of the world.

32

Le grand Empire chacun en devoit estre,	The great Empire, every one would want it,
Un sur les autres le viendra obtenir,	One above the rest shall obtain it;
Mais peu de temps sera son regne & estre,	But his time and reign shall last little,
Deux ans aux naves se pourra soustenir.	He may maintain himself two years in his shipping.

The struggle for the control of an empire is here described, and the prediction that the successful party will exercise its power for only two years.

33

La faction cruelle a robbe longue,	The cruel faction of the long robe,
Viendra cacher souz les pointus poig-nards,	Shall come and hide under the points of daggers,
Saisir Florence, le Duc & le diphlongue,	Seize upon Florence, the Duke and the long skins,
Sa descouverte par immeurs & flang-nards.	The discovery of it shall be by vassals and serfs.

Temporal and spiritual conflict shall ensue in Florence, the city of culture.

34

Gaulois qu'empire par guerre oc-cupera,	A Frenchman who shall occupy an empire by war,
Par son beau-frere mineur sera trahy;	Shall be betrayed by his brother-in-law, a pupil,
Par cheval rude voltigeant trainera,	He shall be drawn by a rude prancing horse,
De fait le frere long temps sera hay.	For which fact his brother shall be long hated.

A true picture, foreseen by Nostradamus, of Napoleon and his numerous relatives, whom he placed on the thrones of Europe. In fact, Napoleon's younger sister, Caroline, was married to Joachim Murat, King of Naples. He later became a traitor to Napoleon in 1814.

35

Puisnay royal flagrant d'ardant libide,	The royal son, heated with ardent love,
Pour se jouyr de cousine Germaine,	For to enjoy his German cousin,
Habit de femme au temple d'Arte-mide;	Shall in woman's clothes go to the temple of Artemis,
Allant meurdry par incogneau du Marne.	Going shall be murdered by an unknown du Marne.

This concerns the son of a King who, very much in love with his German cousin, disguises himself in woman's clothing in order to keep a rendez-vous with her in a church. While going to meet her he is murdered by a person named du Marne.

36

Apres le Roy du Sud guerres parlant,	After the King of the South shall
L'Isle Harmotique le tiendra a mes-	have talked of wars,
pris;	The Harmotic Island shall despise
Quelques ans bons rongeant un &	him,
pillant	Some good years gnawing and pil-
Par tyrannie a l'Isle changeant pris.	laging,
	And tyranny shall change the price
	of the Island.

The direct implication in this verse concerns King Philip II and the defeat of his Spanish Armada by the English Fleet of Queen Elizabeth. It is further predicted that England will go on to greater glories during the reign of this Queen.

37

Grande assemblee pres du lac de	A great assembly of people near the
Borget,	lake of Borget,
Sa ralleront pres de Montmelian;	Will go and gather themselves near
Passants plus outre pensifs, feront	Montmelian,
projet,	Going still further, they shall make
Chambary, Moriant, combat	a project,
Sainct-Julian.	Upon Chambary, Morienne, and
	shall fight at St Julian.

Internal struggles shall cause great disturbances in the above-mentioned towns of France.

38

Amour alegre non loin pose le siege,	Cheerful love lays siege not far,
Au Sainct Barbar seront les garni-	At St Barbar shall be the garrisons,
sons,	Ursini, Hadria shall be sureties for
Ursins, Hadrie, pour Gaulois feront	the French,
plaige,	And many for fear shall go from the
Pour peut rendus de l'Armee, aux	Army to the Grifons.
Grisons.	

A general truce shall be declared between the French and Italians; but a period of general conscription, in France, is to follow, because of the large number of army deserters.

39

Premier fils veufve mal'heureux mar-
  iage,
	The first son will make an unhappy
	  marriage and a widow,

Sans nuls enfans deux Isles en dis-
  cord,
	Without any children, two Islands
	  in discord,

Avant dixhuict incompetant aage,	Before eighteen, an incompetent
De l'autre pres plus bas sera l'accord.	age,
	Of the other, lower shall be the agreement.

Francis II, King of France, was married to Mary Stuart at the age of fourteen; before he was eighteen he died, leaving her a widow.

40

La jeune nay au regne Britannique,	The young man born to the King-
Qu'aura le pere mourant recom- *mande,*	dom of Britain,
Iceluy mort Londres donra topique,	Whom his father dying shall have recommended,
Et a son fils le Regne demande.	After his death, London shall give him a topic,
	And shall ask the Kingdom away from his son.

This is a reiteration of a previous prophecy, namely, the abdication of Edward VIII of England, and the accession to the throne of his brother, George VI. This verse, however, enlarges on the subject and hints at the gossip which was directed at Edward VIII and his future wife.

41

En la frontiere de Caussade & Char-
  lus,
	On the borders of Caussade and
	  Charlus,

Non gueres loing du fond de la valee,	Not far from the bottom of the valley,

De Ville Franche musique a son de
  luths,
	Of Ville Franche shall be heard the
	  music of lutes,

Environnez combouls & grand
  myrtee.
	Great dancing and company of
	  people met together.

Caussade, Charlus and Ville Franche are towns in Provence, all in the same general vicinity; and the event described is quite obviously a festival.

42

Le regne humain d'Angelique geni- *ture,* *Fera son regne, paix union tenir,* *Captive guerre demy de sa closture,* *Long temps la paix leur fera mainte-* *nir.*	The humane reign of an angelic offspring, Shall cause his reign to be in peace and union, Shall make war, captive shutting it half up, He shall cause them to keep peace a great while.

A powerful sovereign, of great goodness, shall have a long reign of peace and prosperity.

43

Le trop bon temps, trop de bonte *royale,* *Faicts & deffaicts prompt, subit, neg-* *ligence,* *Leger croira faux, d'espouse loyale,* *Luy mis a mort par sa benevolence.*	The time too good, too much of royal bounty, Feats and prompt defeats, quick negligence, Fickle shall believe false of his loyal spouse, He shall be put to death for his benevolence.

By trusting those about him, even believing false rumours about his wife, a King shall be destroyed.

44

Par lors qu'un Roy sera contre les *siens,* *Natif de Bloys subjugeura Ligures,* *Mammel, Cordobe & les Dalmatiens,* *Des sept puis l'ombre a Roy estrennes* *& lemures.*	At the time that a King shall be against his own, One born at Blois shall subdue the Ligurians, Mammel, Cordova and the Dalma- tians, Shadow of the seven, both a Royal present and spectre.

Many European countries shall be conquered by a great French leader, but he shall not hold them long.

45

L'ombre du regne de Navarre non vray,	The shadow of the reign of Navarre not true,
Fera la vie de sort illegitime;	Shall make the life of illegitimate chance,
La veu promis incertain de Cambray,	The uncertain allowance from Cambrai,
Roy d'Orleans donra mur ligitime.	King of Orleans shall give a lawful wall.

This deals with the legitimist quarrels of the various contending families for the French throne.

46

Vie sort mort de l'or vilaine indigne,	The living die of too much gold, an infamous villain,
Sera de Saxe non nouveau electeur;	Shall be of Saxony, not the new elector,
De Brunswick mandra d'amour signe,	From Brunswick shall come a sign of love,
Faux le rendant au peuple seducteur.	Rendering a false account, seducing the people.

Industrialists shall seduce the people of Germany, misleading them with many promises, on the strength of which they shall change their government.

47

De Bourze Ville a la Dame Guirlande,	From Bourze, City of the Lady Garland,
L'on mettra sus par la trahison faicte,	They shall by a set treason,
Le grand prelat de Leon par Formande,	The great prelate of Leon by Formande,
Faux pellerins & ravisseurs deffaicte.	False pilgrims and ravishers destroyed.

Paris, City of the Garlands, shall be threatened by a treasonable conspiracy, engineered by a Spanish Prelate.

48

Du plus profond de l'Espagne an-cienne,	From the deepest part of old Spain,
Sortant du bout & des fins de l'Europe,	Going out to the extremities of Europe,
Trouble passant aupres du pont de Laigne,	He that troubled the travellers by the bridge of Laigne,
Sera deffaicte par bande sa grand troppe.	Shall have his great troop defeated by another.

Nostradamus predicts the equipment by Spain of the Fascist Blue Division to fight alongside the Nazi armies at the other extreme of Europe, and their defeat and annihilation at the hands of the Russians.

49

Jardin du Monde aupres de cite neufue,	Garden of the World, near the New City,
Dans le chemin des montagnes cavees,	In the way of the man-made mountains,
Sera saisi & plonge dans la cuve,	Shall be seized on and plunged into a ferment,
Beuvant par force eaux soulphre en-venimees.	Being forced to drink sulphurous poisoned waters.

This startling prophecy of a catastrophic event at a pleasure resort not far from the great new city, predicts a tremendous tidal wave of poisoned waters that shall sweep in from the resort and overwhelm the man-made mountain-like skyscrapers of the city. Atlantic City in the 'garden state' of New Jersey nicely fits this quatrain.

50

La Meuse au jour terre de Luxembourg,	The Meuse by day in the land of Luxembourg,
Descouvrira Saturne & trois en Lurne,	Shall discover Saturn and three in the Lurne,
Montagne & plaine, ville, cite & bourg,	Mountains and plains, town, city and country,
Lorraine deluge, trahison par grand hurne.	A Lorraine flood, treason by a great Heron.

Commerce and learning shall be endangered by a 'flood' of wars, affecting all the peoples of the world.

51

Des lieux plus bas du pays de Lorraine,	In the place of peace of lower Lorraine,
Seront des basses Allemagnes unis,	Shall be a basis of a German unity,
Par ceux du siege Picards Normans, du Maisne,	By reason of the siege of Picards and Normans from Maisne,
Et aux Cantons se seront reunis.	And in the Cantons they shall be reunited.

Germany shall endeavour to unify all Europe under her banners, but shall meet with resistance from all the nations.

52

Au lieu ou Laye & Scelde se marient,	In the place where the rivers Laye and Scelde unite,
Seront les nopces de long temps mainees,	Shall the nuptials be, that were long a doing,
Au lieu d'Anvers ou la grappe charient,	In the place of Antwerp where they draw the grape,
Jeune vieillesse conforte intaminee.	The young unsullied will comfort old age.

An era of peace in Belgium is foreshadowed.

53

Les trois pellices de loing s'entrebatron,	The three harlots shall be long embattled,
La plus grand moindre demeurera a l'escoute,	The greatest less shall remain watching,
Le grand Selin n'en sera plus patron,	The great Selin shall be no more their patron,
Le nommera feu, pelte, blanche, routte.	And shall call it fire, pelt, white, route.

Three corrupt nations shall be defeated; only the weakest of them shall survive even though it will suffer much privation.

54

Nee en ce monde par concubine furtive,	Born in this world from a furtive concubine,
A deux halt mise par les tristes nouvelles,	Set up at two heights by the sad news,
Entre ennemis sera prinse captive,	Shall be taken prisoner among the enemies,
Et amenee a Malines & Bruxelles.	And brought to Malines and Brussels.

This is the story of a noblewoman, born of a concubine, who, by the pretext of sad news, is brought to Brussels and there made captive by those who envied and resented her high position.

55

Les mal'heureuses nopces celebreront	The unhappy nuptials shall be celebrated,
En grande joye mais la fin mal'heureuse;	With great joy, but the end shall be unhappy,
Mary & mere Nore desdaigneront,	Husband and wife shall disdain Nore,
Le Phybe mort, & Nore plus piteuse.	The Phybe dead, and Nore most piteous.

This predicts the marriage, in 1572, of Henry IV, then King of Navarre, and Margaret of Valois. The tragedy of the Massacre of St Bartholomew, in the same year, is also foreseen.

56

Prelat Royal son baissant trop tire,	Royal Prelate bowing himself too much,
Grand flux de sang sortis par sa bouche,	A great flood of blood shall come out of his mouth,
Le regne Anglique par regne respire,	The English reign by reign restored,
Long temps mort vif en Tunis comme souche.	A great while dead, alive in Tunis like a log.

Two separate and completely unrelated prophecies are contained in this stanza. One deals with the death of a dignitary of the Church by a haemorrhage of the throat. The other predicts the saving of the British Isles by the interference on their behalf of a distant nation.

57

Le subleve ne cognoistra son sceptre,	The exalted shall not know his sceptre,
Les enfans jeunes des plus grands honnira,	He shall put to shame two young children of the greatest,
Oncques ne fut un plus ort cruel estre,	Never was one more dirty or cruel,
Pour leurs espouses a mort noir bannira.	He shall put their spouses to the black death.

A great tyrant, raised to the dignity of King, shall misgovern greatly, being especially harsh in his treatment of the poor.

58

Au temps du dueil que le Selin monarque,	In the time of mourning, when the monarch Selin,
Guerroyera le jeune Aemathien;	Shall make war against the young Aemathien,
Gaule bransler, perecliter la barque,	France shall quake, the ship being in danger,
Tenter Phossens au ponant entretien.	Phocens shall be tempted, the real danger in the west.

In the West the Germans shall make their strongest stand; France shall be occupied by enemy forces.

59

Dedans Lyon vingt & cinq d'une haleine,	In Lyons, five and twenty of one breath,
Cinq citoyens Germains, Bressans, Latins,	Five citizens, Germans, Brescians and Latins,
Par dessous noble conduiront longue traine,	Under noblemen shall conduct a long trail,
Et descouvers par abbois de mastins.	And shall be discovered by a barking of mastiffs.

In a time of war, an underground conspiracy against France, fostered by Germans and Italians, shall be shown to be in existence.

60

Je pleure Nisse, Monaco, Pise, Gennes,	I bewail Nice, Monaco, Pisa, Genoa,
Savone, Sienne, Capue, Modene, Malte,	Savona, Sienna, Capua, Modena, Malta,
Les dessus sang & glaive par estrennes,	Upon them blood and sword for a new year's gift,
Feu, trembler terre, eau, mal'heureuse nolte.	Fire, earthquake, water, unhappy ending.

All places mentioned are cities on the Mediterranean; great disasters to befall them are foreseen.

61

Betta, Vienne, Comorre, Sacarbance,	Betta, Vienna, Comorre, Sacarbance,
Voudront livrer aux Barbares Pannone,	Shall endeavour to deliver Hungary to the Barbarians,
Par pique & feu, enorme violance,	By pike and fire, enormous violence,
Les conjurez descouverts par matrone.	The conspirators discovered by a matron.

A conspiracy to betray and surrender Hungary to 'barbarians' shall be uncovered by an elderly woman.

62

Pres de Sorbin pour assaillir Hongrie,	Near Sorbin, to invade Hungary,
L'herauld de Budes les viendra advertir,	The herald of Buda, shall give notice,
Chef Bizantin, Sallon de Sclavonie,	The chief Easterner, Sallon of Sclavonia,
A loy d'Arabes les viendra convertir.	Shall convert them to the Asiatic law.

This stanza has some bearing on the preceding one, inasmuch as it portends the eventual surrender of Hungary to a 'barbarian' form of government.

63

Cydron, Raguse, la cite au Sainct Hierons,	Cydron, Ragusa, the city of St Jerome,
Reverdira le medicant secours,	Shall revive again the medical help,
Mort fils de Roy par mort de deux heron,	The King's son dead, by the death of two herons,
L'Arabe, Hongrie, feront un mesme cours.	Oriental Hungary shall go the same way.

This predicts a plague that will fall on Hungary and which, because of the lack of doctors and medical supplies, will kill off great numbers of people, including the son of the King.

64

Pleure Milan, pleure Lucques, Florence,	Weep Milan, weep Lucques, and Florence,
Que ton grand Duc sur le Char montera,	When the great Duke shall go upon the Chariot,
Changer le siege pres de Venise s'advance,	To change the siege near Venice he advances,
Lors que Colonee a Rome changera.	When Colonee shall change at Rome.

An attempt to change the residence of the Pope from Rome to some place near Venice is predicted.

65

O vaste Rome ta ruyne s'approche,	Oh mighty Rome, thy ruin approaches,
Non de tes murs, de ton sang & substance,	Not of thy walls, but of thy blood and substance,
L'aspre par lettres fera si horrible coche,	The sharp by letters, shall make so horrid a notch,
Fer poinctu mis a tous jusques au manche.	Sharp iron thrust in all the way to the shaft.

Rome is doomed to destruction, not actually, but metaphorically by verbal and literary assault.

66

Le chef de Londres par regne l'Americh,	The chief of London by rule of America,
L'Isle d'Escosse t'empiera par gelee;	The Island of Scotland shall be tempered by frost,
Roy Reb auront un si faux Antechrist,	Kings and Priests shall have one, who is a false Antichrist,
Que les mettra trestous dans la meslee.	Who will put them altogether in discord.

British and American leaders, united in a political venture, shall set up a dictator, who shall in the end betray both leaders and common people.

67

Le tremblement si fort au mois de May,	The earthquake shall be so great in the month of May,
Saturne, Caper, Jupiter, Mercure au Boeuf;	Saturn, Caper, Jupiter, Mercury in Taurus,
Venus aussi, Cancer, Mars en Nonnay,	Venus also, Cancer, Mars in Zero,
Tombera gresle lors plus grosse qu'un oeuf.	Then shall hail fall bigger than an egg.

Confirmation of a previous prophecy, this again signifies May 10th as a fateful day, when the earth shall tremble violently and be bombarded by hitherto unknown weapons.

68

L'armee de mer devant cite tiendra,	The marines shall stand before the city,
Puis partira sans faire longue allee;	Then shall go away for a little while,
Citoyens grande proye en terre prendra,	A citizen army shall then hold the ground,
Retourner classe reprendre grande emblee.	The fleet returning and recovering a great deal.

France shall be blockaded both on land and sea, but a citizens' army will break through on all lines.

69

Le fait luysant de neuf vieux esleve,	The bright action of new old exal-
Seront si grands par midy Aquilon,	ted,
De sa soeur propre grandes alles leve;	Shall be so great throughout the
Fuyant, meurdry au buisson d'Am-	North and South,
bellon.	By his own sister great forces shall
	be raised,
	Fleeing, murdered near the bush of
	Ambellon.

Civil wars are forecast as between the North and South in the United
States in 1860, North and South Korea in 1954, North and South Vietnam
in 1970, North and South India, North and South Yemen, etc.

70

L'oeil par object fera telle excrois-	The eye of the object shall make
sance,	such an excrescence,
Tant & ardente que tombera la neige,	Because so much, and so burning
Champ arrouse viendra en decrois-	shall fall the snow,
sance,	The field watered shall come to
Que le primat succombera a Rhege.	decay,
	That the primat shall succumb at
	Reggio.

A volcanic-like eruption at Reggio in Italy shall cause widespread
destruction.

71

La terre & l'air geleront se grand eau,	The earth and air shall freeze with
Lors qu'on viendra pour Jeudy ven-	so much water,
erer;	When they shall come to worship
Ce qui sera jamais ne feut si beau,	Thursday,
Des quatre parts le viendront honorer.	That which shall be, never was so
	fair,
	From the four parts, they shall
	come to honour him.

Nostradamus here predicts the Pilgrims' first Thanksgiving in New
England in the cold of winter and on a Thursday, no less.

72

L'an mil neuf cens nonante neuf sept mois,	In the year 1999 and seven months,
Du ciel viendra un grand Roy d'effrayeur,	From the skies shall come an alarmingly powerful king,
Resusciter le grand Roy d'Angolmois,	To raise again the great King of the Jacquerie,
Avant apres, Mars regner par bon heur.	Before and after, Mars shall reign at will.

A tremendous world revolution is foretold to take place in the year 1999, with a complete upheaval of existing social orders, preceded by world-wide wars.

Nostradamus shows his mystic knowledge of the great secret of the book of revelations and solves for us the identity of the 'Beast of the Apocalypse' and the time of his arrival which John of Patmos (Rev. XIII: 18) records: 'Here is wisdom. Let him that hath understanding count the number of the Beast: for it is the number of a man: and his number is 666.' By a simple reversal of the numbers and turning 999 upside down we obtain 666.

Also in agreement with the prophetic vision of H. G. Wells and other gifted History and Science-Fiction writers, Nostradamus actually ties in the date 1999 when 'from the skies shall come an invasion . . . and Mars shall reign at will.' Time alone will tell whether this 'War of the Worlds' is to be accepted literally or metaphorically.

'Roy d'Angolmois' is an anagram for 'Roi de Mongulois' (king of the Mongolians). The threat of war will come from the east. Eastern Russia? Tibet? China? Mongolia?

74

Au revolu du grand nombre septiesme,	The year seven of the great number being past,
Apparoistra au temps ieux d'Hecatombe,	There shall be seen the sports of the ghostly sacrifice,
Non esloingne du grand age milliesme,	Not far from the great age of the millennium,
Que les entrez sortiront de leur tombe.	That the buried shall come out of their graves.

The 'great number' refers to X.72 (the year 2000), and here he indicates that in the year 2007 the dead will rise up.

75

Tant attendu ne reviendra jamais,	So long expected shall never come,
Dedans l'Europe, en Asie apparois-	Into Europe, in Asia shall appear,
tra,	One issued of the line of the great
Unde la ligue yssu du grand Hermes,	Hermes,
Et sur tous Roy des Orients coistra.	And shall be over all the Kings of
	the Orient.

A consolidation of nations of the East is forecast, under the leadership of a notable scientist.

76

Le grand Senat decernera la pompe,	The great Senate will bestow a great
A un qu'apres sera vaincu, chasse;	honour,
Des adherans seront a son de trompe,	To one who afterwards shall be
Biens publiez, ennemy dechasse.	vanquished and expelled,
	The goods of his partners shall be,
	Publicly sold, and the enemy shall
	be driven away.

A man, once held in high esteem by his countrymen, shall betray their interests and shall be exiled for his misdeeds. And in 1982 was not Senator Harrison Williams of New Jersey expelled from the Senate? And were not the Abscam conspirators driven away?

77

Trente adherans de l'ordre des Quiret-	Thirty adherents of the order of the
tes,	Quirettes,
Bannis, leurs biens donnez ses adver-	Banished, their goods shall be given
saires,	to their adversaries,
Tous leurs bienfaits seront pour de-	All their good deeds shall be re-
merites,	puted to them as crimes,
Classe espargie, delivrez aux cor-	The feet scattered, they shall fall in
saires.	the hands of the corsairs.

This continues the preceding stanza, going on to relate the similar fate that was meted out to the followers of the above-mentioned traitor.

78

Subite joye en subite tristesse,	Sudden joy shall turn to sudden
Sera a Rome aux graces embrassees,	sadness,
Dueil, cris, pleurs, larm, sang, exce-	At Rome to the embraced graces,
lent liesse,	Mourning, cries, weeping, tears,
Contraires bandes surprinses &	blood, excellent mirth,
troulsees.	Contrary troops surprised and car-
	ried away.

Some newly married couples shall be surprised by a great disaster in the midst of their jollity.

79

Les vieux chemins seront tous embel-	The old roads shall be made more
lis,	beautiful,
L'on passera a Memphis somentrees,	There shall be a passage to Mem-
Le grand Mercure d'Hercules fleur de	phis summarily,
lys,	The great Mercury of Hercules,
Faisant trembler terre, mer, & con-	fleur de lys,
trees.	Making the earth, the sea and the
	countries to quake.

This foretells the time of increased and varied means of communication between the countries of the world.

80

Au regne grand, du grand regne reg-	In the great reign, of the great reign
nant,	reigning,
Par force d'armes les grands portes	By force of arms the great brass
d'arian,	gates,
Fera ouvrir, le Roy & Duc joignant,	He shall cause to be open, the King
Port demoly, nef a fons, jour serain.	being joined with the Duke,
	Port demolished, ship sunk on a
	fair day.

This relates the story of a great naval victory that shall take place when a King and a Duke join forces.

81

Mis thresor temple, citadins Hesper- *iques,*	A treasure put in a temple by Hes- perian citizens,
Dans iceluy retire en secret lieu,	In the same hid in a secret place,
Le temple ouvrir les liens familiques,	The hungry serfs shall cause the
Reprens, ravis, proue horrible au *milieu.*	temple to be open, And take again and ravish, a fearful prey in the middle.

The treasure (gold) placed in a temple (Fort Knox) by Hesperian (Western) citizens. Economic chaos and uprisings shall cause an attempt to storm Fort Knox.

82

Cries, pleurs, larmes viendront avec *coteaux,*	Cries, weeping, tears, shall come with daggers,
Semblanyt faux donront dernier as- *sault,*	With a false semblance they shall give the last assault,
L'entour parques planter profons *plateaux,*	Set around they shall plant deep,
Vifs repoussez & meurdris de prin- *sault.*	Beaten back alive, and murdered upon a sudden.

This relates to the previous stanza and foretells the failure of the attack on Fort Knox.

83

De batailler ne sera donne signe,	Of battle there shall be no sign given,
Du parc seront contraints de sortir *hors,*	Out of the park they shall be com- pelled to come,
De Gand lantour sera cogneu l'en- *seigne,*	Round about Gand, shall be known to the ensign,
Qui fera mettre de tous les siens a *mors.*	That shall cause all his own to be put to death.

A massacre of a surrendered garrison shall take place in a civil war, between two opposing armies of the same blood.

84

Le naturelle a si haut, haut non bas,	The natural to one so high, high not
Le tard retour fera marris contens,	low,
Le Recloing ne sera sans debats,	The late return shall make the sad
En emploiant & perdant tout son	contented,
temps.	The Recloing shall not be without
	strife,
	In employing and loosing all the
	time.

The birth of Princess Diana's child in 1982, heir to the British throne; Prince William shall give joy to even the staunchest antimonarchists.

85

Le vieil Tribun au point de la	The old Tribune, at the end of the
Trehemide,	Trehemide,
Sera pressee captif ne delivrer,	Shall be much entreated not to de-
Le vueil non vueil, le mal parlant	liver the captain,
timide,	They will not will, the evil speaking
Par ligitime a ses amis livrer.	timidly,
	By legitimate to his friends shall
	deliver.

After three months of imprisonment, an old judge shall deliver the captive safely to his friends, in spite of contrary influences.

86

Comme un Gryphon viendra le Roy	As a Griffon shall come the King of
d'Europe,	Europe,
Accompagne de ceux d'Aquilon,	Accompanied by those of the
De rouges & blancs conduira grande	North,
troupe,	Of reds and whites shall conduct a
Et iront contre le Roy de Babylon.	great troop,
	And then, shall go against the King
	of Babylon.

The Griffon, a mythical monster, half lion and half man, was supposed to keep watch over the gold of Russia. Nostradamus foretells a United States of Europe, under the leadership of Russia, opposing the forces of Mammon.

87

Grand roy viendra prendre port pres de Nice,	A great king shall land at Nice,
Le grand empire de la mort si en fera,	The great empire of death shall interpose with it,
Aux Antipodes posera son genisse,	In the Antipodes, he shall put his horse,
Par mer la Pille tout esvanoistra.	By sea all the pillage shall vanish.

An invasion of the southern coast of France shall take place. In the Antipodes (Japan), they shall put their trust in conquest, but they shall be defeated decisively by sea power and lose their ill-gotten empire.

88

Pieds & Cheval a la seconde veille,	Foot and Horse upon the old watch,
Feront entree vastiant tout par la mer,	Shall come in destroying all by sea,
Dedans le port entrera de Marseille,	They shall come into the harbour of Marseilles,
Pleurs, crys, & sang, onc nul temps si amer.	Tears, cries, and blood, never was so bitter a time.

An invasion of Marseilles by a great armada is indicated.

89

De brique en marbre serot les murs reduicts,	The walls shall be turned from brick into marble,
Sept & cinquante annees pacifique,	There shall be peace for seven and fifty years,
Joye aux humains, renove l'aqueduct,	Joy to mankind; the aqueduct shall be rebuilt,
Sante, grands fruits, joye & temps melifique.	Health, abundance of fruits, joys and a mellifluous time.

Nostradamus predicts a golden age for humanity after a great calamitous war among nations.

90

Cent fois mourra le tyran inhumain,	The inhuman tyrant shall die a hundred times,
Mis a son lieu scavant & debonnaire,	In his place shall be put a savant, a kindly disposed man,
Tout le senat sera dessoubs sa main,	All the senate shall be at his command,
Fasche sera par malin temeraire.	He shall be made angry by a rash malicious person.

After the death of one of the world's greatest tyrants, a wise and kindly man shall take his place, and shall fight against the evil laws laid down by his predecessor. This fits the death of Stalin with his successor, Khrushchev, who completely dominated the Party Congress (senate) only to be angered and eventually deposed by Brezhnev.

92

Clerge Romain l'an mil six cens & neuf,	The Roman clergy in the year 1609,
Au chef de l'an fera election,	In the beginning of the year shall make a choice,
D'un gris & noir de la Compagne yssu,	Of gray and black, come out of the country,
Qui onc ne fut si malin.	Such a one never a worse was.

As stated before, Nostradamus dates all events from the Council of Nicaea, A.D. 325. By adding 1609 to this date we have 1934, the year Hitler was granted full power.

92

Devant le pere l'enfant sera tue,	The child shall be killed before the father's eyes,
Le pere apres entre cordes de jonc,	The father shall enter into ropes of rushes,
Genevois peuple sera esvertu,	The people of Geneva shall notably stir themselves,
Cisant le chef au milieu comme un tronc.	The chief lying in the middle like a log.

The League of Nations, its headquarters at Geneva, and its unhappy career, are clearly foreshadowed by Nostradamus.

93

La barque neufue rescuera les voyages,	The new ship shall make a voyage,
La & aupres transfereront l'empire,	Into the place, and thereby transfer the empire,
Beaucaire, Arles, retiendront les hostages,	Beaucaire, Arles, shall keep the hostages,
Pres deux colomnes trouvees de porphire.	Near them shall be found two columns of porphyry.

A government shall change not only its political and economic structure, but shall move to a new city and establish new headquarters there.

94

De Nismes, d'Arles, & Vienne contemner,	From Nismes, from Arles, and Vienna contempt,
N'obey tout a l'edict Hesperique;	They shall not obey the Spanish proclamation,
Aux labouriez pour le grand condamner,	To the laboratories to condemn the great one,
Six eschappez en habit seraphicque.	Six escaped in a seraphical habit.

This predicts a rebellion of the cities mentioned against an edict issued by a tyrannical leader of the Spanish nation.

95

Dans les Espagnes viendra Roy trespuissant,	A most potent King shall come into Spain,
Par mer & terre subjugant au midy;	Who by sea and land shall subjugate the south,
Ce mal sera, rabaissant le croissant,	This evil shall beat down the horns of the crescent,
Baisser les aesles a ceux du Vendredy.	And lower the wings of those of Friday.

The 'horns of the crescent' and those of Friday refer to the Arab (Moslem) allies. The clearest current threat lies with Libya and its aggressive leader, Muammar el-Qaddafi. It is predicted that the Arab confederation will be crushed.

96

Religion du nom des mers viendra,	Religion of the name of the seas shall come,
Contre la secte fils Adaluncatif,	Against the Sect of Caitifs of the Moon,
Secte obstinee deploree craindra,	The deplorably obstinate sect, shall be afraid,
Des deux blessez par Aleph & Aleph.	Of the two wounded by A. and A.

One must delve deeply into these cryptic words in order to grasp their full meaning. The 'Caitifs of the Moon' indicates the Arab nation. The struggle for power and recognition between the Shiites and the Sunnites among the Moslems is noted here. In Islam, the Shiites of Saudi Arabia vie with the Sunnites in Khomeini's Iran.

97

Triremes pleines tout aage captifs,	Triremes full of captives of all ages,
Temps bon a mal, le doux pour amertume,	Time good for evil, the sweet for the bitter,
Proye a Barbares trop tost seront hastifs,	Prey to the Barbarians, they shall be too hasty,
Cupide de voir plaindre au vent la plume.	Desirous to see the feather complain in the wind.

A continuation of the preceding stanza, this relates the bitter struggles that will ensue.

98

La splendeur claire a pucelle joueuse	The clear splendour of the joyous maid,
Ne luyra plus long temps sera sans sel;	Shall shine no more, she shall be a great time without salt,
Avec marchans, ruffians, loups odieuse,	With merchants, ruffians, wolves, odious,
Tous pesle mesle monstre universal.	All promiscuously, she shall see a universal monster.

France shall be closely associated for a while with nations of hitherto enemy status.

99

La fin le loup, le lyon, boeuf & l'asne,	At last the wolf, the lion, ox and ass,
Timide dama seront avec mastins,	The gentle doe, shall lie down with the mastiffs,
Plus ne charra a eux la douce manne,	The manna shall no more fall to them,
Plus vigilance & custode aux mastins.	There shall be no more watching and keeping of mastiffs.

This reiterates previous prognostications of a period of peace and plenty and elimination of war.

100

Le grand empire sera par Angleterre,	The great empire shall be in England,
Le Pampotam des ans plus de trois cens,	The Pempotan for more than three hundred years,
Grandes copies passer par mer & terre,	Great armies shall pass through land and sea,
Les Lusitains n'en seront pas contens.	The Lusitainians shall not be content therewith.

Nostradamus predicts great power and dominance for Great Britain for more than 300 years; also conflict with the Lusitanians (Portuguese). Does he see an English-Spanish (Argentina) conflict in the Falkland Islands?

73

Le temps present avec ques le passe,	The present time together with the past,
Sera juge par grand jovialiste,	Shall be judged by a great jovialist,
Le monde tard luy sera lasse,	The world shall at last be weary of him,
Et desloyal par le clerge juriste.	And shall be thought without faith by churchly critics.

This describes the influence of Rabelais, Voltaire, and Calvin on customs and manners during the time of Nostradamus.

CENTURY XI

[There follow fragments of Centuries XI and XII, the remainder of which have been lost. The original numbering of the verses has been retained.]

91

Meysinier, Manthis & le tiers qui viendra,
Peste & nouveau insult, enclos troubler,
Aix & les lieux fureur dedans mordra,
Puis le Phocens viendrot leur mal doubler.

Meysinier, Manthi and the third that shall come,
Plague and new insult shall trouble them,
The fury of it shall bite in Aix and places nearby,
Then the Phocens shall come and double their misery.

This prognosticates not only the coming of a plague to the city of Aix, in Provence, but also implies that they will have trouble with the inhabitants of Marseilles (Phocens).

97

Par Ville-Franche, Mascon en desarroy,
Dans les fagots, seront soldats cachez,
Changer de temps enprime pour le Roy,
Par de chalon & moulins tous hachez.

By the Ville-Franche, Mascon shall be in disorder,
In the faggots shall soldiers be hidden,
The time shall change in prime for the King,
By dragnets and mills they shall be hewed to pieces.

Civil war will bedevil France in a struggle between the rulers and the people.

CENTURY XII

5

Feu, flamme, faim, furt, farouche, fumee,	Fire, flame, hunger, theft, wild smoke,
Fera faillir, froissant fort, foy faucher;	Shall cause to fail, bruising hard to move faith,
Fils de Deite! toute Provence humee,	Son of God! All Provence swallowed up,
Chasse de Regne, enrage sans crocher.	Driven from the Kingdom, raging and without spitting.

Religious wars, having to do with the struggle for supremacy between faiths, are visualized by Nostradamus.

24

Le grand secours venu de la Guenne,	The great help that came from Gascony,
S'arrestera tout aupres de Poitiers,	Shall stop suddenly at Poitiers,
Lyon rendu par Montluel & Vienne,	Lyon surrendered by Montluel and Vienna,
Et saccagez par tout gens de mestiers.	And ransacked by all kinds of tradesmen.

Help for oppressed France shall be delayed; meanwhile German industrialists shall entrench themselves in the economic life of the nation.

36

Assault farouche en Cypre se prepare,	A savage assault is preparing in Cyprus,
Larme a l'oeil, de ta ruine proche;	Tears in my eye, thy ruin approaches,
Bizance classe, Morisque, si grand tare,	The fleet of Turkey and the Moors so great damage,
Deux differente, le grand vast par la roche.	Two opposing, the great waste by the rock.

Many battles between Moslems and Christians are envisaged by Nostradamus.

52

Deux corps un chef, champs divisez en deux,	Two bodies, one head, fields divided into two,
Et puis respondre a quatre ouys,	And then answer to four unheard ones,
Petits pour grands, a pertuis mal pour eux,	Small for great ones, open evil for them,
Tour d'Aigues foudre, pire pour Eussovis.	The tower of Aigues struck by lightning, worse for Euffovis.

Two nations shall amalgamate, electing one ruler; they shall then be challenged by four other nations, and shall prove their united strength.

55

Tristes conseils, desloyaux, cauteleux	Sad councils, unfaithful and malicious,
Aduis meschant, la loy sera trahie,	By ill advice the law shall be betrayed,
Le peuple esmeu, farouche, querelleux,	The people shall be moved, wild and quarrelsome,
Tant bourg què ville, toute la paix haye.	Both in country and city the place shall be hated.

Here is a picture of the consequences of bad laws and government, and the ills that befall the people thereby.

56

Roy contre Roy & le Duc contre Prince,	King against King, and Duke against Prince,
Haine entre iceux, dissension horrible,	Hatred between them, horrid dissension,
Rage & fureur sera tout province,	Rage and fury shall be in every province,
France grande guerre & changement terrible.	Great wars in France and horrid changes.

Civil war in France is repeatedly predicted by Nostradamus.

59

L'accord & pache sera tu tout rompue;	The accord and pact shall be broken to pieces,
Les amitiez polues par discorde,	The friendship polluted by discord,
L'haine euvieillie, tout foy corrompue,	The hatred shall be old, all faith corrupted,
Et l'esperance, Marseille sans concorde.	And hope also, Marseilles without concord.

A continuation of the preceding stanza, this goes on to give the evil consequences of such debacles.

62

Guerres, debats, a Blois guerre & tumulte,	War and debates, at Blois fighting and tumult,
Divers aguets, adveux inopinables,	Several lying in wait, acknowledgment unexpected,
Entrer dedans Chasteau Trompette, insulte,	They shall get into the Château Trompette, by abuse,
Chasteau du Ha, qui en seront coulpables.	And into the Château du Ha, who shall be culpable.

These last few verses show the concern and uneasiness with which Nostradamus viewed the France of his day, and the France which he foresaw. Here again he warns of the horror of internecine warfare.

65

A tenir fort par fureur contraindra,	He shall by fury compel them to
Tout coeur trembler, Langon advent	hold out,
terrible,	Every heart shall tremble, Langon
Le coup de pied mille pied se rendra,	shall have a terrible event,
Guiront, Garon, ne furent plus horri-	The kick shall return to thee a
bles.	thousand kicks,
	Gironde, and Garonne rivers are no
	more horrible.

The confusion within the League of Nations, and the role of France in its final dissolution, is foretold.

69

Eiovas proche, esloigner Lac Leman,	Eiovas is near, yet seemeth far from
Fort grands appreste, retour confu-	Lake Geneva,
sion,	Very great preparations, return
Loin des neveux, du feu grand	confusion,
Supelman,	Far from the nephews of the late
Tous de leur suyte.	Supelman,
	And all of their suite.

And in this stanza, Nostradamus looks far into the future to predict the coming of a French leader, stern and unyielding, who shall lead his people out of bondage.

71

Fleuves, rivieres de mal seront obsta-	Brooks and rivers, shall be a stop-
cles,	ping to evil,
La vieille flame d'ire non appaisee,	The old flame of anger being not
Courir en France, cecy comme d'ora-	yet appeased,
cles,	Shall run through France, take this
Maisons, manoirs, palais, secte rasee.	as an oracle,
	Houses, manors, palaces, sects
	shall be razed.

This final prediction by Nostradamus points to the fact that not until complete political and economic equality is realized in France, shall there be an end to the spirit of unrest.

Index